THE
SCANDAL
OF HOLINESS

THE SCANDAL OF HOLINESS

RENEWING YOUR IMAGINATION IN THE
COMPANY OF LITERARY SAINTS

Jessica Hooten Wilson

BrazosPress
a division of Baker Publishing Group
Grand Rapids, Michigan

© 2022 by Jessica Hooten Wilson

Illustrations © Kelly Latimore

Published by Brazos Press
a division of Baker Publishing Group
PO Box 6287, Grand Rapids, MI 49516-6287
www.brazospress.com

Printed in the United States of America

Library of Congress Cataloging-in-Publication Data

Names: Wilson, Jessica Hooten, author.

Title: The scandal of holiness : renewing your imagination in the company of literary saints / Jessica Hooten Wilson.

Description: Grand Rapids, Michigan : Brazos Press, a division of Baker Publishing Group, [2022]

Identifiers: LCCN 2021041826 | ISBN 9781587435249 (cloth) | ISBN 9781493435340 (ebook) | ISBN 9781493435357 (pdf)

Subjects: LCSH: Holiness. | Imagination—Religious aspects—Christianity. | Christians—Books and reading. | Books and reading—Religious aspects—Christianity. | Learning and scholarship—Religious aspects—Christianity.

Classification: LCC BT767 .W555 2022 | DDC 234/.8—dc23

LC record available at https://lccn.loc.gov/2021041826

The author is represented by WordServe Literary Group, www.wordserveliterary.com.

Baker Publishing Group publications use paper produced from sustainable forestry practices and post-consumer waste whenever possible.

22   23   24   25   26   27   28   7   6   5   4   3   2   1

To my children Evelyn, Zade, and Lucette,
who encourage my daily sanctification

The only real sadness, the only real failure, the only great tragedy in life is not to become a saint.

—Léon Bloy, *The Woman Who Was Poor*

Contents

Foreword

For over twenty years, I've been quarreling in my head with something a college history professor said to me shortly after I graduated. This was a woman I revered (and still revere), a woman whose books and teaching made an enormous impact on me, a woman who opened her kitchen table to me regularly, and whose life seemed elegant and generous and beautiful. I took to heart much that she said over the years, and only about this have I persistently quarreled.

The quarrel concerns fiction: "I don't read it anymore," she said. "It takes too long to get to the heart of the matter." I was stunned. Taken aback. I knew this woman had once read a great deal of fiction—novels were constantly coming up in conversation, Tom Jones and Jo March often adduced to illustrate a point. Furthermore, it was hard for me to grasp that a life as beautiful as hers didn't include novel-reading.

I asked my professor what she read in bed at night. "Scholarly articles in other disciplines," she said. This was the only time a glimpse of my professor's routines seemed other than enviable.

———

Hers was the first argument I encountered against reading fiction; it wouldn't be the last. Shortly after that professorial conversation, I was baptized, and I began learning my way around Christian texts, and I soon saw that the Christian tradition has long worried about reading fiction.

In the *Confessions*, Augustine remembers being absorbed in the tale of Dido and Aeneas. "I was made to master the wanderings of some fellow called Aeneas (meanwhile neglecting my own wanderings), and to weep for Dido's dying, just because she killed herself for love. And all the time—pitiable though I was—in such matters I endured my own dying away from you, O God, my life; and I shed not a single tear."[1] In other words, I cried, I wept, I wept over Dido's death—but, in fact, it was all made up, and I should have been weeping over my sins.

Leap ahead more than a millennium to the literary landscape of the novel (so called because the genre of long-form fiction that derived its plot from something other than a classical tale or fable was, when it emerged in the eighteenth century, new). In 1802, Quaker physician, abolitionist, and minor founding father Benjamin Rush took a page from Augustine: novels nurtured "abortive sympathy . . . [that] blunts the heart to that which is real."[2] Many of Rush's contemporaries worried especially about the ways that fiction might distort the affections of young female readers. In 1798, a writer in the *Weekly Magazine* offered a representative warning:

> I have heard it said in favour of novels, that there are many good senti-
> ments dispersed in them. I maintain, that good sentiments being found
> scattered in loose novels, render them the more dangerous, since, when
> they are mixed with seducing arguments, it requires more discernment
> than is to be found in youth to separate the evil from the good . . . and
> when a young lady finds principles of religion and virtue inculcated in
> a book, she is naturally thrown off her guard by taking it for granted
> that such a work can contain no harm; and of course the evil steals
> imperceptibly into her heart.[3]

Those critics, from Augustine to Rush, worried that the fiction-reader would be forever spoiled for real life, so busy weeping for

Dido that there would be no time to develop the habit of weeping for her own depravations. So busy fantasizing about the adventures of a fictional heroine that she would fail to discipline herself to the constraints of her own more humdrum reality. Note the 1798 writer's word choice: "seducing." Novels didn't just tell the stories of rakes and scoundrels—they *were* rakes, texts that had the power to lead the reader down the primrose path of debauchery.

To Rush and Augustine, the book you're now holding proposes a magisterial counterargument. Like Rush et al., Jessica Hooten Wilson recognizes that fiction can mold our imaginations—but she shows that exactly because fiction so powerfully engages our imagination, novels and short stories can lift our gaze from the stream of simulacra in which we constantly swim and show us truths that neither treatises nor Twitter can show us. And in particular, fiction can show us truths about the Christian life—about life with God and life with neighbor—that theological treatises cannot show. In this book, you'll keep company with all manner of fictional characters—a thirty-year-old priest dying of cancer who understands something about the ubiquity of grace; the biblical Moses recast as "a superhero for the Black community"; a medieval Norwegian woman whose quotidian life is revealed, over hundreds of pages, to participate in the life and sufferings of Jesus. The fictional heroes about whom Wilson writes exemplify certain virtues; they are all saints, of a sort, and Wilson means to show us how keeping company with them might give us an imagination for sanctity.

But novels like *Kristin Lavransdatter* and *Moses, Man of the Mountain*, Wilson suggests, do more than inspire us to live more saintly lives (which is to say, lives more intimate with Jesus). It seems to me that Wilson thinks reading novels is actually efficacious. That is, reading novels might not merely motivate us to do something holy-making *after we finish reading*. Rather, in Wilson's hands, novels become a kind of sacramental. The very act of reading can work holiness into us.

I see one flaw in Wilson's plumping for fiction: Wilson wants to show us how fiction can stimulate the imagination, but her book—this book—is nonfiction, and it stimulates the imagination, too. It has stimulated mine to all sorts of wonderings—among them:

- How central is *narrative* to imagination? How is the stimulation of imagination worked by narrative, by story, like or unlike the stimulation of imagination worked by abstract painting or by tableaux?
- How are hagiographies—Christian lives of the saints—different from novels? Wilson quotes Dorothy Day criticizing hagiography as treacle, but, even if I share Day's aesthetic aversions, needn't I somehow place my precious literary tastes underneath the centuries-long devotion of Christian readers to hagiography and ask what that history of devoted hagiography-reading has to show me about my own peculiar readerly preferences?
- Is reading one of the zillions of middle-brow mystery novels I adore more like watching television or more like reading the strenuous novels Wilson puts before us? Or are the better categories of comparison not television versus novels, but instead strenuous, challenging art, whatever medium, versus entertainments that follow a predictable path?

Just as I have argued in my head with my professor all these years, I'll be conversing with, riffing on, and returning to *The Scandal of Holiness* for months and years to come, because, although it is not fiction, like the best fiction, *The Scandal of Holiness* prods the imagination. It opens out. It exceeds itself.

Happy reading,
Lauren F. Winner
Durham, North Carolina

Introduction

If our civilization is to be saved . . . it will not be by Romans but by saints.

—Thomas Cahill, *How the Irish Saved Civilization*[1]

A CROWD OF WELL-DRESSED LADIES, men with graying beards, and young people flew at the author as he descended from the podium, exclaiming, "You're our prophet! We've become better people since we read *The Karamazovs*."[2] Fyodor Dostoevsky was taken by surprise at this response to his novel, which had just been released the previous year. Yet he had dedicated his life to writing for this very reason—to stir people to become better.

Stories are capable of inspiring people to change their lives. When I was an awkward, shy kid, two disparate novels emboldened me— Mark Twain's *The Adventures of Tom Sawyer* and T. H. White's *The Once and Future King*. Both told the story of kids becoming heroes, about bravery and standing apart from the current of the culture. Combine those books with an unhealthy diet of the television show *Teenage Mutant Ninja Turtles*, and you'll understand why I spent most of my Saturdays as a kid balancing along fenceposts or running around our cul-de-sac with a jump rope as my weapon, fighting tree giants and looking for treasure.

When I read fiction now, I no longer pretend to be a hero, but I do practice something higher. As an adult, I echo those graybeards who cried out to Dostoevsky, for his novels have changed me for the better. *The Brothers Karamazov* taught me what the word "love" means, not in theory but in practice. Flannery O'Connor's stories showed me how to face my sins, to see how parasitic, how demonic, they are. C. S. Lewis's Ransom trilogy reminds me that my lack of love is tied to my lack of obedience. I could add many stories to this list. I'm sure you could too. Stories that have made you better. The best stories are read not to escape our world but to better prepare us for living in our world. They shape our imaginations.

While Christians love talking about how to live better, how to help people, how to fight injustice, and so on, we too often do so as an intellectual exercise. We push imagination to the side as fantastical and unnecessary: fiction offers an escape and has nothing to do with the practice of faith. But the imagination has everything to do with our faith: how we imagine our God, his world, and ourselves affects how we live and how we die. Our imaginations reflect the story in which we assume we are participating. What story are we part of? Who's telling it? Does it end happily ever after?

The Importance of Imagination for Knowing God

C. S. Lewis is the twentieth century's primary defender of the imagination. When he published his spiritual autobiography, *Surprised by Joy*, many people were disappointed that he spent so much time discussing the imagination and so little time explaining how he "passed from Atheism to Christianity."[3] Readers wanted the author of *Mere Christianity* to focus on the apology for his conversion, to give reasons for his faith. Yet most of the book focuses on Lewis's early life, specifically the life of his imagination. For Lewis, God first draws us to himself via our imagination, our way of seeing ourselves in the world.

The climax of Lewis's conversion itself is rather dull. He observes near the final page of the book that he drove to a zoo with his brother, Warnie: "When we set out I did not believe that Jesus Christ is the Son of God, and when we reached the zoo I did."[4] Neither the arguments that compelled his intellect nor the dramatic change of his will becomes the center of Lewis's conversion story. Instead, Lewis traces backward to his childhood, telling how seeds were planted in his imagination, how those seeds were cultivated by imaginative stories in adolescence, and then how his imagination was baptized by an encounter with the work of George MacDonald. Through works of the imagination, God converted Lewis's soul before his mind could make sense of the move.

Lewis reflects on how such imaginative stories prod at the human soul "only when your whole attention and desire are fixed on something else."[5] To be merely entertained by a story is to use it for pleasure. Yet, reading Beatrix Potter's *The Tale of Squirrel Nutkin*—and Lewis experiences similar glimpses in other literature—he becomes absorbed by an "intense desire" for "another dimension."[6] Lewis has unvolitionally practiced total surrender to the imaginative reality of the children's story. For Lewis, these experiences with literature become the groundwork for an imaginative knowledge of God.

Lewis defends his dependence on the imagination as a way of knowing God. He explains to his skeptical reader, "I do not think the resemblance between Christian and the merely imaginative experience is accidental. I think that all things, in their way, reflect heavenly truth, the imagination not least. 'Reflect' is the important word. This lower life of the imagination is not a beginning of, nor a step toward, the higher life of the spirit, merely an image."[7] Imagine God's light stronger in some parts of creation than others—"As kingfishers catch fire, dragonflies draw flame," as Gerard Manley Hopkins begins one poem—but then imagine the immense light that shines forth in a person who "acts in God's eye, what in God's eye he is—Christ."[8] Writers for ages have drawn on this idea of the imagination as a way of perceiving these images and reflections here on earth.

In some ways, Lewis is speaking to himself as a young man as much as to his skeptical reader. Whereas he begins his story in childhood, when he was dwelling often in the fantasy worlds he created, by the time of his adolescence he had constructed a false divide between his "imaginative life" and his "intellect." He laments, "The two hemispheres of my mind were in the sharpest contrast. On the one side a many-islanded sea of poetry and myth; on the other a glib and shallow rationalism. Nearly all that I loved I believed to be imaginary; nearly all that I believed to be real I thought grim and meaningless."[9] Literature versus science, poetry versus facts—or, as he puts it, "gods and heroes" versus "atoms and evolution and military service."[10]

The disjunction between these ways of knowing collides while Lewis rides a train as a young man. Reading George MacDonald's *Phantastes*, Lewis has his imagination "baptized." Whereas the world of the Norse gods offered him in his youth an escape from the nihilistic, drab material reality that surrounded him, this book plunged him deeper into the real world. Before, he did not enjoy closing a book and returning to our world—yet after *Phantastes*, Lewis reflects, "I saw the bright shadow coming out of the book into the real world and resting there, transforming all common things and yet itself unchanged."[11] In Lewis's *The Voyage of the Dawn Treader*, Aslan explains that he has brought the children to Narnia "that by knowing me here for a little, you may know me better there."[12] So, too, the young Lewis experienced some truth in *Phantastes* that he could bring forth as a new lens by which to view our familiar landscape.

Too many of us commit the same fallacy as Lewis did as a young man—dividing imagination from intellect. We consider imagination as fancy or fantasy, disconnected from truth. Lewis clarifies the connection between the two in his book *The Discarded Image*. In the medieval world, imagination meant how you imagined the world that you were in, the story that you were part of. Our imagination includes more than cognition; to imagine means to know in our affections, memories, habits, desires, attitudes. We participate in our world based on how we see ourselves situated within it, what it is, how it functions, how it began, to what end we have been called, and so forth. In other words, we imagine ourselves within a story in a certain way that affects our disposition, loves, and behaviors. As Alasdair MacIntyre famously puts it, one cannot answer the question "What ought I to do?" before knowing "Of which story am I a part?"[13]

Lewis's story about his own imagination becomes compelling for understanding how to read our own lives apart from the leading cultural narratives. Our imagination becomes the realm where God meets us first and *shows* us more than *tells* us who he is and to what life we have been called.

Forming the Imagination by Reading

From Lewis we also learn that we must be mindful of how we train our imagination, for it will be formed whether or not we attend to it. In a lecture titled "Learning in War-Time," Lewis warns the students, "If you don't read good books, you will read bad ones."[14] We are cultural creatures who will read *something*. Of course, Lewis was living in a different era than the digital reality of the twenty-first century. More people today stream media content rather than read books.[15] If we are spending half our day consuming the world's narratives about who we are, what we want, and how to love, then we are being formed by an idolatrous imagination.

In Lewis's novel *That Hideous Strength*, the legions of darkness are generaled by the floating head of a criminal's corpse. Quite literally, death rules those who scramble to climb the ranks in his service, and it is later uncovered that a demonic entity puppets this head in vying for world control. When I consider the millions of people who spend hours a day watching mountain bike tricks, or children karaoking Disney songs, or advertisements for new skin products, I fear we are serving a disembodied head. Not that media in and of itself possesses some power, but the addiction to it is frightening. We seem unable to look away, and suddenly half a day has gone by. If we do not take care, this level of enslavement to media absorption will steal from us all perception of joy, longing, and desire that extends beyond this world.

If we are to counteract the diseased imaginations that we inherit and that daily influence us, we must be revolutionary in how we spend our time. The apostle John warns first-century Christians, "Don't love the world or the things in the world. If anyone loves the world, the love of the Father is not in them. Everything that is in the world—the craving for whatever the body feels, the craving for whatever the eyes see and the arrogant pride in one's possessions—is not of the Father but is of the world" (1 John 2:15–16 CEB). I would argue that reading beautiful literature forms a person in a much deeper way than watching content that has been catered to our lowest common denominator. Unfortunately, a handful of books cannot compete with the influence of hundreds of hours of media. We must turn off the screens more often and open up the books.

Somehow, the call to read great books has become a rebellious mantra. Once an innocuous pastime, reading literature in our current culture is a way of protesting. Can you imagine anything more countercultural in this society than to say, "No, thank you!" to Netflix? To not let a program select a movie for you to watch next, but to choose a novel instead, one that may not fit an algorithm's prediction about your preferences? And what if, instead of streaming alone in your home, you read the book and joined a book club where you discussed the book with others? If enough of us commit to these radical demonstrations, we may hold off the brave new world for another decade or so.

Choosing to read rather than occupy our minds with an endless stream of digital content—and choosing particularly to read great books—may strike people as odd. For the church, though—called to be in the world but not of it—we must be ready to appear weird to our culture. A transition from watching to reading might be uncomfortable for a season, like retraining a weak muscle, but the results will be worthwhile. If we change our disposition toward reading, considering it not as entertainment but as a spiritual practice, we will be more willing to dedicate time to the activity.

The Models Our Culture Gives Us

The cultural content around us forms our imagination more than we may realize. In his 2007 commencement speech at Stanford University, poet Dana Gioia proposed an experiment "to survey a cross-section of Americans and ask them how many active NBA players, Major League Baseball players, and *American Idol* finalists they can name." He would then follow up by asking "how many living American poets, playwrights, painters, sculptors, architects, classical musicians, conductors, and composers they can name."[16] While many of us can name many in the former category, our culture has deprived us of the ability to name many—if any—in the latter. Gioia argues that the loss is twofold: we neither honor those whose work is long lasting and transcendent, nor do we uphold models for "a successful and meaningful life that [is] not denominated by money or fame. Adult life begins in a child's imagination, and we've relinquished that imagination to the marketplace."[17]

In concert with Gioia, I wonder if the curators of our imagination are not training us away from virtuous living toward autonomous evaluations of value. Many of the stories that we regularly absorb only increase our delusion about who is writing the story and who is the hero. In children's films, the heroes gaze into mirrors to find all the help they need (see *The Nutcracker and the Four Realms* or *Mulan* or *Ralph Breaks the Internet*, among a host of others), while billboard slogans and inspirational posters encourage us: "You do you," "Be all that you can be," "You can do it!" Self-help books outsell most other categories, with juvenile fiction not far behind, by feeding the lie that you create your own identity.

As Christians, we are sensitive to obvious worldliness—explicit language, pornography, superfluous violence—but we often miss vicious philosophy. We're concerned when our children see violent zombie movies, but less so when their princess coloring books proclaim, "Choose your own destiny!" We are not meant to be the heroes of our story, we are not meant to be anything we desire, and we are definitely not meant to be the *author* of our tale. If, from our culture, we are imbibing stories that tell us we are the hero of our own story—or worse, we are the author of our own story—then we will confront a swarm of problems: frustration when other characters or events do not act as we want them to, confusion in our attempts to create meaning; and a lack of control over beginnings and endings. If we believe we are the authors of our story, we will be blind to our potential as the villain, and our failed attempts at being heroes will cause us guilt and heartache.

Worst of all, when we believe our culture's narrative that we are the author or hero of our story, we fail to desire a relationship with the true Author and the true Hero of this story. The real narrative is much more exciting. Our Creator is writing a story that begins with, "Let there be light." It has a triumphant middle with the incarnate God being swaddled in a trough in the middle of a tiny town in Roman-occupied territory. Each of us is invited to be a character in this Hero's story. In Psalm 139, the psalmist praises his Author:

> Like an open book, you watched me grow from conception
>   to birth;
>   all the stages of my life were spread out before you,
>   The days of my life all prepared
>   before I'd even lived one day. (MSG)

And this story will continue after we live our last day.

We Need Models, Particularly Holy Ones

Our ways of being and imagining ourselves in the world come from how we have seen others live. While the hair on our neck might bristle at the notion of imitating, we have never done anything but imitate. The idea of absolute originality is a lie. Think of how you learn language, how you decide what foods you like, what college football team you support, what you enjoy wearing, or what hobbies you take up.

You did not decide to learn your native language, nor did you make up a language all on your own and have great success employing it out in the world. Imitation is written into reality, and it has been since God created us in his image. In the Genesis narrative, "God created human beings in his image" (1:27 NCV). The dust was crafted by a particular mold. After the fall, when this shape became distorted, God descended as Jesus Christ to show us our rightful image. The incarnate God asks us to follow him, to do what he does, to live like he lives. His disciples imitate him, which is exactly what makes them disciples.

The reality is that, whether or not we realize it, we all have models. If we do not deliberately choose whom to imitate, we will slavishly follow someone or something without recognizing it. Every culture has heroes; every culture chooses whom to remember and to revere. As Christians, we have not lost our capacity to adore heroes, but we are uncomfortable venerating anyone—unless it is an NFL player, the latest Christian guru, or a superhero.

In twenty-first-century America, we exalt political leaders to the point of worship. We consume stories about celebrities whom we have never met and whose ethics are, shall we say, loosely defined, without giving a thought for how it affects our own behaviors. Each year, we gorge on films aimed to sell to a mass market, intending us to empathize with the victories or defeats of superheroes, without re-flecting on whether these figures display eternal verities. If the church decides not to uplift saints, its members will worship the alternative heroes offered by culture. Our impulse to exalt or imitate others will not be lessened if we choose to neglect the saints. Either we model saints, or we imitate substitutes.

Modeling Saints Because We Are Called to Holiness

I recommend that we spend more time reading stories about those who *pursue* holiness, for we too are called to be saints. When I use the word "saint," I am not referencing those canonized by a specific church, but more generally all Christians, who have a universal call to be saints. In his letter to the church at Corinth, St. Paul reminds his listeners of their vocation to be saints. He addresses his letters to the "saints." The call to be a saint is to become holy, to be set apart. In the Old Testament, God declares the Sabbath a holy day, one set apart for himself. Throughout the laws of the Torah, God commands his people to be likewise holy, an admonition echoed repeatedly in the New Testament: "Be holy, for I am holy" (1 Pet. 1:16 NRSV). Holiness is a call to be not of this world but to be set apart for the next one. As overwhelming as it might seem, God has called his people to be holy. To be a Christian is to be called to be a saint.

We should find it reassuring, however, that sanctification does not occur under our direction. No longer must we subscribe to all the dictates of Leviticus, and we are not required to keep the Ten Commandments on our daily calendars, for Jesus Christ has fulfilled all of these laws for us. Rather than a list of tasks to achieve, sanctification occurs because of God's provision in his Son. His grace refines our nature, converting our desires into his and changing our likeness to reflect his. When people hear this call to sanctification or holiness, they fear perfection depends on them. Yet this error would be to once again commit the sin of autonomy, as when Adam and Eve fashioned their own coverings in the garden.

Colleen Carroll Campbell confronts the sin of perfectionism in her memoir, *The Heart of Perfection*. Campbell writes, "Christian perfection is not just different from perfectionism. It's diametrically opposed."[18] "Perfect" is defined by God, taught by God, and effected in us by God. We are not responsible for perfecting ourselves, so we need not stock our shelves with self-improvement books in an endless and disquieting quest to make ourselves into who we think God wants us to be. Sanctification is when God works on us; we cannot fake it or check enough boxes to make it happen.

Campbell admits to learning the difference between "real holiness" and its "self-righteous counterfeit" by reading saints' lives, or the "great cloud of witnesses," as the writer of Hebrews puts it (12:1).[19]

The call to sanctity is directed to all of us. In our response to that call, we can be uplifted by the stories of others who lived and died faithfully. Paul writes in Romans 1:12, "We can be encouraged by the faithfulness we find in each other, both your faithfulness and mine" (CEB). We are not the first human beings to attempt to be holy, nor will we be the last. The way these saints embodied the gospel invites us to imitate them, to pass on an inheritance of faithful following.

Reading Stories of Holy Lives

We cannot concoct holiness on our own, decide what it looks like without examples, or try to become holy without other people. The goal is to be remade into God's likeness, and we do so by imitating models of holiness. When we read stories of holiness, we live vicariously through those stories, then we body them forth in our reality. The models become part of our imagination, our way of seeing how to live a holy life. For me, when I try to imagine how to be holy, I have a cloud of witnesses—from Dostoevsky's Father Zosima, to Walker Percy's Father Smith, to Willa Cather's Archbishop Latour, to Toni Morrison's Baby Suggs.

You'll notice in the novels that I have chosen to explore that these characters are not perfect; they are not goody-goodies, and their stories are not hagiographies. Rather, these figures exhibit the reality of our common sinfulness as they chase after holiness with greater and lesser diligence. Some characters encounter saints along their journey and share the experience with the reader, that we may long for such sanctity. Others attain holiness at the end of their long, wayward lives. But none of these figures are satisfied with their self as it is; all of them desire holiness. It is the story of a life lived in longing for the holy that I most want to emulate.

In Dostoevsky's last novel, *The Brothers Karamazov*, his rebellious nihilist Ivan Karamazov sets forth a convicting argument against God, complete with a host of newspaper accounts of suffering children as evidence against a good, omnipotent Creator and a narrative poem that illustrates Christ's impotency. How is Dostoevsky to defeat such a robust intellectual attack against God? He does so by recounting the life of a saint, his fictional Father Zosima, whose life was as full of sin and suffering as Ivan's, yet who chooses love over winning the argument. His story bears fruit in the soul of his novice Alyosha, who has patiently listened to his brother's account but finds his elder's life more convicting. So many questions cannot be answered in life, yet Dostoevsky's story asks, Which life do you want to live? Do you want to imitate Ivan, whose world becomes smaller, narrower, more confused, and despairing as the novel continues? Or do you want to imitate Zosima, whose life freed others to cry out in gratitude at the beauty of the stars, to embrace and kiss the earth, and to shout "Hurrah!" at the hope of resurrection?

Worldviews, debates, and apologetics have their place in Christian faith. No one wants a church without the legacy of Thomas Aquinas or Karl Barth. But stories convert our desire for well-versed explanations. After we read Dostoevsky's novel, we first hope to be like Zosima. Then we can think about why. When we read Lewis's Chronicles of Narnia, we love Aslan before we ever analyze what the lion reveals about God.

In Dante's *Paradiso*, the pilgrim witnesses a dance of two circling groups of saints in the realm of wisdom, the sphere of the sun. The rings are made up of twelve saints each, intensely bright, crossing one another in a circling dance. One group represents those who reasoned through doctrines of the Trinity, the relationship between body and soul, and so on, epitomized by St. Dominic, a great doctor of church thought. The other group, whose prime example is St. Francis, loved through how they lived, with dramatized nativity scenes, stories of hermetic asceticism, and even the stigmata. In Dante's description, these rings of saints flash

> each other's radiance like glass
> each turning but in the opposite career,
> circling together as they cross and pass.[20]

Not only do they reflect one another's light, but each group tells the story of the other: Aquinas (who is Dominican) uplifts not his Dominican father but instead Francis, while Bonaventure (who is Franciscan) praises Dominic.

Their dance shows the reciprocal relationship between imagination and intellect, how these parts move with one another, not separately. Dante commands his reader three times at the start of canto 13 to "imagine" what he himself feigns to witness. As a student of both Dominican and Franciscan education, Dante could portray both in his poem. Dante could not have penned this work of imagination without having studied both the disputations of Aquinas and the life of St. Francis. Because of Dante's poem, I understand this relationship between intellect and imagination better than I might have through reason alone. When I consider the roles of these spheres, I imagine those bright dancing saints from *Paradiso*.

As we try to imagine a life of holiness, we need more than a definition, philosophical argument, or to-do list. We need an image. We need the stories that will compel us to follow the saints, that we might become saints ourselves. When Dorothy Day, founder of the Catholic Worker Movement, was once seeking inspiration, she picked up two hagiographies and "closed them both with horror." She records in her diary the sickening and false descriptions of the saints that she found and declares, "No wonder no one wants to be a saint. But we are called to be saints—we are the sons of God!"[21] Great fiction will not sugarcoat the internal work within the saint's soul, her struggles, the grit and grime of everyday reality. When we are allowed to see through these saints' eyes, we experience their desires and thus practice holiness alongside them.

Reading these literary accounts of sanctity provides an antidote to our preoccupation with our autonomous selves. We live through another's eyes and experience their struggles and victories in following Jesus Christ. We fill our hearts with stories of holy exemplars with whom we relate, love, and make friends: Flannery O'Connor's crazy prophets, Eugene Vodolazkin's holy fool in *Laurus*, Zora

Neale Hurston's Moses, and Georges Bernanos's faithful country priest. These stories of holiness may not be *real* in the empirical sense of the word, but they are more true than some of our knowledge of history or science. Their holiness attracts us and trains our imagination.

In the Eastern Orthodox liturgy, the priest prays for sinners but also for the publican and for the prodigal son from Jesus's parables. These characters from Jesus's stories have become invested with an unexplainable reality in the prayers of the church. So, too, have the saints whom I have met in novels. I pray I can learn from their faithfulness and live out such holiness in my own life, that my story of becoming a saint might be true.

An Ecumenical, Unified Church

When we consider what it means to learn from saints' stories, we draw from our specific church background. The Orthodox are surrounded by the saints in the icons; Catholics celebrate saints' days and share their stories as regularly as Bible stories with their children; Protestants often overlook these historical figures because of their association with pre-Reformed tradition but will occasionally read *Foxe's Book of Martyrs* or focus on the sacrifice of beloved missionaries, such as Jim and Elisabeth Elliot. I have sought to overcome these divisions by assembling holy figures from a diverse array of writers from each tradition. I am not conflating the differences between these divergent faiths, but I am hoping to focus on our commonality for the present pages. What might we learn from the Orthodox writer Eugene Vodolazkin; Roman Catholic writers such as Sigrid Undset, Julia Alvarez, Georges Bernanos, Flannery O'Connor, Walker Percy, and Graham Greene; Protestant authors C. S. Lewis and Walter Wangerin Jr.; or even agnostics such as Ernest Gaines, Zora Neale Hurston, and Willa Cather? God's truth is universal and does not privilege one race, one gender, nor one church.

While there are a host of authors from Homer to Dante to Bunyan that I could have also drawn from to consider the virtues of faithfulness, suffering, and other scandalously holy traits, I limited my choices to twentieth-century novels, those that have been proven good, true, and beautiful by at least a quarter of a century, or by a host of awards, or by the authority of those with good judgment. I refrained from scanning our thousands of years of tradition, though I do hope this book becomes a lens and a guide. After you finish the book, you may apply this way of reading outward to other great stories. Also, I chose only novels so that I would not have to explain how other genres relay stories and affect our imagination, but these novels should merely be an introduction, not an end to the quest for cultivating a holy imagination. Each chapter concludes with questions for reflection, a short devotional drawn from the themes of the stories that you might practice regularly as you desire, and a list for further reading. Consider these chapters an invitation to read the books that are new to you so that you may either begin or persevere in a lifelong journey of reading as a spiritual practice. I hope that you fall in love with these stories, that you close these pages desiring more beauty and goodness, and that these stories, most significantly of all, will increase your love for the one writing your story, the Author of us all.

1

Holy Foolishness

The world has its own center: fallen, lost, though many ways good. Christians have a different center. Christ is our center. That makes us stand out if we're faithful in ways that are odd. That's who the saints are. The saints are the odd wads who have stood out from society—cultures they would have been predicted to conform to.

—Ralph C. Wood[1]

WHEN I FIRST READ Eugene Vodolazkin's novel *Laurus*, I was pregnant with my third child. The year prior, I had been pregnant two other times and lost both babies. We buried the second in our yard in a jewelry box. He had been so much bigger than I had expected, which made the loss that much heavier. I read *Laurus* when I was thirty weeks along, and I had endured fifty weeks of pregnancy without yet holding a baby. I was temporarily living in Southern California with my four-year-old daughter and two-year-old son while my husband remained for those four months at our home in Arkansas. I was on a sabbatical fellowship at Biola University, renting an apartment that continuously smelled of my neighbor's bulgogi and laundry lint.

Because I shared a room with my two children, I would read on my Kindle at night so as not to wake those saints-in-progress from their dreams. I'd rub my rounded belly, skin tight from expanded womb, trying to catch my baby's foot when she'd kick me. It was in this state that I read *Laurus*—how Arseny, the hero of the story, lost his lover and their son in childbirth. Weeping along with him, I also knew how much pregnancy entailed being open to death as much as to life.

In *Laurus* readers receive a gift, a vision from another vantage point, where death is viewed from the perspective of the eternal. Life thus takes on a reordering. We see in *Laurus* a life lived in Christ. For me, this novel awakened a desire to be more than an ordinary Christian, to move toward the extraordinary, to be open to the mystery and the mystical, to celebrate God's providence even in suffering and pain. G. K. Chesterton says, "The Christian ideal has not been tried and found wanting. It has been found difficult and left untried."[2] In *Laurus* we experience the Christian ideal in all its difficulty. The novel transmits knowledge by the experience of reading it, such that one cannot say *Laurus* is "about" any certain plotline or reduce the novelistic truth to a sound bite. Instead, reading the novel introduces you to holiness; it becomes palpable in the life of this fictional character. His extreme sanctity increases our desire for holiness.

The story is set in fifteenth-century Russia, where the realities of sin and faith permeate all of life. Because the plague has killed both of his parents, our protagonist Arseny is raised by his grandfather Christofer, an elderly and devout healer who resides beside a graveyard so that it will be easy to carry his dead body a short distance for burial. Christofer trains Arseny in the art of healing. When Christofer dies, Arseny takes over as the medicine man for his village, Rukina Quarter. He falls in love with an abandoned woman Ustina, and she becomes pregnant. Ashamed of their unholy union, Arseny refuses to allow her to go to confession or to have a midwife at her birth, and thus she dies without forgiveness of her sins, and the baby dies as well. Arseny thereafter surrenders his life for the one he feels that he robbed from her, traveling the country to heal others, risking his life during the plague, spending time as a holy fool, pilgrimaging to Jerusalem, and finally dying back in Rukina Quarter as a different man than the one who left. Some might even say a saint.

Laurus as an Icon

Protestant writer Frederick Buechner defines holiness in relation to how much we see God active in a person's life. "Only God is Holy," Buechner reminds us. "To speak of anything else is to say that it has something of God's mark upon it. Times, places, things, and people can all be holy, and when they are, they are usually not hard to recognize."[3] When we see holiness in the life of Arseny, later named Laurus, we are seeing God at work. The character becomes what we have all been called to be—a living icon. While we are made in the image and likeness of God, the Russian Orthodox Church believes that the fall distorts this likeness. To imitate Christ is to restore the likeness. A Russian saint whom I admire, Maria Skobtsova, says we will become "the very incarnate icon of God in the world."[4] Christ's likeness will be enfleshed in us in such a way that God's holiness shines through.

If you're not familiar with icons, they are more than mere illustrations or decorations in a church. In the icon tradition, the two realities of God and the world come together; the "icon transmits historical fact, an event from Sacred History or an historical personage, depicted in his physical form, and again, like the Holy Scriptures, it indicates the revelation that is outside of time, contained in a given historical reality."[5] For the Eastern church, an icon bears the Holy Spirit as the saint depicted in the icon did in life, becoming a window to the sacred world, an invitation to participate in the divine light manifested in the holy person's biographical life. Each icon likewise manifests "the presence of the all-sanctifying grace of the Holy Spirit"; encountering an icon is thus an experience of the divine.[6] In the icon, the saint's visage offers an encounter with God.

We reflect on ourselves as seen by the one who knows us better than we know ourselves. In a mysterious way, the icon provides a portal through which we envision God gazing at us.

For those who are skeptical, let me explain in a less mystical way. We have all met people who have revealed to us how God loves us— strangers whose attention never wavered when they listened to us speak, parents who patiently served us when we were sick and bed-ridden, friends who wept beside us when we mourned those we lost. We've experienced God acting through other people. The Russian Orthodox tradition would say such people are living icons, incarnate portals of God's holiness.

If readers approach *Laurus* as a "fictional icon," we might grasp again the old truths that Vodolazkin inscribes there. The phrase "fictional icon" would be antithetical to the Orthodox church, and I do not want to blur the distinction between mystical and aesthetic realities. *Laurus* should be read similar to how one reads an icon, yet the novel cannot be venerated as one would an icon because the "saint" narrated is not a real person. However, I do not think it is heretical to hope that through this artistic depiction of a saint, we may experience the transformative power of the Holy Spirit. *Laurus* is like a hagiographic icon, which, in the Russian Orthodox tradition, displays the saint, usually in the center, with the scenes of his or her life from left to right, top to bottom across the icon, so that readers may experience the story of sanctification simultaneously with the presence of the saint who faces them. What dominates is the providential order of events, the sense of a divine author or artist.

In Russian Orthodox iconography, each saint's life is depicted in resemblance to other icons. Often the saint's particular stories—no matter the time or place—are set within biblical scenery or ancient costume. The objective of depicting the saint is not individuality but transfiguration. In the mystical theology of the Eastern church, there is no notion of imitating models, but each saint participates in the divine life. Holiness is gauged by how much one's life resembles the life of the incarnate Jesus Christ; humans are living icons of God, and the icon written is then an "external expression of this transfiguration, the representation of a man [or woman] filled with the grace of the Holy Spirit."[7] When you read an icon, you may notice certain features that communicate whether this saint was a desert father, mystic, holy fool, and so forth, but many of the features will be identical—thin noses, small mouths, large eyes. Harmony and unity are emphasized over individuality. Within the icon tradition, *Laurus* reads like an assemblage of saints.

Living by Providence

Arseny's story begins in the 6,948th year since the creation of the world and the 1,440th since the birth of our Savior Jesus Christ. He is born on the feast day of Arsenius the Great. In every way that he can, Vodolazkin reorganizes our imagination to see time according to the Christian perspective. Arseny's story is part of a larger story, in which he is a character. From our place in the middle of our own stories, we often cannot understand what is going on, what God is doing with us. The beauty of reading a story like *Laurus* is seeing the whole picture, the life of the saint from beginning to end, a narrative in which the author has created order and meaning. In *Laurus* we vicariously experience the path to sanctification pursued by the title character, whose life journeys from healer to sinner to penitent to ascetic to holy fool to pilgrim to monk to hermit to saint.

Vodolazkin is an Orthodox believer, a historian, and an expert in medieval folklore who has worked for nearly thirty years in the department of Old Russian Literature at Pushkin House in St. Petersburg. He sets his novel in the Middle Ages so that he can depict a counternarrative to those of the twenty-first century regarding identity and purpose, the world's order or disorder, and the relationship to the divine. In his own words, *Laurus* "describes the life of a saint and is written according to the rules of medieval poetics." Rather than prioritize the role of the author in the creation of the text, médieval writers saw themselves as humble scribes recalling old truths to the current culture, passing on traditions. In hagiography, the writers "would include in their texts fragments from other saints' lives" without recourse to historical accuracy, any modern sense of cause and effect, or even consistency of fact within the narrative. For medieval writers, providence mattered more than time, the vertical plane more than the horizontal, and the unseen reality was more real than the empirical world. At the heart of medieval writing was Holy Scripture, which "set the tone for the majority of medieval compilations." While the story may appear to be a collection of fragments, the divine reality gives the narrative its order.[8]

In the medieval world, Holy Scripture "gave meaning to the signs that were generously scattered in daily life," and life was "a text written by God that excluded the ill-considered and accidental." Knowledge of this truth has been lost, so the world may now have "any number of individual meanings. . . . Think of the blogger who describes, minute by minute, a day that has passed."[9] Contemporary readers lack the sense of an overriding narrative, or they choose meaning according to their dissonant beliefs, or perhaps some no longer permit themselves to desire a cohesive order.

To practice seeing our life as Laurus saw his own—as an ordered mosaic—I would recommend either journaling or practicing the daily examen. In twenty-first-century America, people lose interest in journaling when they exit eighth grade, but diaries provide a witness of how God has authored your life. From within certain seasons and moments, it is hard to see how that time fits within the whole story. Yet when you read a journal entry from several years prior in comparison to where you are now, you are able to see prayers that have been answered or justly received silence. You see that God was at work even when you doubted his presence. Similarly, the daily examen can provide a structure to your journals, or it can be silent reflection. If you follow the St. Ignatius method of daily examen, you will adhere to five steps at the end of each day: become aware of God's presence, review your day in gratitude, attend to how you feel about the day, pray over one feature of that day, and then look forward in hope to the morning.

Vodolazkin explains how medieval writers would draw together stories from various saints' lives into one, often borrowing from the lives of saints who shared the same name—since names are not accidental, "why shouldn't their fates resemble one another? And why not draw on the one to illuminate the other?"[10] In his own novel, he alludes to these sources, quoting Arsenius the Great as the inspiration for Arseny's silence when he lived as a holy fool. The young healer also steals away from a prince's home, much like Arsenius the Great fled his palace life, and both the fictional hero and the desert father become hermits. Like the great saint before him, Arseny becomes renowned for his "ascetic struggle, spiritual detachment, prayer and tears."[11] Later Arseny more closely resembles St. Arsenius of Komel, who copied books at a monastery and by prayer tamed wild beasts. We see Arseny as a young boy with a domesticated wolf, and as an old man he listens to a bear's complaints about the cold and temporarily shares a cave with it. The stories of Laurus's healings echo not only saints' narratives but also the biblical miracles of Elijah, Jesus, and the Lord's apostles healing the lame, the diseased, and the possessed. Vodolazkin ties in fragments of apocrypha and other tales, all weaved into one, or written into one icon.

Arseny as a Holy Fool

Arseny originally departed the home of his birth because he desired to surrender his life on behalf of the woman whom he loved and murdered, Ustina, as well as the baby who died because of his pride. Vodolazkin intends to counter our contemporary narratives of success and individuality with a story about sacrifice. Within our secular culture, we have similar stories of one person living on behalf of another who has died: think of *Titanic*, where Rose lives in place of Jack, or *Saving Private Ryan*, where the saved Ryan is commanded to "earn this" by the dying Captain Miller. To be worthy of the sacrifice of another, these characters need to accumulate experiences that the dead missed: Rose rides horseback on a beach, and she attains the wealth and privilege she tried to give up; Ryan is surrounded by his family at Miller's grave, a sign of his having achieved earthly happiness. What differs significantly in Arseny's attempt to live for Ustina is that he, on her behalf, is attempting not satisfaction but *sanctification*. Only after living a life of sacrifice does Arseny conclude, "I wanted to give up my life for her, or rather to give my life *to her* for the life I took from her," but "the fruits of my labors turned out to be so small and ridiculous that I have experienced nothing but shame."[12] He confesses his inability to *earn* the gift of another's sacrifice, a lesson he learned by the practice of sacrifice.

As readers we experience the rightness of Arseny's renunciation of his life for Ustina as well as the realization that sanctification does not come as a result of effort. When Elder Nikandr accuses Arseny of murdering Ustina, he suggests that Arseny give his life for her. Arseny may not *will* his sanctification by effort, but his practice of asceticism, "the strength of his love," "the strength of his prayer," and the disowning of his very identity lead him to the place where he may receive mercy, both for himself and mystically for Ustina: "Mercy should be a reward for effort," the elder says.[13] When Arseny converses with Ustina after her death, he is not praying to her. He prays to the Lord; he prays before icons; he prays to saints. His conversations with Ustina should remind literary readers of Dante's poetic figuring of Beatrice, his departed love. In these similar imaginations, love on earth draws us toward divine love. Through enfleshed icons of those we love, we experience the incarnate Christ. We see the face of the divine in others; we experience Christ's love for us and practice our love for him in loving our neighbor as ourselves. Arseny demonstrates this to an extreme degree.

Arseny must learn that he does not belong to himself. His grandfather Christofer taught him that people are but instruments of God's grace. Instead of seeing himself as the designer of his own story,

Arseny must disown his identity. He must be so humble as to see himself as a character in God's story, as a tool of healing and redemption, participating in God's work. At first, pride gets in his way when he will not provide a midwife for Ustina or take her to church to receive the sacraments. After her death, luxury prevents him from feeling her presence, and his fame keeps him from talking with God. While we often see asceticism from a distance as strange and unnecessary, when we read about Arseny's inner thoughts, we understand why he must forego the pleasantries of life. They distract him from his work as a healer. Hyperbolically, Jesus commanded us to cut off our hands or blind our eyes if they caused us to sin. Is it really so strange, then, to give up the wealth and fame of this world to focus on the unseen one?

Arseny arrives in Pskov having been bludgeoned in the head, wearing raggedy clothing, and speaking little—the Russian townspeople assume such a spectacle means that Arseny is a holy fool. When the ferryman asks Arseny for payment, the people respond, "Do not ask him for money . . . for this is a person of God before you, can you not see?"[14] From our vantage point in the twenty-first century, we would think Arseny homeless or in need of asylum, but who would jump to the conclusion of holiness? Yet Russians in the fifteenth century held to a tradition of holy fools, those zealots for God who did not run off to the desert but dwelled in society, prophesying and reminding them of the realities of sin and grace. There are already two such fools in Pskov, and the townspeople categorize Arseny accordingly. His asceticism and silence are characteristic of holy fools.

Holy fool Foma, who resides in the town, declares Arseny a fellow holy fool. He defines the role as a life "wild and disparaged by people." He encourages Arseny to embrace this calling: "Be outrageous. Being pious is easy and pleasant, go ahead and make yourself hated."[15] In opposition to how we normally consider the Christian walk—that of easy and pleasant piety—Foma describes holy foolishness as wild, outrageous, and hated. To be recognized by others as a person of God will mean that Arseny must live without the luxury and fame that he ashamedly enjoyed in the town of Belozersk. This means that Arseny pelts demons with stones, talks to angels, attends christenings, and nearly dies several times from mosquitoes, freezing temperatures, and the violent attacks of sinners. He publicly struggles against the flesh, and the city cares for his needs. Through his practice as a holy fool, Arseny learns that good deeds may not be "enacted within oneself" but "are only for other people, and praise the Lord that He sends us these people."[16] Even the sanctification of a holy fool occurs in a community.

Stories like this of extreme holiness stoke the fire in my heart for Christ. The holy fool is a tradition in Russia, but it is not a universal calling. When we read *Laurus*, we are not meant to walk away from the book and become such an extreme saint. Dostoevsky's Underground Man says of himself, "I have merely carried to an extreme in my life what you have not dared to carry even halfway."[17] That is the challenge: Can we move more than halfway toward that extreme sanctity? Reading the story of such holy fools as Laurus should compel us to reexamine our lives for how we may have settled.

We are scandalized when belief in Jesus Christ is shown to be transformative and all-encompassing, even when we cognitively know it to be true. In one of his most famous passages, C. S. Lewis writes, "We are half-hearted creatures, fooling about with drink and sex and ambition when infinite joy is offered us, like an ignorant child who wants to go on making mudpies in a slum because he cannot imagine what is meant by the offer of a holiday at sea. We are far too easily pleased."[18] In a novel such as *Laurus*, there is no room for half-hearted creatures. This challenge, though, is not a call for us to lead lives of extreme asceticism and hermitage but for us to recognize the ways we have become too easily satisfied with our comfortable faith. If God is holy and we are called to be holy, we have a long road ahead of us.

The pursuit of holiness is a way, a journey, a lifelong endeavor. Reading Laurus's life, we experience Arseny's choices—to hide Ustina, to save the princess, to leave Kseniya, to perform as a holy fool in Pskov—and a thousand other small choices of prayer, abstinence, and charity. Our small, seemingly insignificant choices are creating a story, an icon that either leads the kingdom to flourishing or de-tracts from it. Every moment that we choose God's glory over our own moves us toward holiness. Are we choosing the world's wisdom or his foolishness? Have we dared to pursue holiness even halfway?

Death as Liberation

In Pskov, Arseny resides in a cemetery, similarly to how he lived next to one in his grandfather's house as a boy. His life is lived always with an awareness of the dead. During the plague, he had seen death hovering with its wings over the door of his parents' home. He can see when it is coming, and he weeps over those it takes. His grand-father has taught him not to fear death, "for death is not just the bitterness of parting. It is also the joy of liberation." When seen from God's perspective, "all are living," Christofer reminds him.[19] In this imagination, death frees the soul from the confines of the body and its earthly limitations.

When C. S. Lewis lost his friend Charles Williams, he wrote a let-ter to his widow explaining that he now believed fully in eternal life: "We now verified for ourselves what so many bereaved people have reported; the ubiquitous presence of a dead man, as if he had ceased to meet us in particular places in order to meet us everywhere. It is not in the least like a haunting. . . . It is vital and bracing."[20] Arseny likewise experiences the dead always around him. In *Laurus*, Vodol-azkin plays across life and death as often as he plays across time and space, these created realities that differ from eternal reality and our participation in the divine. Arseny is raised beside a graveyard; the black plague haunts the landscape with death; as a holy fool, Arseny resides in a cemetery; and there are stories in *Laurus* that use death as a character.

When Arseny visits the cave of St. Anthony and the caves of Theo-dosius, he speaks with the dead: "The saints were not exactly moving or even speaking, but the silence and immobility of the dead were not absolute. There was, under the ground, a motion that was not completely usual, and a particular sort of voices rang out without disturbing the sternness and repose. The saints spoke using words from psalms and lines from the lives of saints that Arseny remembered well from childhood."[21] Notice that the saints speak through Arseny's memory. They are not merely chattering away at him with individual voices. Here Vodolazkin toys with the line between believable and mystical.

Although Vodolazkin implies that death is an illusion, it is only so when perceived from this side of death—when we view death as a final end in which the person disintegrates into nothingness. Rather, from Vodolazkin's Orthodox perspective, death has been overcome, so that life continues, though in a new way. Vodolazkin confronts contemporary readers with death's reality and our false hunt for the "elixir of immortality," which only exists in the triune and resurrected God.[22]

The novel scandalizes readers who view time as a linear progression of events, for it trumps such conceptions with an iconic vision of time. How do you view time according to a God who exists outside of it? Might you pray for the salvation of people who have *already* died? Can you pray for events that have already occurred? The whole plot of the novel hinges on an eternal perspective of time. After Ustina dies, Elder Nikandr informs Arseny, "There is no already where she is now. And there is no still. And there is no time."[23] Arseny does not comprehend these great mysteries, though he learns more about the possibility of this truth over the course of his life. Initially, Arseny trusts the authority of the elder. On his journey to Jerusalem, his friend Ambrogio (whose name, significantly, comes from *ambrosia*, the nectar of the immortals) opines, "I think time is given to us by the grace of God. . . . A person is not born ready-made. He studies, analyzes his experience, and builds his personal history. He needs time for that."[24] Ambrogio can prophesy the future hundreds of years ahead of him, so that history and future play back and forth with the present. As the narrator tells readers in the prolegomenon, Arseny "did not always understand what time ought to be considered the present."[25] For us twenty-first-century readers absorbed in our present moment, this novel counteracts our limited vision with a more fluid experience of past and future.

Only when Arseny enters a monastery does he learn the rhythm of time—the monastic hours of prayer, the Christian calendar designating the practices of each day, saints' festivals. In this world, he begins to sense that time is circular. His elder corrects him, likening the motion of time to a spiral: "This involves repetition but on some new, higher level. Or, if you like, the experience of something new but not from a clean slate. With the memory of what was experienced previously."[26] The elder explains how the Bible exhibits the spiraling of time: for example, in the Old Testament is the first Adam, and then Christ in the New Testament is the second Adam. We see this idea played out in medieval literature: for instance, in *The Divine Comedy*, we see the pilgrim ascend in a circular motion but ever higher onto a new plane, spiraling in his ascent to God. The elder teaches Arseny that such an ordering of time, in its spiraling and repetitious nature, is for our benefit: "Repetitions are granted for our salvation and in order to surmount time."[27] This insight provides the key to understanding the ending of the novel.

Hope and Redemption

As a hermit in the woods, Arseny, now called Laurus, comes to exist so much in God's will that he functions according to eternal reality, which is outside of time. The narrator observes, "Laurus now sensed only cyclical time" and refers to events as occurring "one day" without other designations.[28] Drawing from hagiographic models, Vodolazkin clarifies, "Lives of saints consist of small storylines strung one after another along a time-based axis. With rare exceptions, they do not cause one another. . . . The cause of events is found in the realm of the providential."[29] Without intention, Laurus wanders from the monastery to a cave located near Rukina Quarter, where he is from. A new lost soul comes to him, much as Ustina had; her name is Anastasia, and she is pregnant with someone's child but will not name the father. We begin to intuit the similarities between the episodes: the beginning is repeated at a new register, as the elder had told him. The names are significant: Ustina connotes "justice," and Anastasia means "resurrection." The girl who did not receive justice is resurrected here in a new form, and her justice will be, for Laurus, a final mercy.

In the initial episode of his life, Arseny sinned in multiple ways against his love, Ustina: he hid her from the town, did not bring her a midwife as she requested, kept her from confession and Communion, and did not confess his sin of impregnating a woman whom he had not yet made his wife. In this second version in his story, Anastasia is a young girl and, although the child is not Laurus's, he claims it as such and publicly suffers disgrace. The pregnant girl cannot believe Laurus's sacrifice for her, that he is willing to be humiliated, to tell an "untruth" to protect her life. Laurus questions, "Did I really tell them an untruth?"[30] On the literal level, he is not the father of her child. On a spiritual plane, she is the resurrected Ustina, and he is receiving a great mercy by being allowed to repeat this moment in his life at a higher register. Earlier in the narrative, when the elder referred to time as a spiral, Arseny had asked, "Do you mean to say I will meet Ustina again?"[31] Only now, in claiming Anastasia and her child, does Arseny imagine time as a spiral. The repetition has been granted to him for his—and Ustina's—salvation.

Readers may see hope for Laurus's salvation in the way that his body does not show signs of decomposition after his death. Contrast this scene to a similar one in another Russian novel, *The Brothers Karamazov*. Elder Zosima's flesh begins to rot because the faith of the people needs to be tested; they have trusted in the wrong ends. Poor Alyosha Karamazov, a novice under Zosima's authority, had hoped for the kingdom to come with Zosima's departure, that this man's holiness would bring about some sort of utopia. Yet he returns to the church where the miracle of Cana at Galilee is being read over the departed and receives a vision of the transfigured saint, emanating in the light of Jesus Christ. Miracles still occur, but only after Alyosha has rescinded his false dreams of earthly vindication. In the *Laurus* narrative, the saint's body does not stink, but not because the novel is less realistic than Dostoevsky's masterpiece. Rather, the lack of decomposition is a sign of Ustina's, and the baby's, redemption. After Ustina and the baby died, Arseny became self-absorbed in his grief and did not attend to their bodies. Because of his sin, their bodies were disgraced in decomposition—bloating and filling with maggots. It's a heartbreaking opening to the novel. Only within this narrative does the miracle of Laurus's stenchless corpse become a beautiful sign of God's grace. Arseny entered Pskov covered in scabs and lice; his wretchedness contrasted with the grandeur of the city and made it appear more beautiful.[32] The miracle must be understood within the logic of the novel; viewed against the wretchedness of the man's sins, we can experience the beauty of God's mercy to him.

The life of Laurus appears to be a series of unrelated scenes, fragments of stories that do not make sense. At the conclusion of the novel, the saint confesses to an elder, "I no longer sense unity in my life. . . . I was Arseny, Ustin, Amvrosy, and I have just now become Laurus. . . . Life resembles a mosaic that scatters into pieces."[33] We have been prepared for this moment since the novel's prolegomenon. The first line of *Laurus* reads, "He had four names at various times. A person's life is heterogeneous, so this could be seen as an advantage. Life's parts sometimes have little in common, so that it might appear various people lived them."[34] Rather than introduce our hero with a clear and absolute knowledge of his identity, the narrator begins with mystery followed by axiomatic knowledge about life, of which our hero will be an example. Before the narrative even begins, the reader is prepared to read a cohesive rendering of what seems to be several lives.

If we read the novel as an icon, we will understand how all the fragments cohere in a divine rendering. St. Dionysius the Areopagite says, "All that was disorder in [Jesus Christ] becomes order; what was without form acquires form, and his [the saint's] life . . . becomes fully illumined by light."[35] For readers to perceive the divine light, we must practice seeing life through the eyes of Christ. At the end of the book, as Laurus receives his final name, the elder offers a way of interpreting the seeming disorder:

> Being a mosaic does not necessarily mean scattering into pieces, answered Elder Innokenty. It is only up close that each separate little stone seems not to be connected to the others. There is something more important in each of them, O Laurus: striving for the one who looks from afar. For the one who is capable of seizing all the small stones at once. It is he who gathers them with his gaze. That, O Laurus, is how it is in your life, too. You have dissolved yourself in God. You disrupted the unity of your life, renouncing your name and your very identity. But in the mosaic of your life there is also something that joins all those separate parts: it is an aspiration for Him. They will gather together again in Him.[36]

For the contemporary reader who does not believe in a grand narrative, a divine author, or a cohesive meaning to life, this exegesis sounds shocking. Yet because the words are not presented as didactic discourse, but rather occur in a dialogue and are contextualized within a setting, they retain the potential to be accepted as truth by even the most obstinate reader. Who is seeing rightly—Laurus, who feels life in its fragmented mosaic, or the elder, who presents the divine imagination? And which vision of life is more satisfying—the scattering of pieces or the gathering together in God?

Pursuing Holiness

In spring 2014, I lived in Prague with my husband and our then-four-month-old daughter; we were on a Fulbright Fellowship. I was teaching religion in American literature at Charles University in the self-proclaimed most atheistic country in Europe. During my time there, I had the startling and discomfiting realization that my Americanness stood out far greater than my Christianness. Whereas Czech people, because of years of oppression by the Soviets, guard themselves from revealing to strangers what they think or feel, my American friendliness and generally open demeanor marked me as different. In my classes, the students found it perplexing that someone so educated could believe in things like a virgin birth, resurrection, and miracles, but they witnessed nothing in my life that seemed out of the ordinary. Never once did they, or any of my Czech colleagues, question how I lived. Why not? Wasn't I supposed to be living in a way that was foolish to the world? Shouldn't they have been looking at me and saying, "Something's different about her," or "I want what she has"? Except for my lack of Czech and my inability to keep a poker face in conversation, I never felt like an oddball.

After this season abroad, I started voraciously reading books on Christian living, such as Lauren Winner's *Wearing God: Clothing, Laughter, Fire, and Other Overlooked Ways of Meeting God* and works that I had previously had little attraction to, such as Jen Hatmaker's *7: An Experimental Mutiny against Excess*. I wanted to find practical methods of living differently that surpassed the tamed-down ethos of the greatest commandment: "Be nice to others, so they will be nice to you." In my search through these books, I discovered two things: First, what I was seeking was holiness (or sanctification); and second, in order for it to become compelling, I needed to imagine holiness embodied in a life.

Laurus taught my heart how to pursue holiness because the novel surrounded me with a company of saints. When Arseny reads *Alexander Romance*, the ancient story of Alexander the Great, he becomes its "most grateful reader" by memorizing it and living out his own narrative in response to the story that has become a part of him. His great-grandfather transcribed the narrative, writing on the first page, "It is I Feodosy, a sinner, who made a copie of this book in memory of brave people, that their deeds not go unremembered."[37] We must remember the stories of the heroes and saints who preceded us so that their lives may guide our own. As Arseny recalls Alexander, Christofer, and other saints, so we should saturate our lives with their stories. *Stories of the Saints: Bold and Inspiring Tales of Adventure, Grace, and Courage* by Carey Wallace is a beautiful collection for children. *All Saints* by Robert Ellsberg offers stories of even noncanonical saints, one per day, to reflect on. And whether or not you are Eastern Orthodox, icons are more substantial reminders to imitate Christ than decorative, painted crosses or T-shirts that equate him with consumable goods ("I love Jesus and coffee"). I want to be an imitative reader of *Laurus*, to saturate my reading life with biographies of heroes and hagiographies of the holy, and to enclose myself with their images so that their way might become my way.

Devotional

From *Laurus*: "If history is a scroll in the hands of the Creator, does that mean everything I do and think is my Creator's thinking and doing, rather than mine?"

"No . . . the Creator is good but not everything you think and do is good. You were created in God's image and likeness, and your likeness consists, among other things, of freedom."[38]

Scripture: "We are fools for Christ's sake, but ye are wise in Christ; we are weak, but ye are strong; ye are honorable, but we are despised" (1 Cor. 4:10 KJV).

Wisdom from the Saints: A certain monk once asked Saint Arsenius the Great what he should do when he read the Holy Scriptures but did not comprehend their meaning. Arsenius answered, "My child, you must study and learn the Holy Scriptures constantly, even if you do not understand their power. . . . For when we have the words of the Holy Scriptures on our lips, the demons hear them and are terrified. Then they flee from us, unable to bear the words of the Holy Spirit Who speaks through His apostles and prophets."[39]

Prayer: Providential Author of History and the Word, enslave us to your freedom that we may not be conformed to the ways of this world but fit the contours of your Holy Scriptures. May we pursue more than halfway that holiness to which you have called us, even if it makes us appear to be fools in the eyes of the world.

Discussion Questions

1. What practices from Arseny's life seem strange or unadoptable to you, and why? Silence? Fasting? Homelessness?
2. If your church tradition does not envision the dead in the same way as Arseny does, how do you think of the dead who have gone before us?
3. What are some stories that have made an impression on how you live? Think of those from your childhood, from the Bible, or perhaps repeated legends of family members.
4. Could Arseny's story have been told in the contemporary world, or does it necessarily belong to the past? Is it possible to have holy fools in twenty-first-century America?
5. What are ways that you might practice a more extreme or zealous faith? How might you try to appear foolish to the world in imitation of Christ?

Further Reading

Frederick Buechner, *Godric*
Flannery O'Connor, *Wise Blood* and *The Violent Bear It Away*
Kirstin Valdez Quade, "Christina the Astonishing"
John Kennedy Toole, *A Confederacy of Dunces*

2

Communion of Saints

"Holy solitaries" is a phrase no more consistent with the Gospel than holy adulterers. The Gospel of Christ knows no religion but social; no holiness, but social holiness.

—John Wesley, *Hymns and Sacred Poems*[1]

IN HIS ACCOUNT OF HIS TIME in the concentration camps in World War II, Elie Wiesel witnesses his father's death. For a week, his father grows weaker and more delusional, unable even to climb out of his bed to relieve himself. The others in the camp beat him and steal his ration of bread. The elder of the block of cells advises the fifteen-year-old Wiesel, "In this place, it is every man for himself, and you cannot think of others. . . . In this place there is no such thing as father, brother, friend. . . . Let me give you some good advice: stop giving your ration of bread and soup to your old father. You cannot help him anymore. . . . In fact, you should be getting *his* rations."[2] The young boy listens as one who has experienced the worst kind of suffering—abuse, sickness, starvation, hopelessness. For a split

second, he considers hoarding his father's ration for himself. Even mulling over the possibility leaves him feeling guilty.

Why? Why does Wiesel's hesitancy in this moment cause him guilt? To take his father's ration is reasonable: the old man will soon die; he'll be oblivious to his son's theft; in his right mind, he may even encourage his son to take the ration for himself. Not to mention that Wiesel needs the food: his body is starving. This brief moment in Wiesel's memoir reveals that human beings are more than mere minds or appetites. There is something in us that cannot be contained within the body-mind dichotomy, something else where filial piety, generosity, magnanimity, and guilt are manifest.

Humans with Chests

Only a year before Wiesel's deportation to Auschwitz, C. S. Lewis— seemingly a world away in England—gave a series of talks about this middle sphere of the human person, which he calls "the chest—the seat of Magnanimity, of emotions organized by trained habit into stable sentiments."[3] This part of the person is what makes us human beings. It is our heart, the place where morality is felt and willed. According to Lewis, "It may even be said that it is by this middle element that man is man."[4] Whereas the world allows us only two options—we are either beasts ruled by our guts or we are brains who rule by the power of our intellect—Lewis prioritizes this third part as the true indicator of humanity. He published these talks in 1943 as *The Abolition of Man*.

The book centers on education and culture, seeking to answer the question, How do we cultivate human beings with chests? Not every person in the concentration camps responded to suffering with the character—or chest—of Elie Wiesel. In *Night*, the young Elie watches one son abandon his father and prays to not be like him. While it may seem like a strange undertaking for Lewis to have written a book about education and culture in the midst of war and the

Holocaust, Lewis knew the necessity of such a work. Nazis did not rise up from hell to impose their viciousness on Europe. They were formed by the schools that were controlled by the government, the cowardly withdrawal of many churches, and the misuse of language that encouraged masses of people to swallow evil as though it was a palliative. Lewis explains that the formation of Nazis may begin with something as seemingly benign as a textbook that unwittingly dismantles objective beauty and discards our emotional responses as irrelevant.

As a storyteller, however, Lewis knew that the most compelling work was not a collection of essays on education but a novel (though I highly recommend everyone read *The Abolition of Man* regularly if you care about a flourishing human culture). Lewis had already published *Out of the Silent Planet*, the first in his space adventure trilogy. He and J. R. R. Tolkien had agreed to write the kind of stories they themselves enjoyed, what Lewis calls in the dedication of the book a "space-and-time-story." At the end of that story—a rather crazy romp on planet Mars—the main character, Dr. Ransom, a philologist (who seems to be based on Tolkien), decides to publish his experience as *fiction*. For one, his story seems unbelievable and would not be heard as fact. Second, fiction has "the incidental advantage of reaching a wider public."[5] In this decision, we glean from Lewis his desire to proselytize, to ensure that a large audience change after reading his book. By the time Lewis writes the third novel in the series, *That Hideous Strength*, he informs his reader in the preface that the book is a storied version of *The Abolition of Man*: "a 'tall story' about devilry though it has behind it a serious 'point.'"[6]

What is that serious point Lewis hopes readers draw from *That Hideous Strength*?

In *The Abolition of Man*, Lewis argues that good education must not merely tear down jungles but also irrigate deserts. He means by this metaphor that, more than dismantling false conceptions of the world, we must teach people what they are to love. In the novel, Lewis disillusions readers of their mistaken assumptions about evil while showing us a beautiful picture of the good. Good and evil do not exist as entities "out there" but rather are planted and grow within a community through small and gradual actions that assent to or dissent from warring powers. In other words, the small decisions matter. For instance, if we lie to the DMV about whether we drove our car after the registration was expired (not that I'm speaking from experience), we have increased the strength of evil. And if we offer a room in our home to a student for a semester while she figures out finances for college, we have participated in increasing the strength of God's kingdom. It's like the Netflix show *Stranger Things*: the darkness grew stronger or weaker based on people's actions.

Even better than a show or film that portrays reality with truthfulness, *That Hideous Strength* teaches readers the necessity of being formed by good culture. Those with all the head knowledge in the world still don't stand a chance against evil if they have not cultivated a strong chest. Without chests, even those who fashion themselves as "heads" will devolve into beasts. In *That Hideous Strength* we witness both a community that nurtures a culture of holiness and its opposite, an infernal world that drags down the most dedicated of humanists. Lewis offers an illustrative warning based on Paul's Letter to the Corinthians: "Bad company corrupts good character" (1 Cor. 15:33). But he also shows us what the church, in its highest ideal, could look like.

Lewis's Aim for *That Hideous Strength*

In Lewis's space trilogy, the first novel is an allegorical representation of a Christianized version of Plato's *Republic* set on Mars. The second is a rewrite of Milton's *Paradise Lost* set on Venus. The third book brings the theological drama home to Earth. We are the silent planet under the rule of a fallen angel, to use biblical language, or what Lewis calls in his imaginary world a "bent Oyarsa." Because of this fallen angel, no longer can we hear the music of the spheres, and those outside of our planet cannot hear any singing from us. With contemporary readers, the first two novels were more successful than *That Hideous Strength*. When George Orwell reviewed *That Hideous Strength*, he lamented, "One could recommend this book unreservedly if Mr. Lewis had succeeded in keeping it all on a single level. Unfortunately, the supernatural keeps breaking in."[7] For me, the breaking in of the supernatural makes the novel much more interesting, and more people read the third novel now than they do the other two. However, I do agree with Orwell's contention that the supernatural breaks into the action "in rather confusing, undisciplined ways."[8] What begins as a story about an unhappy marriage in a sleepy college town turns into a story of demons and angels, and of bears mating in old manors, with a cameo by the wizard Merlin, who returns to life after fifteen hundred years asleep underground. No wonder people left feeling rather confused by the book.

But, if you enter the reading experience expecting the supernatural and abnormal, perhaps you'll appreciate the book more. Lewis calls the story a "fairy tale" and a "tall story."[9] By doing so, he coaches his readers not to read the story as they would Evelyn Waugh's *Brideshead Revisited* but as they might Orwell's *Animal Farm* (both also published that year). Instead of complex realism, Lewis's story is more like one of Aesop's fables, complete with a didactic moral. The characters are rather two-dimensional: heroes versus villains. And the ending ties up all the loose threads with a bow. Some have even accused the book of deus ex machina, God intervening to bring the problem to a resolution. All that to say, do not read this story as much for the beauty of intricate character development and complex metaphors, but read according to Lewis's intention for the work: to understand, through the pleasurable experience of the story, why we need communities that cultivate holiness.

While the first two novels follow Ransom, in the third novel, he does not appear until midway through the narrative. Instead, Lewis begins the story with Mark and Jane Studdock, a newly married couple who are unhappy in their marriage. Jane is trying to write a dissertation, while Mark is rising up in the esteem of the faculty at his college. The spouses ignore one another for their vocational ambitions. Then Mark is lured to join a secret organization called N.I.C.E. (National Institute of Coordinated Experiments) at Belbury, an abandoned estate, where he becomes a resident among a group of obvious villains and writes fake news. Meanwhile, Jane has been experiencing visions that turn out to be true. A parallel group of good characters, who have been drawn together at a manor named St. Anne's, invites her to share her visions with them that they may somehow stop the destructive forces of Belbury. Ransom is the director of this other group, having now become the Fisher King and representative of Christ on earth. If any figure is saintly in this story, it is Ransom. Rather than examine his character, though, I'd like to look at the culture he creates around him, how he inspires others to crave holiness, and what methods we might gather from this example.

Holiness as a Communal Virtue

In Leviticus, the Lord details for Moses all the laws for the Israelites to follow to set themselves apart as God's people. What we sometimes overlook is that these commands are communal in nature, not to be pursued as individuals. The Lord commands Moses to say "to all the community" and uses the plural form of "you": "You must be holy, because I, Yahweh your God, am holy" (Lev. 19:2 LEB). Saints are never saints by themselves any more than a person can practice virtue on an island. Even St. Anthony, who spent twenty years as a hermit in Egypt fighting off devils, was followed around by others who imitated his life and colonized the desert. Many saints from church tradition have chosen to live in religious communities, where the rhythm of their days is dictated according to prayers, worship, work, and service. For the vast majority of twenty-first-century Christians, however, our days feel chaotic and sporadic. Whenever I read stories about saints such as Hildegard of Bingen or Teresa of Ávila, I wonder whether it was easier to be holy if you didn't have toddlers screaming at you. Then I remember: my children are my community. They are the family with whom I am pursuing holiness, as are my neighbors, my friends, my church, as well as the strangers with whom I daily interact.

We all suffer from a radical individualism, one that may have even encouraged the purchase of this book: *I* want to self-improve; *I* want to be more like Jesus. But none of us are on these journeys alone. We were born to parents; we carry the history and genes of generations; we speak the language of those who taught us. In our daily lives, we are drawn to churches, educating alongside others, participating in institutions. Yet our culture is removing human-to-human engagement, especially coming out of the pandemic. Your groceries can be delivered, so you never see others at the store, not even a cashier. You can watch church from the comfort of your home. During the pandemic, households everywhere got a taste of what schooling from home looked like. (Because of this stressful new experience, Jimmy Fallon joked that this would be known as the generation taught by day drinkers.) Separation from one another causes us to put unrealistic expectations on our relationships—others are there to serve our needs. When people disappoint us, annoy us, or require more investment than they seem to be worth, it is easy to label them as "toxic" and pull away.

However, as Lewis said of books—if you're not reading good ones, you're reading bad ones—so too with community: if you don't have a good community, you will have a bad one. Solitary confinement is a punishment or is symptomatic of a disorder. It is not the ideal. The good and right community flourishes together so that no one stands alone. Jesus did not pursue his ministry as a one-man show: he called twelve disciples and sent out seventy-two. The Godhead itself is relational between Father, Son, and Spirit. And the early church is an example of the necessity of community for sanctity. We are all called to be saints together.

Marriage in *That Hideous Strength*

Lewis's story begins with a marriage because that is the starting place of human community. We all came from the joining of two, even if it was not from an orthodox marriage. The plot of the novel follows these two married characters, Jane and Mark Studdock, as they move away from one another, joining opposing sides in a supernatural conflict, and then eventually return to one another. As a medievalist, Lewis writes of marriage as the ultimate happy ending. In the biblical book of Revelation, the wedding of the Bridegroom and the church begins the new creation. Every "happy" ending in the medieval paradigm means a joining of lover and beloved. It should thus strike the reader as concerning that the book opens with Jane Studdock meditating gloomily on her marriage vows and how unfulfilling they have been. This is the first indication that we are not in paradise. Like all good storytellers, Lewis signals the coming conclusion of the story within the first lines, for marriage will be the paradisal ending.

Neither Jane nor Mark is a saintly model for readers. Really, they're rather bland personalities. They offer to the reader case studies for the effects of two different communities. Both Jane and Mark are well-educated, middle-class, white, English citizens. Besides their gender, the only difference that surfaces later in the story is that Jane was raised in the church and left it, while Mark never believed nor received any instruction from the church. Mark is a professor at Bracton College before his induction into the questionable organization N.I.C.E. at Belbury. As Mark is descending deeper into this group, Jane is recruited to reside at St. Anne's Manor with a very different set of people. The distinction between the two worlds becomes the parable for the reader: *How does a community lead a person toward holiness or damnation?*

Belbury and the Disembodied Head

We'll begin with the cautionary tale, with Mark's descent into inferno. As Mark tours the grounds of Belbury, he notes that these are not the sort "anyone could walk in for pleasure." There's iron, brick, trees surrounded by pebbles, misshapen flower beds, and slabs of metal. "The whole effect was like that of a municipal cemetery."[10] At Belbury, they prize utility. They distrust the organic and things connected to the earth, preferring the artificial, the man-made, the constructed. Everything has an industrial feel, like Sauron's Mount Doom churning out orcs and weapons, but more subtle. You might be thinking of schools shaped like warehouses. Consider how much that affects the students' and teachers' imagination for the work that occurs in the building. If the building looks like a warehouse, is education merely about output, products, and standards? Or is it about planting seeds, growing character, and flourishing community? Setting greatly influences imagination.

Belbury also houses a zoo of animals, but these are intended for vivisection and experimentation. As Mark returns to the building from the grounds, he hears "a loud melancholy howl," then "all manner of trumpetings, bayings, screams," which die "away into mutterings and whines."[11] I remember visiting Barcelona Zoo in 2001, where the animals were locked in glass closets with walls painted to resemble their natural habitats. It repulsed me, and I left feeling so distressed over their lives. I had no way of changing their situation. Unlike my visceral reaction, Mark does not hear this infernal racket as a warning. He does not recognize the sterile grounds as a sign for what kind of place N.I.C.E. is.

Mark becomes a member of N.I.C.E. because he views the leaders of the organization as having power. Mark overlooks all the signs that these people are villainous. For example, Lord Feverstone has "a mouth like a shark," "flash manners," and "never looked you in the face."[12] Only later, when his life is at stake, does Mark realize that he should have seen Lord Feverstone for the "crook" he is. And

Professor Frost is so frightening that "any child would have shrunk away from him and any dog would have backed in the corner with raised hackles and bared teeth."[13] But Mark was immune to this intuition. Unlike his wife, who never would have trusted any of these people, Mark overrides his feelings about them with his rationalism. For the reader, Lewis gives names to these characters as if they are villains in a comic book so readers will not miss that they are evil: Feverstone, Steele, Straik, Hardcastle, Wither, Frost. Their names denote hardness, death, winter. Nothing can grow, flourish, or spring from this group.

Without any clear sense of the purpose of N.I.C.E., Mark joins their vague efforts to increase dominion. The name of the organization should have been Mark's first clue of its hollowness. We think of "nice" in a positive way, but it is a word that I do not allow my children to use. The word comes from the Latin *nescire*, meaning "to not know." Historically, the word meant "ignorant" or "know nothing." As a medievalist and one familiar with language, Lewis is playing with this meaning of the word. He is especially drawing attention to the ignorance of those in the town of Edgestow who misuse the word to mean "kind" and thus miss the real treachery of the organization. Only someone with a proper education that valued words, as we'll discuss later in the chapter, would have felt an inkling that something was rotten in Denmark, so to speak.

Like the name of their organization, the leaders of N.I.C.E. speak vacuously but positively. In his first conversation with the director, Wither, Mark feels confused: "What are we both talking *about*?" he wonders.[14] But he senses "a perfectly direct question would have sounded a crudity in that room." Like the ultimate politician, Wither speaks in verbose sentences with idioms that circumvent reality: "You will find us a very happy family"; "I am very glad you have raised this issue now in a quite informal way"; "not, of course, speaking of an Appointment in the quasi-technical sense of the term."[15] When the whole organization later unravels and the face of the institute speaks gibberish, Wither does not initially catch on because he "had never expected speech to have any meaning as a whole."[16] The abstract nature of the group and its way of speaking should have been another sign of its immorality.

Early in my career, I was teaching at a university, and the speaker brought in by the administrators for faculty professional development spoke for an hour on ten words that together spelled D-I-F-F-E-R-E-N-C-E. When he finally revealed his acrostic, you could see the pride on his face, like Peter Pan crowing, "Oh, the cleverness of me!" But what inspiration did he believe he had offered us? "To make a difference!" he intoned. The problem is that the word "difference" is noncommittal, like "interesting" or "change." I could make a difference in the lives of my students by spraying them with cold water, watching movies every class period, or failing all of them in an attempt at a poor life lesson. If a person enlists in a group that believes in "change," that word may lead them to commit as many negative changes as positive ones. Hopefully readers, unlike Mark, begin to listen for the evidence that N.I.C.E. lacks any substance, that they are, as their name suggests, nothing.

After Mark enters N.I.C.E., he is told to "make yourself useful."[17] Utilitarianism, progress, and an abstract human utopia are the watchwords of N.I.C.E. When Lord Feverstone recruits Mark, he plays on Mark's pride to be part of the ruling elite: "Man has got to take charge of Man. That means, remember, that some men have got to take charge of the rest."[18] Lewis had warned in *The Abolition of Man* that those who try to evolve human nature forward will become "the power of some men to make other men what *they* please."[19] The groups who claim to be part of such progress—the communists and materialists, as Mr. Straik positively identifies them—will expedite the fulfillment of their utopian vision by killing off those who do not fit, what Feverstone describes as "sterilization of the unfit, liquidation of backward races, selective breeding."[20] It's a familiar story to those of us in the twenty-first century, yet we would do well to watch out for signs of its coming: architectural choices that prize efficiency over beauty, the mistreatment of animals for scientific experiments or even for increased meat or commodification, the exaltation of "use," and the appreciation of *power* as though it is a good in itself.

We should also witness in Mark a warning for how good people can assent to bad deeds or allow evil organizations to increase in influence. Mark is what we would call a "people pleaser." The narrator remarks of him, "Mark liked to be liked."[21] I recognize this vice in myself. For Mark, his guiding drive is to be in what Lewis calls "the Inner Ring."[22] This temptation to be on the inside of a group and not be left out will lead him to act in ways not usually part of his character. Lewis discovered the allurement of the inner ring during his years in all-male boarding schools, which you can read about in his autobiography *Surprised by Joy*. If we look back on our childhood, most of us can recall a moment when we betrayed a friend so we could move into the cool group or when we slighted our parents to fit in with the popular kids. Mark remembers how he traded in the things he really enjoyed—"John Buchan and stone ginger"—for the activities that other teens deemed "in": "the hours that he had spent learning the very slang of each new circle that attracted him, the perpetual assumption of interest in things he found dull and of knowledge he did not possess, the almost heroic sacrifice of nearly every person and thing he actually enjoyed."[23] With self-pity and contempt, Mark realizes that he has pretended to be someone he is not in order to get ahead. He has been a "public self" without any knowledge of his private self.

For Mark, the persistent desire to be "in" lands him in prison, and he faces potential execution. What began as a harmless pretense to be in with a group of the prestigious set at his college became his complicit involvement with the criminal acts of N.I.C.E., an organization that is anything but what it pretends to be. At first, Mark enters the institute as a sociologist, then he agrees to write articles that are a bit of a sham, and then he knowingly participates in the riots led by N.I.C.E. The moment that Mark decided to commit his first criminal act "slipped past in a chatter of laughter, of that intimate laughter between fellow professionals which of all earthly powers is strongest to make men do very bad things before they are yet, individually, very bad men."[24] The narrator broadens the scope of Mark's decision to include other men or human beings, those who do "bad things" because they get carried away by the group they are in.

Perhaps Lewis was thinking about the Nazis, those who participated in what Hannah Arendt describes as "the banality of evil."[25] A decade or so after Lewis's novel, Arendt was reporting on the trial of Adolf Eichmann, one of the primary organizers of the "Final Solution" in Germany. The Jerusalem court convicted him, and he was hung for his crimes against humanity in 1962. Arendt was disturbed by how "terribly and terrifyingly normal" Eichmann appeared. He was not a monster, not a demon, but an ordinary man. Writing on Eichmann, Arendt uncovers how a person can go from a bureaucrat overseeing the emigration of people—in this case, Jews—to creating ghettos in major cities, to arranging a large-scale Holocaust as if it were any other job. Scholars have debated whether Arendt misunderstood Eichmann as a robot who merely followed orders or whether he took pride in his role in the mass destruction of people. But she hits on a truth that matches well what Lewis illustrates in *That Hideous Strength*: evil functions systematically, drawing people in and seeping out through culture in mundane ways.

In *The Abolition of Man* Lewis contrasts the conditioners (exemplified by Frost and Wither) with those who have a proper education, comparing the scientists of contemporary culture with those wise sages of the past. Enamored of their own abilities to apply science, contemporary conditioners look for "how to subdue reality to the wishes of men: the solution is a technique."[26] The goal for N.I.C.E. is a utopia of floating heads, automatons, computerized brains—perhaps it is a world where every need is satisfied by a computer in our hands. Dr. Filostrato of N.I.C.E. says that humans must "learn to make our brains live with less and less body: learn to build our bodies directly with chemicals."[27] For Lewis, such nightmares about the future begin in the miseducation of our youth. As Mark debates choosing between N.I.C.E. and St. Anne's, he laments, "Why had his education been so ineffective?"[28] Apparently, Mark has been conditioned by those who desire to abolish our humanity. They have thrown out the place of the heart altogether, finding such sentiment useless or even distracting from their greater goals of rational achievement. In the story of Mark's descent, Lewis brings the distant wickedness of 1940s Nazism close to home. He shows that, with the wrong education, poor culture, and a hollow community, any decent person can commit evil.

How St. Anne's Cultivates Those with Chests

Lewis himself was educated and taught differently than those modern conditioners. As a student in the home of his tutor, William Kirkpatrick, whom he calls "the Great Knock" or "Kirk," Lewis translated Homer from Greek and Virgil from Latin, read old and new fiction insatiably, and later went on to receive three firsts at Oxford, a rare achievement. As a scholar, he studied Spencer, Milton, Dante, and the great tradition. From those writers of the past, Lewis learned, the problem was "how to conform the soul to reality and the solution had been knowledge, self-discipline and virtue."[29] In opposition to the scientism of the modern world, which dominates reality for its own ends, Lewis puts forth Ransom and his group at St. Anne's as those who try to conform their souls to reality with knowledge, self-discipline, and virtue. He even captures the essence of the Great Knock in a character named MacPhee.

When I teach *Surprised by Joy*, I perform Lewis's first meeting with the Great Knock, one of my favorite passages in Lewis's work. Here's this sixteen-year-old Irish lad showing up to meet the imposing figure who stands six feet tall with mustache and side whiskers "like the Emperor Franz Joseph."[30] Lewis attempts to make small talk with Kirkpatrick, commenting that the scenery of Surrey "was much 'wilder' than I had expected." Suddenly Kirkpatrick stops and demands, "What do you mean by wildness and what grounds had you for not expecting it?"[31] Contrast this conversation with that between Mark and Wither, whose words mean nothing and whose entire conversation is meaningless. Kirkpatrick demands that people mean what they say and know what they mean. I tell my students I want to be like the Great Knock when I grow up.

I only mean that in part, for the Great Knock was only good for training a strong head, a necessary component to a fit chest. Poor Mark suffers from a rather soft head as well as no chest. Yet, as Lewis himself discovered after his years with Kirkpatrick, one needs a chest as well. The rest of Lewis's story of education follows the thread of joy—what delights did he find that pointed him beyond this world to something that gave meaning to life? He recalls reading Beatrix Potter's stories and Norse myths, and he begins to recognize that all of these signals of joy are designs of "the Adversary," as he terms it, or God. Lewis's experience is the same path that Jane herself will follow in her moves toward the Adversary.[32]

While Mark wanders the treacherous grounds of Belbury, Jane enters a garden at St. Anne's "like the garden in *Peter Rabbit*. Or was it like the garden in the *Romance of the Rose?* . . . Or the garden in *Alice?*"[33] In contrast to the cemetery-like space of Belbury, St. Anne's offers a world that is alive and growing, and brings forth memories of enchantment and joy. As she walks the gardens, Jane experiences the same longing Lewis had when reading Beatrix Potter. There is something whimsical, enchanted, and mysterious about this place. After her initial visit among these guests, Jane returns on a train to her home, but she sees everything with delighted vision. Seeing rabbits and cows, "she embraced them in her heart with merry, holiday love" and determines to go home to "listen to many chorales by Bach on the gramophone that evening. Or else—perhaps—she would read a great many Shakespeare sonnets." She would eat "a great deal of buttered toast." She recognizes these are all intimations of "joy."[34] Whereas the place Mark has chosen anesthetizes him to pleasure, Jane's visit to St. Anne's awakens within her the love of beautiful things—animals, music, poetry, and buttered toast.

Unlike the mannequins of Belbury, the residents at St. Anne's sound like storybook characters. Mother Dimble connotes nurturing, softness, and the childish delight of nursery rhymes. One fancies her with a roundness of face and form and a certain jolliness. Arthur and Camilla take their names from mythic warriors—the King Arthur legends and Camilla from the *Aeneid*. They are names that recall tradition and speak as much to the past as to the present. Most of all, the director, Ransom, greatly affects Jane. Three times the narrator comments that after meeting him, "her world was unmade."[35] The experience is a bit like falling in love, not at all parallel to Mark's encounters with the leader of N.I.C.E.—the decapitated and revived head of the criminal Alcasan. Instead of horror and revulsion, Jane feels comfort and peace. She sees a wounded man who looks neither young nor old. This is the same Ransom who traveled to Malacandra and Perelandra in the other novels, but who becomes, in this third book, both marginalized (in plot) and central (as a Christ figure) to the story. He is the Pendragon, the inheritor of King Arthur's role protecting the spiritual community that lives in Britain. These diverse persons in this community share common loves for hearth, friendship, and beauty. What Jane comes to realize is that this adventurous world at St. Anne's is somehow connected to the religion she had put behind her. In fact, it's a world more faithful to the vision of the church than the "smell of pews, horrible lithographs of the Savior, . . . the confirmation classes, the nervous affability of clergymen."[36]

One might imagine the world of St. Anne's like Lewis's world. If you've never visited his home at the Kilns, it lies within walking distance from Oxford. Vines draw up around the white, many-plated windows, and gardens surround it. The roof is red and cheery, as are the brick walls. Inside, each room is cozy with intimate-sized spaces, with various stairs (as Lewis describes St. Anne's), and it is of course full of bookshelves. In addition to his home, Lewis had rooms at Magdalen College, as does Dr. Dimble in the novel. It was in these on-campus rooms that he met with the Inklings, including Tolkien, Owen Barfield, Charles Williams, and others. The community he imagines for St. Anne's might have been drawn from the real community he experienced with these friends, who read fantastical stories and shared their works-in-progress with one another. They discussed the King Arthur legends, debated the meaning of words, and talked of elves, angels, and Númenor.

It's worth a moment to look at St. Anne's structure of power as opposed to that of N.I.C.E. Ransom acts as the director, fulfilling the calling that Maleldil (or God) has placed on him. He willingly assents to this role but does not rule the group or lord over them. In fact, as leader, he endures the most suffering, instead of reaping the most benefits. Like Perceval in the Graal legends, Ransom has a wound that cannot be healed. There is no inner ring at St. Anne's. Everyone has a different role within the home, shares responsibility for cooking and cleaning, and pays no attention to class distinctions (which, at first, bothers Jane). They submit to "old-fashioned" morals, pass down stories to one another, and exalt history, tradition, and myths as much as Belbury omits them.[37]

Tower of Babel versus Pentecost

When Jane intimates that St. Anne's might be a more exciting, adventurous version of a church community, she is catching on to Lewis's intention. He is juxtaposing two communities that have their roots in the Bible—the Tower of Babel (Gen. 11:1–9) and Pentecost (Acts 2). The title *That Hideous Strength* is drawn from Sir David Lyndsay's early-sixteenth-century poem *Ane Dialog* describing the Tower of Babel, quoted in the book's epigraph: "The shadow of *that hideous strength*, six miles and more of its length." Ransom himself alludes to this story when he informs Merlin, "For the Hideous Strength confronts us and it is as in the days when Nimrod built a tower to reach heaven."[38] The story from Genesis uncovers the roots of the problems of N.I.C.E. and offers a beautiful course for healing.

In the Genesis account, people begin to build a tower that reaches into the heavens. What motivates these efforts? They reason, "so that we may make a name for ourselves" (Gen. 11:4). They use the gift of "one language and a common speech" (11:1) for their own purposes, to exceed the limits that God placed on them as human beings, those who came from and belong to the earth. The Lord's response is a little confusing: "If as one people speaking the same language they have begun to do this, then nothing they plan to do will be impossible for them" (11:6). The Lord prophesies that these fallen creatures will perpetrate evil if they succeed in building their version of utopia. As one friend pointed out during our Bible study of this passage, the Babel builders mistake themselves as architects of their own glory instead of seeing themselves as "living stones" (1 Pet. 2:5) for God's glory.

Like the builders of the Tower of Babel, those who construct Belbury do so under the guise that it is for the benefit of humanity. Feverstone hires Mark to "camouflage" their intentions: "For instance, if it were even whispered that N.I.C.E. wanted powers to experiment on criminals, you'd have all the old women of both sexes up in arms and yapping about humanity: call it reeducation of the maladjusted and you have them all slobbering with delight. Odd thing it is—the word 'experiment' is unpopular, but not the word 'experimental.' You mustn't experiment on children: but offer the dear little kiddies free education in an experimental school . . . and it's all correct."[39] When I hear this speech, I want to shout out like Big Daddy from *Cat on a Hot Tin Roof*, "Mendacity! Mendacity!" These are all lies. Mark falls for every lie because he believes the premise that human beings may innovate their own good, that we are evolving ourselves, and thus we can make words mean whatever we need them to. Lewis warns against this deception in *The Abolition of Man*: "The belief that we can invent 'ideologies' at pleasure and the consequent treatment of mankind as mere . . . specimens, preparations, begins to affect our very language. Once we killed bad men: now we liquidate unsocial elements."[40] We may hide our violence, or camouflage our evil, as Mark does for N.I.C.E. But when words adjust to the purposes of the user, we are living under the rule of Babel.

As the Lord did at Babel, in his mercy, he does again in fiction, confusing the speech of those in N.I.C.E. to keep their evil schemes from unfolding. The novel concludes at a banquet of pretense in which all those at N.I.C.E. have gathered with reporters watching and celebrating their abstract achievements. Yet the key speaker produces nothing but gibberish. Frost thinks he may be drunk. Mark notices gradually. At first, Wither misses it. Then, as he stands to smooth over the situation, "to him his own voice seemed to be uttering the speech he had resolved to make. But the audience heard him saying, 'Tidies and fugleman—I sheel foor that we all . . .'"[41] None of them can control their words, expressing instead "meaningless syllables." After years of considering words without meaning, these figures realize too late the necessity of meaning for communication. The scene ends in bedlam and violence.

In a previous and contrasting episode, those at St. Anne's experience the descent of the gods, or *eldils*, who grant those gathered in the manor the gifts of the spirit. As the Dimbles, Dennistons, Maggs, Jane, Ransom, and Merlin await the visitors from the heavens, those downstairs speak in muted tones. Yet when the *eldils* descend, suddenly "they all began talking loudly at once, each, not contentiously, but delightedly. . . . A stranger . . . would have thought they were drunk." What the *eldils* say they cannot remember, but they recall them being "extraordinarily witty. If not plays upon words, yet certainly plays upon thoughts, paradoxes, fancies, anecdotes . . . skyrockets of metaphor and allusion."[42] The lord of meaning had graced them with his gift, and they were immersed in the beauties of true language.

The scene resembles Pentecost, the parallel story that redeems the Tower of Babel. In Acts 2, following Jesus's ascension, the disciples are "together in one place" in Jerusalem (v. 1). What seem to be "tongues of fire" descend on them: "All of them were filled with the Holy Spirit and began to speak in other tongues as the Spirit enabled them" (vv. 3–4). Here we see that Pentecost is not a return to *one* language, but the Spirit provides polyphony that we may comprehend each other's languages. The Spirit enables the disciples to communicate and to be understood by those outside of their community, including, in this moment in history, "Parthians, Medes and Elamites; residents of Mesopotamia, Judea and Cappadocia, Pontus and Asia, Phrygia and Pamphylia, Egypt and the parts of Libya near Cyrene; visitors from Rome (both Jews and converts to Judaism); Cretans and Arabs" (vv. 9–11). The Lord shows forth the universal call of the Spirit at Pentecost; there is no inner ring.

In the story of Acts, some are amazed while others think the disciples have drunk too much wine. Lewis alludes to this confusion in the scene at St. Anne's when the *eldils* descend. Lewis shows that the silent planet need not be filled with the cacophony of animal cries and the gibberish of ill-meaning humans, but can be a place where communication fosters community, where poetry and true speech provide communion between us. In *That Hideous Strength*, Lewis depicts how the Tower of Babel might be overcome by the faithfulness of Pentecost.

Overcoming the Inner Ring

When I was an undergraduate, I often attended conferences with notable writers and famous thinkers. As an undergraduate, I didn't receive much attention from the big-named speakers at the event, not to mention all the important people who attended. I didn't mind much that I spent most of the time those weekends alone, awkwardly standing by the booksellers' tables, trying to talk to people I admired. In one embarrassing moment, I spotted a renowned poet at the Eighth Day Books display. Without introducing myself, I began to recite his poem to him. I was such a nerd. What influenced me the most over those weekends were the teachers who took the time to sit down and talk with me or eat with me so that I was not an alone twenty-one-year-old overlooked by celebrity Christian writers. They saw me standing apart from the "inner ring" and invited me to their table.

Now when I attend such events, I look for those on the outer ring. Where are the bright-eyed undergraduates and overeager graduate students? Who looks as though they know no one at this event and need a friend to sit with them? I've been able to love people who care about poetry and the arts but who will never be known in the eyes of the world. Over dinner, we have shared our enthusiasm for Chagall and Yo-Yo Ma (I even met a fellow who studied at Juilliard with him). Only by keeping our eyes open to those who need community will we overcome the temptation to push ourselves up to the front, on to the stage, or next to the most powerful person in the room. It's a temptation that does not disappear but, by grace and practice, may weaken.

In an effort to cultivate good community, how do we live? Do our homes resemble St. Anne's or Belbury? With our families, do we read Shakespearean sonnets or Dickinson or Countee Cullen or Marilyn Nelson? Do we listen to Bach more than podcasts? What kind of education are my children receiving—do they know the great tradition of Homer, Dante, and Austen, as Lewis did? Do they learn languages in school, such as Latin or Spanish? Or are they learning to prize rationalism, progress, and utility? What habits are being cultivated by my home, my children's school, and my church, and what kind of community are they forming? We may feel lost when we read headlines about large-scale changes in culture, but we confront worldly waywardness best by investing in our local communities. In attending to how we raise and educate our children—or the children of our neighbors—in tending our own gardens, and in encouraging the persons in the pew behind us, we become a culture where holiness flourishes like fruit from his vine.

Devotional

From _That Hideous Strength_: The Lord "doesn't make two blades of grass the same: how much less two saints, two nations, two angels. The whole work of healing Tellus depends on nursing that little spark, on incarnating that ghost, which is still alive in every real person, and different in each."[43]

Scripture: "Pursue the things over which Christ presides. . . . All the old fashions are now obsolete. Words like . . . insider and outsider, uncivilized and uncouth, slave and free, mean nothing. From now on everyone is defined by Christ, everyone is included in Christ. So, chosen by God for this new life of love, dress in the wardrobe God picked out for you: compassion, kindness, humility, quiet strength, discipline" (Col. 3:2, 10–14 MSG).

Wisdom from the Saints: C. S. Lewis: "If you can ask for the prayers of the living, why should you not ask for the prayers of the dead? . . . We are all agreed about praying *with* [the saints]. 'With angels and archangels and all the company of heaven. . . .' It is only quite recently I made that quotation a part of my private prayers. . . . One always accepted this *with* theoretically. But it is quite different when one brings it into association of one's own little twitter with the voice of the great saints and (we hope) our own dear dead. They may drown some of its uglier qualities and set off any tiny value it has."[44]

Prayer: Lord, teach us to nurse the spark and incarnate the ghost. May we gradually, patiently, and continuously participate in the coming of your kingdom by joining the saints in the small good works you have called us to do. Instead of chasing the inner ring, teach us to look for those outside and to draw the friendless and needy into the fold. Dress us in your wardrobe of kindness and humility. May it be said of us as Ransom says of the faithful at St. Anne's: "You have done what was required of you. You have obeyed and waited."[45]

Discussion Questions

1. What would have lured you to N.I.C.E.? Would Feverstone's arguments have worked on you? ("Man has got to take charge of Man. That means, remember, that some men have got to take charge of the rest.") Why or why not?

2. In what ways does St. Anne's look like the church? How might the church do well to model St. Anne's?

3. How has Mark's education failed to prepare him to stand up against N.I.C.E.? Do you see any disturbing similarities between his modern education and twenty-first-century American education?

4. If you were Mark and Jane's marriage counselor, how might you get them to understand each other better after the events of the novel? What counsel might you offer them?

5. Choose a passage from the story that reads like a prayer. What did you learn about holiness from rereading those lines?

Further Reading

Walker Percy, *The Thanatos Syndrome*
Muriel Spark, *The Prime of Miss Jean Brodie*
J. R. R. Tolkien, *The Lord of the Rings*
Charles Williams, *War in Heaven*

3

Creation Care as a Holy Calling

It is the story of all life that is holy and is good to tell, and of us two-leggeds sharing in it with the four-leggeds and the wings of the air and all green things; for these are children of one mother and their father is one Spirit.

—Black Elk, *Black Elk Speaks*[1]

THE QUESTION OF HOW we treat the earth is not merely—as has been too often asserted by our culture—a political or ethical obligation. Rather, the question should stir us to reflect on our identity as creatures and our vocation on earth. So much of our imagination has been malformed by the past few centuries, when we have viewed nature as a resource and the environment as controllable data. In the church, we are to blame for thinking of this world as an object for human use and that we are to dominate over animals, vegetation, and the very soil in whatever way we deem fit. Fallaciously, we've reasoned that we can misuse this world because God will destroy

it at the end of time anyway. Those who choose to worry over the state of the world are hippies, mystics, or granolas. But what if we are wrong? Not just a little bit wrong, but so wrong that this error leads us away from rightful worship, toward idolatry of human beings, and toward the destruction of what God loves? Can we pursue holiness if we do not care about his world?

When I was a kid, I started an "Environmental Club." I pulled a red wagon down my suburban street collecting people's aluminum cans and plastic bottles. I started a newsletter with facts about the world's water supply, air contagions, and waste disposal. In junior high, I petitioned for the school to keep bins in each room to recycle homework and excess paper. By the time I was in high school, I had lost my fervor but not my awareness. I donated money to 1-800-SAVE-WHALE and harped on my parents if they discarded glass or bought plastic baggies instead of recycled Tupperware. As an adult, I invest regular attention to our couple of acres, where we've planted trees and hope to provide a home for chickens and goats in the future. All of these small goods produce immense benefits for our earth, but are they holy? What would a saint look like who cared about our earth?

The first saint to come to mind is St. Francis of Assisi, the twelfth-century Italian who relinquished all his wealth to live as a mendicant friar and preached to the birds. Francis even made the sign of the cross over a wolf that was terrorizing the town of Gubbio and convinced him to cease his predatory ways. In 1979 Pope John Paul II named Francis the patron saint of ecology: "The poor man of Assisi gives us striking witness that when we are at peace with God we are better able to devote ourselves to building up that peace with all creation which is inseparable from peace among all peoples."[2] The pope—now canonized a saint himself—incorporates peace with creation as part of God's peace, what the Hebrews called *shalom*. In 2015 Pope Francis, whose namesake is the founder of the Franciscan order, titled his encyclical letter with an allusion to a song written by the saint: *Laudato Si'*, meaning "Praise be to you." Holiness, in St. Francis, looks like a person who thought of all creation around him as alive and lovable, who sang out, while wandering through the woods, praise to the Creator for Brother Sun and Sister Moon, for Brother Wind and Sister Water. Francis shows us that all of creation is our kin, our family. His way of loving the earth was more than merely responsible or dutiful. Because of the joyful and gracious ways that Francis pursued shalom, his love for creation was holy.

For many people, such a way of imagining the world feels scandalous. They worry about becoming too mystical. In his biography of St. Francis, G. K. Chesterton differentiates between mysticism and mystification, the latter being prone to "melt away the edges of things and dissolve an entity into its environment."[3] Instead of mystification, the church celebrates the mystics, those who see clearly the world as it is, rather than through the tainted eyes of culture. When our vision has been formed by the world, we reduce a tree to a source of wood, a pleasant-looking object to lift our spirits, or a conveyer of oxygen. But mystics like Francis "see each tree as a separate and almost a sacred thing, being a child of God and therefore a brother or sister" of human beings.[4] The mystic lives within a different imagination than the one cultivated by the world, whether it be the prevalent nominalism of Francis's twelfth century or the postmodern materialism of the twenty-first century. It might be time to reclaim mysticism in the church, that we may see the oaks as well as the hummingbirds and daffodils as our kin, to see ourselves surrounded by God's family, and thus to increase our capacity to love this creation we are part of.

Throughout the Middle Ages, theologians thought God revealed himself through the book of Scripture as well as through a second book, that of the created order. This metaphor of the book of nature can be found in writings from the church tradition, from the systematics of Hugh of St. Victor to the mystical reverie of Hildegard of Bingen.

If we consider that the world around us offers another form of God's revelation, the book of nature, what story is this second book telling us? All of creation tells us a story that began long before we were born—before human beings existed—and in which we play a small, humble role. There are trees behind my house that are older than my grandparents. The Rocky Mountains were not formed by human beings. We do not control the tides. The book of nature reminds us that God created us but that we are not the center of the story.

Instead of being center stage with the world as our backdrop, humans are called to be fellow characters, those who lead and serve and behold with awe the other characters in the magnificent drama of creation. When Job questions God in the ancient story, God responds with a litany of his other creatures for whom the Lord cares: the wild ox, the mountain goats, horses, hawks, ostriches. If God intended the strongest to rule, it would be the lions or elephants. If the oldest were intended to lead the way for others, it would be trees or mountains. But God chose human beings to be caretakers of his creation: we have the unique privilege of being his image bearers. In his magnificent theater of creation, our role is to stand in for God. He intends for us to "inherit the earth," but not by domination. When Jesus sat on a hill in a position of humility, he taught, "Blessed are the *meek*, for they will inherit the earth" (Matt. 5:5 NRSV). Or, in Eugene Peterson's exposition of this verse, "You're blessed when you're content with just who you are—no more, no less" (MSG). To understand our place in creation is to become meek, to be content with God's calling on you, and to play a part in the holy communion of living creatures.

In *From Nature to Creation*, theologian Norman Wirzba stresses "the development of an imaginative capacity because it has become evident that more knowledge or information about the earth is not, by itself, going to be of sufficient help."[5] We need to imagine creation differently via literature. Wirzba draws on Cormac McCarthy's *The Road*, for instance, as an apocalyptic narrative that shows us what is at stake if we fail to change our ways of living on this earth. In this novel, the world is destitute, extinguished by some unnamed disaster that we caused: "nights dark beyond darkness and the days more gray each one than what had gone before. Like the onset of some cold glaucoma dimming away the world."[6] One of the human survivors, the main character of the story, reflects on this gray, barren earth:

"Perhaps in the world's destruction it would be possible at last to see how it was made. Oceans, mountains. The ponderous counter-spectacle of things ceasing to be."[7] As readers, we see the darkness of *that* world and contrast it with our own. After reading apocalyptic novels, we should revere the oceans, mountains, and even the sun's brightness and the grass's greenness, for they could be lost. Yet, though apocalyptic novels may induce fear about the consequences of our negative behaviors, they might not always provide models of holiness to increase our love for this place.

When Christians talk about literature that increases their love for the world, they tend toward agrarian narratives. Wendell Berry is at the top of most lists, as a novelist, poet, farmer, and ecological activist. He sets many stories in the fictional town of Port William, where even as an author he can invest in the community there and attend closely to the people amid their flora and fauna. "I have made the imagined place of Port William, its neighborhood and member-ship, in an attempt to honor the actual place where I have lived. By means of the imagined place, over the last fifty years, I have learned to see my native landscape and neighborhood as a place unique in the world, a work of God, possessed of an inherent sanctity that mocks any human valuation that can be put upon it."[8] By telling fictional stories about his world, Berry unveils the true holiness of the place and shares it with the world. Through his stories he hopes that read-ers likewise learn the blessing of their places.

Berry defends the imagination as the agent of change for those desiring to better care for their place:

> If we are to protect the world's multitude of places and creatures, then we must know them, not just conceptually but imaginatively as well. They must be pictured in the mind and memory; they must be known with affection, "by heart," so that in seeing or remembering them the heart may be said to "sing." . . . To know imaginatively is to know intimately, particularly, precisely, gratefully, reverently, and with affection.[9]

Through stories, we gain more intimate knowledge of places and creatures, learning to attend to the world with gratitude, reverence, and affection. However, most of us do not have the privilege or opportunity to live on a farm or return to a world without electricity. The majority of Berry's stories occur from the Civil War to the mid-twentieth century in America, without the distractions and habitual conveniences of our culture. But for those of us who live in cities, suburbs, or places wholly unlike Berry's world, how shall we live?

In Defense of Animal Stories

Let us consider an unusual genre for increasing our love for this earth: animal stories. In J. R. R. Tolkien's 1938 defense of "fairy stories," he distinguishes between fantasy, which he himself published (*The Hobbit* and *The Lord of the Rings*), and the "beast fable." The latter connects with the former. In both worlds, the animals speak like human beings. Tolkien writes, "In some part (often small) this marvel derives from one of the primal 'desires' that lie near the heart of Faerie: the desire of men to hold communion with other living things."[10] In other words, Tolkien says that the heart of fairy stories and beast fables alike is the desire to commune with creation, a desire too often dulled by our partiality for efficiency or ease. For Tolkien, the beast fables differ because no human beings appear, or the humans are "mere adjuncts," and thus "*Reynard the Fox*, or *The Nun's Priest's Tale*, or *Brer Rabbit*" cannot be categorized properly as fairy stories.[11] He nearly makes an exception for the stories of Beatrix Potter because of "their inherent morality."[12] While Tolkien recognizes that beast fables inspire our desire for communion with other creatures and offer a moral rendering of the world, he overlooks the ways they enchant our vision of the world and instill in readers meekness that prepares us to inherit our earth.

Tolkien lists historical examples of animal stories, showing humans' lengthy history with the genre. Tolkien also mentions "The Monkey's Heart," a Swahili story, and he could have listed Aesop's fables, Buddhist Jataka tales, Hindu Panchatantra, or Native American myths, in which animals are even the first creators of the world. These stories may have been adopted for children's education, but they were intended for adult readers. In the first century AD, Apollonius of Tyana praises Aesop for choosing "humble incidents to teach great truths" and for telling the truth "by announcing a story which everyone knows not to be true."[13] Apollonius expounds on the paradox that fiction may instruct us in wisdom, that stories may be truer than our experience.

By relegating animal stories to the shelves of children's literature, we miss their deep lessons for our hearts. Tolkien and his friend C. S. Lewis adored the animal stories of Beatrix Potter; Tolkien read them to his children, and Lewis read them for himself alone. In *Tolkien's Modern Reading*, Holly Ordway suggests that these trousered, pipe-smoking rabbits like Peter and Benjamin Bunny influenced the creation of hobbits. In *Surprised by Joy* Lewis credits Potter's *Squirrel Nutkin* with an initial experience of joy that gradually led him to Christianity, and we notice how he imitates the Potter books in his creation of talking animals in Narnia. Both Tolkien and Lewis "often played with the idea of a pilgrimage to see her [at her home in the Lake District] and pictured what fun it would be to shoulder aside the mobs of people who want to show you all the Wordsworth places with a brief rejoinder 'We are looking for Miss Potter.'"[14] For many Christians, Tolkien and Lewis are heroes of the church. Should we not also learn from their admiration for animal stories and see what these tales hold in store for our faith?

The Book of the Dun Cow

In 1978 novelist Walter Wangerin Jr. adapted the aforementioned "Nun's Priest's Tale" from Chaucer into a novel titled *The Book of the Dun Cow*. Although no one would mistake Chaucer's story for children's literature, Wangerin's novel received the *New York*

Times Best Children's Book of the Year. He also won the National Book Award for science fiction, but the book was never meant to be categorized as either children's literature or sci-fi. In his afterword to the twenty-fifth-anniversary edition, Wangerin explains why his work needs to be read outside of such groups: while "the beast fable has ever been a moralizing thing, an instructing thing . . . the modern novel requires greater complexity and less overt moralizing." Wangerin draws from all the beast tales we've mentioned, as well as the bestiaries of the Middle Ages, ancient sermons on the six days of creation, medieval cosmologies, Milton's epic, Mallory's *Le Morte d'Arthur*, *Beowulf*, *Watership Down*, and Norse myths. Instead of us reading the story as an allegory, *The Book of the Dun Cow* "invites experience," Wangerin writes.[15] It is an event that changes the reader's way of imagining herself in the world.

The novel is set before human beings have been created, so animals rule the created order. Wangerin intended for the protagonist to be the "Community of the Meek," the Rooster Chauntecleer and those creatures near his coop of thirty hens. God grants these simple ones a purpose, though "few of them recognized the full importance of their being, and their being *there*," which is to be "Keepers. The watchers, the guards. They were the last protection against an alarming evil."[16] When a nearby coop invites the evil, a monster deep underground called Wyrm, the evil births new evils, Cockatrice and his basilisks. These perverted creatures destroy that coop, and their evil spreads toward Chauntecleer's Coop. Like the great shadow reaching its hand from Mordor outward in *The Lord of the Rings*, Wyrm's strength grows and threatens to conquer everything good and beautiful in creation. An epic battle between good and evil must be fought by these animals, with the intervening grace of God.

As an animal story, *The Book of the Dun Cow* tempts readers familiar with Aesop's fables to be satisfied with simplistic answers to complex questions. Protestants, trained well by their schooling under John Bunyan, have a tendency to seek one-to-one correlations between their reading and the story's meaning. But Wangerin pushes against readers' predilection to reduce *The Book of the Dun Cow* to an allegory. One cannot conflate Wangerin's protagonist Chauntecleer with the apostle Paul, for instance, though his testimony shares elements of Paul's conversion. As opposed to allegories or didactic writing, such as sermons, which are meant to exposit correlations between images—the lost coin in the parable or the seeds scattered among various soil—novels must be lived within to transform their reader.

Wangerin's predecessors, Tolkien and Lewis, vigorously argued against allegory for one primary reason—it removes freedom from the reader.[17] In Tolkien's foreword to *The Lord of the Rings*, he protests, "I think many confuse applicability with allegory, but the one resides in the freedom of the reader, and the other in the domination of the author."[18] Following this example, Wangerin explains that he intends for his novel to shape the reader's experience with the "internal integrity of *all* the elements of the narrative." "Should I, the author," Wangerin says, "ever state in uncertain terms what my book means, it would cease to be a living thing; it would cease to be the novel it might have been, and would rather become an illustration of some defining, delimiting concept."[19] We learn from the experience of *The Book of the Dun Cow* because the cosmology, characters, and narrative shape our imagination. However, in this discussion, I seek to draw out explicitly some of those implicit lessons.

Like Tolkien and Lewis, Wangerin returns contemporary readers to the sacramental cosmology of the medieval world. *The Book of the Dun Cow* spells out its cosmography:

> For in those days the earth was still fixed in the absolute center of the universe. It had not been cracked loosed from that holy place, to be sent whirling—wild, helpless, and ignorant, among the blind stars. And the sun still travelled around the moored earth. . . . The clouds were still considered to flow at a very great height . . . and God still chose to walk among the clouds, striding, like a man who strides through his garden in the sweet evening.[20]

Although this cosmography does not correlate with our scientific discoveries of the world, Lewis would argue that its smallness, enchantment, and the very presence of God provides its holiness. Within this medieval world we can locate ourselves. Every creature can be perceived on multiple levels of meaning. Implied within Wangerin's description is an alternative, which Chesterton himself questioned as a young atheist: "Is it God's bright house we dwell in or a vault of dark confusion?"[21] As contemporary readers, we may imagine that we live in a futile environment of scientifically explained phenomena, but *The Book of the Dun Cow* invites us into a world where our divine Maker strides through his garden, enjoying its sweetness.

In his afterword, Wangerin defends his cosmography as drawn from medieval sources and from the church when it still lauded the created world as a place of beauty and delight. Wangerin explains, "Medieval cosmologies did more than give me a well-constructed metaphor for the world of my novel; they established a *weltanschauung*, a thematic vision of elemental relationships spiritual, communal, natural: a cosmic order to things."[22] The narrator describes the world in *The Book of the Dun Cow* thus: "The earth had a face, then: smiling blue and green and gold and gentle, or frowning in furious gouts of black thunder. But it was a *face*, and that's where the animals lived."[23] To adopt this way of viewing the world, Wangerin read the sermons of the early church fathers on creation because this material assumes "that the mind and the purpose of the Creator might be read in creation itself."[24] He also read medieval bestiaries and cosmologies.

Although medieval bestiaries are not as common as hymnals in church pews, we should consider bringing them back into vogue. These books read animals spiritually, within the context of Scripture, so that Christians could read the book of nature in ways that taught us to see our Creator by his creation. For instance, in the description of the cock from *The Aberdeen Bestiary*, the anonymous author writes, "When the cock crowed assiduously for the last time, Peter himself, the rock of the Church, washed away his guilt." In this same entry, the author quotes St. Gregory, who says, "The cock gets its understanding . . . so that it can first dispel the night-time hours, then at last utter the cry that awakes, in the same way that a holy preacher first considers the circumstances of his congregation, and only then develops a preaching style suitable for instructing them."[25] Reading the bestiary, we hear layers in nature: the cock that crowed at Peter's denial and a cock like a holy preacher. The entry continues, but we need not go on for the point to be made. Whereas we moderns strip away all meaning apart from the scientifically verifiable, the medieval writers blended all significances—even those that disagreed—to enrich our ways of imagining creation.

The Book of the Dun Cow invites its reader into this prolifically meaningful reality. Although the novel's truth can be felt without a teacher pulling apart all the layers, the experience is hopefully sharpened and thickened when you do. The evil Wyrm caged under the earth draws its form from the *Miðgarðsormr* or "World Serpent" of the Norse myths, the offspring of Loki, god of mischief. We can only imagine what kind of beast the villain would generate. Christians will hear of his serpentine form and his whispered lies and think of the serpent in Genesis. Wangerin extracts the name "Wyrm" from the Old English word for "dragon" found in *Beowulf*. In Tolkien's 1936 lecture on *Beowulf*, he transfigures the pagan figure into "almost a Christian knight" because the evils that Beowulf contends with have been poetically rendered as "inmates of hell," "offspring of Cain," "enemies of mankind."[26] These resonances should be retained when we read Wyrm in *The Book of the Dun Cow*. The evil Wyrm speaks in Latin, roaring repeatedly (almost mechanically) the phrase "*Sum Wyrm . . . sub terra!*"[27] And yet there is some underlying humor, some dark comedy. The repetition of the phrase renders the evil dumb, ignorant of the mighty wisdom, beauty, and power of the God who created the stars as well as the chickens and the mosquitoes. How can this monotoned beast compete with that?

The way that Wangerin presents his world teaches us to read with more depth, and we can apply this practice of reading his novel outward to how we read creation. When Wyrm seduces the old Rooster

Senex to produce Cockatrice, a hen named Pertelote, who later marries Chauntecleer, tells everyone the name Cockatrice rhymes with "hissssss," the same sound the legions of fallen angels produce in Milton's hell.[28] The final battle between Cockatrice and Chauntecleer resembles Beowulf's fight with the dragon. In the medieval bestiaries, Cockatrices could be killed by a rooster's crow or by seeing their own reflection—in other words, by seeing a real rooster. These layers demonize the beast and foreshadow how Cockatrice will die. By raping the flock of hens in Senex's coop, Cockatrice produces thousands of basilisks. Some readers have viewed these basilisks as temptations, and we witness in their overwhelming number the way that, by our participation in evil, sin multiplies into a legion.[29] These basilisks overrun the river, polluting creation, and the animals near the coop are unable to stop it.

Order in the Coop

Before readers witness the source of evil, the novel establishes the order of grace in the circumscribable world of Chauntecleer's Coop. The book does not open with the story of creation, but *in medias res*, like an epic; literally "in the middle" are the first words of the novel. When we meet Chauntecleer, the rooster is a master to be feared but also to be loved. His most significant responsibility is to crow, and for this task he was named "Lord" of the coop. His crows sound like psalms; there are those for thanksgiving and those for lament: "Crows for laughter and crows for grief; a whooping crow for joy, which made joy come alive and dance right there in the Coop; a soft, insinuating crow for shame at which the Hens would hide their heads under their wings."[30] The crows, like the psalms, unite the community. Whether the hens are experiencing joy or shame, the whole group, like the church, expresses those feelings on behalf of one another. In Ecclesiastes, the wisdom author reflects on the various times in life, and the description sounds like that of Chauntecleer's crows:

"a time to weep, and a time to laugh; a time to mourn, and a time to dance" (3:4 NRSV). As though immersing his coop in wisdom literature, Chauntecleer crows to train the passions of his coop. Later, Chauntecleer reflects on the sneakiness of his weasels and how he "catechized" even them into "meekness."[31] By Chauntecleer's crows, the community punctuates its ecclesiastical seasons.

In addition to his emotive crows, Chauntecleer crows to keep time, what the narrator calls "canonical crows." For Christians through much of church history, canonical hours marked the day for prayer, so we can imagine that segment of time as holy. Chauntecleer's canonical crows "told all the world—at least the section of the world over which he was Lord—what time it was, and they blessed the moment in the ears of the hearer. By what blessing? By making the day, and that moment of the day, familiar; by giving it direction and meaning and a proper soul. . . . It was comfort to be able to measure the day and the work in it."[32] As we've seen in other novels, holy figures of the past kept time according to the faith, not by their to-do lists. The creation story in Genesis speaks to this ordering of time and calls it good. The psalmist prays, "Teach us to number our days, that we may gain a heart of wisdom" (Ps. 90:12). In the novel, Chauntecleer's canonical crows maintain peace for his coop.

Chauntecleer's Coop reads like a parable for understanding the "God-wrought world"[33] of Genesis. In the chapter that elucidates the cosmography of the world, God is emphasized as the one who strides among the animals, notices them, lets them be ignorant of their purpose, sends messengers, damns Wyrm to his locked place below, and concludes "that's the way it was, because God had chosen it to be that way."[34] Although the text does not offer an account of creation, all the facts about the world point back to God. More than that, not only have the natural and moral realities been established by God, but the narrator also justifies these observations with no reason other than God's omnipotent authority over creation. Theologian Steven Bouma-Prediger unpacks what we can learn about creation from the Genesis narrative, highlighting the orderliness of creation, its status as "home" for "all living things," a place where "peace is primordial," with Sabbath as the climax.[35] Within the novel, readers will not witness Sabbath until the denouement, yet the opening scenes of *The Book of the Dun Cow* envelop readers in a world described by the revelation of Genesis.

Autonomous Individuals versus Neighbors

Part two of the novel introduces readers to the horrors of the neighboring coop, though neither coop was aware of the existence of the other. The description of this destroyed coop sounds like McCarthy's apocalyptic narrative, illustrating a warning of what can occur if we do not live as a community of the meek: "The wasted land, the shattered society, the bodies dead and festering, were all Wyrm's triumphs."[36] How did such a flourishing creation become a desacralized place? After the unnatural manufacturing of Cockatrice, who murders his father Senex and abandons his corpse to the maggots, the foul smell of Cockatrice infects everything. The beast rules the land like a malevolent dictator, prohibiting the congregating of animals and silencing them. He holds court at Terebinth Oak, a tree known to produce the volatile, pungent oil turpentine. In Scripture, the terebinth tree is connected with idols, heathenism, and sin (Isa. 1:29; 1 Sam. 17:2; Hos. 4:13). Cockatrice relishes the name of the tree, as well as the rotting of Senex's flesh and the terror of the animals around him.

Instead of rooting this enemy from out of their midst, most of the animals succumb to Cockatrice's villainous rule. Like the Israelites in the book of Judges, who each did what was right in their own eyes, at Senex's coop, "Each began to make his own way in the world." The more they keep to themselves, the more each family grows "narrow eyed and suspicious over-against its neighbors." The world sounds similar to those under totalitarian rule, where people fear for their lives, looking over their shoulders for who may be listening and waiting to turn them in for insubordination. The narrator observes that such individualist and divisive behavior, neighbor against neighbor, results in the animals descending "from speech to snarls, barks, roars, and bleated accusations."[37] By not acting as neighbors in their place, these animals mutate into beasts. The warning applies to humans as well: if we live by the so-called dog-eat-dog world, we degenerate into wolves who devour one another.

Only a couple of animals survive this devastation and report it to Chauntecleer, one of whom, Pertelote, he marries. Their marriage is at the center of the community. In opposition to the autonomous division in Senex's coop, Chauntecleer draws all of the creatures together to depend on one another as one family. Chauntecleer knows the interconnectedness of all things and thus the necessity of their unified community. Against the legion of Wyrm, Chauntecleer calls out to his gathered, fellow creatures: "We've got to be as one as we have been one! For he is many."[38] Only their unity can defeat the evil, which seeks to divide, break creatures apart, and destroy the vision of the whole.

As these animals gather together, they grow to understand their interdependence. The ants are needed to build the walls of protection because they can go unseen, and they are strong workers. The weasel family is destined to kill the basilisks. The mosquitoes can travel quickly and act as a communication network between all the animals. And Chauntecleer can crow powerfully as their leader. "Every animal in the yard learned a duty," and "every creature needed desperately every other creature at his side."[39] The animals show readers the truth about the world we live in, each of us called to our own particular role. Chauntecleer observes at the gathering of the "rabbled congregation": "These were every one of them the meek of the earth. They were meek by inheritance."[40] These animals are meek because they know their place within the ordered whole.

If meekness means to be content with one's calling, how much do animals demonstrate this meekness to human beings? An ant who longed to be a bear would cease to do the work of an ant, and our creation would not have as much aerated soil, water drainage, the necessary soil chemistry, or the dispersal of seeds to proliferate plant life. These animals with their varying gifts contributing to the community show us a picture of the metaphor of the body of Christ that Paul describes in his Letter to the Corinthians:

> If the foot would say, "Because I am not a hand, I do not belong to the body," that would not make it any less a part of the body. And if the ear would say, "Because I am not an eye, I do not belong to the body," that would not make it any less a part of the body. If the whole body were an eye, where would the hearing be? If the whole body were hearing, where would the sense of smell be? But as it is, God arranged the members in the body, each one of them, as he chose. If all were a single member, where would the body be? As it is, there are many members, yet one body. (1 Cor. 12:15–20 NRSV)

As I often counsel my sweet children with their differing gifts, they should not wish to be created like so-and-so but rather to celebrate who God has made them to be. When we read in *The Book of the Dun Cow* how each animal devotes their gifts to the community to unify against evil, we experience why such meekness is necessary and how it fits within the created order. Reading the book of nature shows us the interconnectedness of all things, and this novel highlights such interdependence in its narrative of the animal community.

Pertelote's Song and the Music of the Spheres

In an effort to communicate to the creatures the coming evil and the necessity of working together to fight it, Chauntecleer delivers a riveting—but ineffective—sermon. Despite the thousands of animals gathered there and what should sound like a cacophony, complete silence follows his words. Chauntecleer observes that "their ears had been stone."[41] Along with Chauntecleer, readers witness the limitations of didactic prose. As the silence thins, a song breaks forth from his wife Pertelote: "The song was beautiful, a new thing in this place and unexpected. The voice was like a single shaft of cool light through so much gloom."[42] Through her singing, Pertelote expresses the same story and utters the same cause as Chauntecleer, but her song rouses the hearts of the creatures in a better way. "Her ballad hid nothing of their dread," the narrator observes. "But the music itself spoke of faith and certainty; the melody announced the presence of God."[43] The music calms the animals, dissolves their ears of stone, and touches something true within each of them.

Why does music draw these creatures toward a common purpose, and how does this scene teach us to love creation better? Beautiful music that draws up the soul aligns us with the harmony of all creation. The ancients called this "the music of the spheres." Pythagoras thought that the sun, moon, earth, and other planets emit their own hums. Drawing on these ideas, seventeenth-century scientist Johannes Kepler wrote *The Harmony of the World*, arguing that this inaudible music may be perceived by the soul and imitated in human music.[44] In *Only the Lover Sings*, philosopher Josef Pieper describes music as capable of forming people into contemplatives who behold and praise the visible and invisible alike. "In this existential depth of the listener," Pieper writes, "far below the level of expressible judgements, there echoes—in identical immediacy—the same vibration articulated in the audible music."[45] Our souls desire to sing the song the creation sings, and certain music moves us toward that harmony. We have lost this sense that we should attune ourselves to the world's song.

This perception of the world as singing influenced both Tolkien's and Lewis's creation accounts when they imagined how Middle-earth and Narnia came to be. In Tolkien's *The Silmarillion*, God (Ilúvatar) first creates angelic beings called Ainur who sing his thoughts into existence, creating the universe (Eä):

> The voices of the Ainur, like unto harps and lutes, and pipes and trumpets, and viols and organs, and like unto countless choirs singing with words, began to fashion the theme of Ilúvatar to a great music; and

a sound arose of endless interchanging melodies woven in harmony that passed beyond hearing into the depths and into the heights, and the places of the dwelling of Ilúvatar were filled to overflowing, and the music and the echo of the music went out into the Void, and it was not void.[46]

Although there are various singers, the voices weave together to become one. Their songs are endless, connected, and countless, much like the infinite variety of good things in our creation. By depicting creation as fashioned by song, Tolkien highlights the creativity of the Creator. In the words "filled to overflowing," Tolkien stresses the abundance of this music. The gratuitousness of the song points to God's grace.

As friends, Tolkien and Lewis influenced one another in their creative works, and the creation of Narnia in *The Magician's Nephew* showcases a scene similar to that of *The Silmarillion*. From the darkness, "A voice had begun to sing."[47] What begins as one voice becomes many, "more voices than you could possibly count. They were in harmony with it, but far higher up the scale: cold, tingling, silvery voices."[48] These voices are accompanied simultaneously by the creation of stars, and the human observers feel "certain it was the stars themselves who were singing." In response to this beautiful song and its reflecting creation, one observer, a cabby from London, exclaims, "Glory be! . . . I'd ha' been a better man all my life if I'd known there were things like this."[49] The cabby does not notice the irony that our created home is "like this." Witnessing creation firsthand, the cabby notices its beauty for the first time in his life. As readers, we are placed in this moment, that we may return to our reality and listen for its song.

These creation accounts that emphasize the harmony of the world show why Pertelote's song affected the animals as it did. As Chauntecleer listens to her sing, he praises her creator: "O God! Where was there a faith in all the land to match the faith of Pertelote?" She expresses her faith in song, and all creation responds: "The clouds broke; and then the visible sun . . . turned the white Coop golden . . . and all the ears were filled with light and understanding." Pertelote restores the pandemonium of the coop to its harmony with the natural order of things. Rather than applaud the performance of the singer, all the animals recognize that the song comes not only from her voice but also from a source outside of her. As the song ends, "the multitude whispered together one massive word: 'Amen,' as if it were an exhalation from the earth to the spheres. The moment was peaceful and good. In the days to come, Chauntecleer would remember it often and draw strength from it."[50] The primordial peace has been reestablished in a moment, and like the Lord says of his creation repeatedly in Genesis, "It was good." Although the animals are soon to face evil, this memory of how things are meant to be will fortify them in their fight.

Sabbath

To end "happily ever after" would be to tell only a partial truth. Depending on how happiness is defined, it could be to tell a lie. *The Book of the Dun Cow* ends with the evil power defeated by the good creatures; Mundo Cani, like a Christ figure, sacrifices himself to kill Wyrm. But Pertelote accomplishes the final act: "She had been successful. She slept peacefully."[51] Though the sentences refer to literal sleep, figuratively they could be carved into one's tombstone. At the conclusion of good work, one rests in peace. The grand finale of any good story is that the heroes rest. When Augustine says our hearts are restless until they rest in God, he only does so after praising the Lord: "You have made us for yourself, O Lord."[52] Once we fulfill our calling as creatures who praise their Creator, the end is Sabbath.

Scripture reveals this happy ending to us in the first book of the Bible. Genesis tells a story of creation that concludes with Sabbath. By resting, God the Creator prescribes this telos as the proper ending for all his creatures. In *God in Creation*, Jürgen Moltmann corrects humans' "anthropocentric worldview," replacing our mistaken view that humans are the crown of creation with the true crown, the Sabbath. Instead of reading that God, the omnipotent Creator, after six days of creating, was tired out, Moltmann assures us, "On the contrary: the whole work of creation was performed for the sake of sabbath."[53] Sabbath, shalom, peace—these are the purposes of creation, and we demonstrate our love for the Creator by resting, singing, praising, and loving what he has made.

Devotional

From *The Book of the Dun Cow*: "The land, and the time, and the children—these are the Lord's doing! . . . The Lord has permitted you to be what you were born to be. Then bless the Lord—And let the creatures of the Lord say Amen! . . . By the Lord was a land made good! . . . I am a witness! The Lord loves you with an abiding love."[54]

Scripture: "Then the angel showed me the river of the water of life, bright as crystal, cascading from the throne of God and the Lamb, right smack-dab through the middle of this gardened city. On the banks, on both sides of this azure-pure river, grew trees. From seeds sown from the very tree of life, this flourishing forest, well watered and leaf-full. . . . These trees are for life" (Rev. 21–22).[55]

Prayer from the Saints: "The Canticle of the Creatures" by St. Francis of Assisi:

> *Most High, all-powerful, good Lord, yours is the praise, the glory and the honor and every blessing. To you alone, Most High, do they belong, and no one is worthy to speak your name. . . .*
>
> *Praised be you, my Lord, through our Sister, Mother Earth, who sustains us and directs us bringing forth all kinds of fruits and colored flowers and herbs. . . .*

*Blessed are those who endure in peace, for by you, Most High,
they will be crowned. . . . O praise and bless my Lord, thank him
and serve him humbly but grandly!*

Discussion Questions

1. What fears do you have about caring for creation? Why do we hesitate to love the earth in all the small ways available to us?

2. How often during the day do your hands or feet touch bare ground? Do you notice plants, animals, or the skyline? What do you feel or consider when you notice the natural world around you?

3. In *The Book of the Dun Cow*, none of the characters are perfectly good (not to mention, they are not human!). How then can we learn anything about holiness through their example?

4. What aspects of the medieval cosmology might be true—in spite of being empirically false? How does this affect your way of situating yourself in the world?

5. How does keeping the Sabbath align with holiness? Where do you see Sabbath in the Bible and in the novel? How do you guard the Sabbath in your own life?

Further Reading

Wendell Berry, *Jayber Crow*
James David Duncan, *The River Why*
Diane Glancy, *The Reason for Crows: A Story of Kateri Tekakwitha*
Cormac McCarthy, *The Road*

4

Liberating Prophets

> . . . Justice can rise up,
> And hope and history rhyme.
>
> —Seamus Heaney,
> *The Cure at Troy*[1]

AS A YOUNG GIRL, I read *The Diary of Anne Frank* and became obsessed with it. I wanted to record all my thoughts and feelings for posterity. But within a few months of writing in my diary, I realized that I experienced none of the dramatic tension that would make people care about my crush on the neighbor or the fight with my parents. I was dismayed, in a way Anne never would have been, that I was not being called to stand strong against a regime. I worried my writing would only matter if people could hear it against the backdrop of totalitarian evil. My interest in these stories of heroism did not wane with time. In college one night, when all the other freshman girls in my suite dolled themselves up to go out drinking and dancing, I chose to stay in my dorm to finish reading Julia Alvarez's *In the Time of the Butterflies*. The Mirabal sisters in that novel fascinated

me; to me, they were who Anne Frank would have been if she could have grown up and taken on the Nazis. Later I read biographies of Dietrich Bonhoeffer, Thea Bowman, Aleksandr Solzhenitsyn, and other witnesses who refused to be cowed by evil. Their lives made me question, What would I have done if I had been confronted by terrorist powers?

I have discovered that you can answer that question by looking at how you respond to widespread injustice now. Whatever action you have taken when you have seen demonstrations for civil liberties and headlines about egregious crimes against humanity, genocides, innocent victims imprisoned, inequitable legislation, or persecution of your neighbors will show you what you would have done at any other wicked time in our past. Our protests may not even be against large-scale persecution or violent reigns of terror, but perhaps merely against "narcoticized insensibility to human reality," to borrow the language of Walter Brueggemann.[2] We fight against conformity to consumerism, autonomous individualism, satiation by material reality, earthly utopias, immunity to injustice, apathy, ignorance, volitional blindness, and a demonic desire for power that makes us enemies of the gospel. By reading about the lives of those saints who resisted and fought against totalitarian evil, we may be transformed by an imagination set apart from the pervasive consciousness ruling our own current culture.

Prophetic Imagination and the Disinherited

America's great twentieth-century prophet and revolutionary Martin Luther King Jr. used to carry a copy of Howard Thurman's *Jesus and the Disinherited* with him when he traveled. In this scandalizing book, Thurman highlights Jesus's particularity as a youth in occupied Palestine: "The urgent question was what must be the attitude toward Rome."[3] Jesus grew up in a Jewish community under the dominion of the Roman Empire. Thurman summarizes the situation: "Rome was the enemy; Rome symbolized total frustration; Rome was the great barrier to peace of mind. And Rome was everywhere."[4] The situation parallels the life of African Americans in the United States in the 1940s. Thurman writes, "The masses of men live with their backs constantly against the wall. They are the poor, the disinherited, the dispossessed."[5] Christianity was never meant to solidify worldly power; instead, it was to share the grief of those with their backs against the wall. In order to offer an alternative to the Roman imagination, God chose not to become incarnate as an emperor, but he lived and died as one of the disinherited.

In fact, the whole biblical story narrates the travails of the disinherited: Moses frees the Hebrews from under the yoke of Egyptian rule; the Israelites suffer in Babylonian captivity; they submit to Persian authority; they are dominated by Rome. In his 1978 *The Prophetic Imagination*, Protestant theologian Walter Brueggemann explicates the imagination of the biblical prophets and their dissent from the reigning powers of their time to bring forth revelation and to model lives of hope and holiness apart from the worldly despair laid on them by the ruling elite. "The resurrection of Jesus made possible a future for the disinherited," Brueggemann writes. "In the same way, the alternative community of Moses was given a new future by the God who brought freedom for slaves by his powerful word."[6] Brueggemann charts these precursors of Jesus, beginning with Moses, Jeremiah, Isaiah, and Daniel, but he also shows how Jesus Christ fulfills their prophetic blueprint with his ministry.

For Brueggemann, the prophetic imagination counters the ruling culture's way of seeing the world, which he calls "royal consciousness." Within this imagination, one is limited to the *now*, to enslavement to trends, to talk of "production and schedule and market."[7] Think of the Egyptian slave masters driving the Hebrews to build monuments to Egyptian glory, the Soviet Communists imprisoning their own citizens to work, and our current American culture that values a thing by its use, a person by their success, an idea by its market viability, or a work of literature by its relevance. Brueggemann insists that we not align this royal consciousness with any particular political party, by denominational lines, or even with language like "liberals" or "conservatives." He shows the limits of both sides: "Liberals are good at criticism but often have no word of promise to speak; conservatives tend to future well and invite to alternative visions, but a germane criticism by the prophet is not often forthcoming."[8] Instead, those called to resist the ruling social and political myths must submit themselves to "the alternative religion of the freedom of God."[9] We should not subsume political prophets under our banner, for true prophets speak for universal and deep truths, rather than according to temporal sides in our polarized world. Nor should we limit our conceptions of prophets as future-tellers and soothsayers, or as those who revel in conspiracy theories and expose political or corporate powers as counterfeits. The prophetic imagination receives truth from a much higher authority—from the Holy Spirit, who communicates revelation. This ultimate truth frees the prophet from the wearied culture of the dominant imagination.

Although Christians are called, as were the prophets before us, to be set apart from the royal consciousness, merely talking about the need to change will rarely free our imaginations. After all, as Brueggemann points out, "We also are children of the royal consciousness. . . . So, the first question is: how can we have enough freedom to imagine and articulate a real historical newness in our situation?" The imagination is the key. Brueggemann emphasizes the poetry and lyric employed by the prophets: "Poetic imagination is the last way left in which to challenge and conflict the dominant reality. . . . The *imagination* must come before the *implementation*."[10] We must imagine a new narrative and participate in a better story. Through novels, for instance, we vicariously experience an alternative way of seeing the world. With clearer sight of what *is* now and what *ought* to be, we might become actors of change toward realizing that hopeful vision.

Of her intentions for *In the Time of the Butterflies*, Alvarez writes, "I wanted to immerse my readers in an epoch in the life of the Dominican Republic that I believe can only finally be understood by fiction, only finally redeemed by the imagination. A novel is not, after all, a historical document, but a way to travel through the human heart."[11] The novel becomes the locus of transforming the imagination, of participating in the redemptive kingdom. By these stories, we are awakened to more truth and set freer from the reigning consciousness. As a relevant sidenote, Brueggemann reminds us, "Thus every totalitarian regime is frightened of the artist."[12] There is a reason the Nazis burned books and the Communists exiled their writers, for these imaginative prophets challenged the status quo of the false powers.

If we look at two novels written in the twentieth century, Zora Neale Hurston's *Moses, Man of the Mountain* (1939) and Alvarez's *In the Time of the Butterflies* (1994), we read about prophets resisting the royal consciousness, following God's call to help others, and, in the case of the latter, even dying for the sake of others' freedom. Hurston's novel returns readers to the powerful example of Moses from the Bible, and Alvarez's story shows us the ongoing ministry of the Spirit in the world. Both novels are based on real characters in history, a fact that should be convicting and empowering, for we too have access to a Spirit who can aid us in fighting injustice, attending to the poor, and playing roles in the vast story God continues to tell. While Moses prefigures Christ, the Mirabal sisters follow his example. As readers, we should witness these stories and remember them in how we live.

Moses: Precursor of Jesus

Moses is the first prophet called by God to free his people from reigning evil. For too many Christians, the story of Moses and the Hebrews is overly familiar. Brueggemann worries we are "so used to these narratives that we have become insensitive to the radical and revolutionary social reality that emerged because of Moses."[13] However, Moses was an Egyptian prince, perhaps even a general;[14] he exhaled power. Yet he forwent all of the power of Egypt to become an exile. Moses returns to Egypt to free the Hebrews because the Lord intervenes, calling him out of his safe, secure world at home to take "sides with losers and powerless marginal people."[15] How might we reimagine the power of this story so that it becomes real to us, so that it renews our imagination? In Moses, we should see a forerunner of Jesus. His call is our calling: to always look out for the underdog and not be in the rally of the mighty.

In 1939 Hurston published her rendition of the Moses story in a novel titled *Moses, Man of the Mountain*. Hurston was the daughter of a Baptist pastor and knew her Bible well. After achieving literary success with her novels *Their Eyes Were Watching God* and *Jonah's Gourd Vine*, Hurston toiled on this retelling of the Moses story; she spent five long years trying to perfect it. She researched how Black people from Africa, America, and the West Indies read Moses. Among these people "scattered by slavery," Hurston writes in her author's introduction to the novel, "there is acceptance of Moses as the fountain of mystic powers. . . . For he is worshipped as a god."[16] Hurston creates Moses as "a kind of jive godfather," in Andrew Delbanco's words. He describes how Hurston, "with a kind of antic reverence," expropriates "the story of the Jews' redemption under Moses as an exemplum for contemporary black life."[17] Hurston's Moses is a hoodoo priest and a superhero for her Black community to see themselves in and take pride in.

Hurston evaded the world of Jim Crow South but suffered plenty of persecution as a Black woman in a culture that imagined the categories "white" and "male" to be superior. In spite of the racism infecting the royal consciousness of her time, Hurston rejected hate, anger, and the common language of protest employed by her contemporaries, such as Langston Hughes and Richard Wright. In her 1928 essay "How It Feels to Be Colored Me," Hurston deposits slavery and the rest of the tragic timeline behind her: "I am off to a flying start and I must not halt in the stretch to look behind me and weep."[18] Her fiction protests injustice by offering an expansive image, one that shows the universal, timeless nature of prejudice and broadens it beyond the category of race.

In *Moses, Man of the Mountain* the Hebrews in the story, which many read as allegorical to the experience of American slaves, are not dark-skinned but pale with red hair. Moses, as an Egyptian prince, is tanned brown. And it is insinuated by other characters that Jethro and Zipporah are the ones with darker complexions, sharing features associated with African Americans. By her own admission, Hurston did not want to "write about the Race Problem," but she does address her concerns that people create hierarchies between one another, and she questions in her narrative why we decide that some people are better than others.[19] Published at the start of Hitler's Aryan nation-building and his genocide of the Polish people, Hurston's novel ties the racial biases in America with European bigotries, showing that prejudice is not limited to skin color.

Despite exaltation by later writers, such as Alice Walker, who hails *Moses, Man of the Mountain* as "one of the rarest, most important books in black literature,"[20] the book received little praise when it came out and garners even less attention now. Of the novel, Hurston wrote to a friend, "I have the feeling of disappointment about it. I don't think that I achieved all that I set out to do."[21] Hurston wanted to showcase Moses as the powerful conjurer like the one she discovered in Haitian folklore. She wanted to transform people's imaginations from seeing Moses as a white man with a foot-long white beard as Theodore Roberts, the actor from Cecil B. DeMille's 1923 *Ten Commandments*, to envisioning the godlike hero from the cultures that she had surveyed.[22] In the worlds where she encountered Moses, he was a darker-complected, muscular, confident figure who wielded a rod of power and exuded terror from "THAT MIGHTY HAND."[23] Hurston fails in her project to create the Moses that she desires to read because she misses the audacious figure that the Bible shows him to be.

Hurston's novel will trouble readers not only because Moses is such an inconsistent hero, but also, for Christian readers, because

Moses, in this novel, claims power for himself that, in the biblical accounts, comes from God. If, as Brueggemann explains, the royal consciousness controls our imagination so much that we cannot break free from it by ourselves, how did Moses ever conceive to free the Hebrews? Brueggemann writes in awe of the biblical Moses, for his breach with the reigning "social political reality is so radical and inexplicable that it has nothing less than a theological cause."[24] In other words, how would a fish suddenly evolve into a frog? It cannot, but by the grace of God, be prepared to breathe air instead of water. Prophets must receive a counternarrative free from the water they swim in and have become accustomed to. One must encounter a flaming bush and kneel before it on holy ground and accept its death-defying, dangerous command to accomplish the unheard of—free thousands of slaves. By not recognizing the necessity of divine intervention, Hurston creates a character who controls the elements with his bare hands and yet, disconcertingly, fears a fiery shrub.

Seeing and Hearing the Disinherited in the Moses Story

In spite of its artistic and theological faults, *Moses, Man of the Mountain* accomplishes great good for the believer eager to follow in Moses's footsteps, for the novel defamiliarizes the biblical story. Hurston frees the narrative from our domestication of it, breathing new life into it and intensifying its power away from white filmmakers and back into the hands of the disinherited. A few years after this novel, playwright Dorothy L. Sayers adapted the Gospels into a radio play for the BBC called *The Man Born to Be King*, in which she colloquialized characters to sound like British laborers of the 1940s. Similarly, Hurston alters the biblical language of her King James translation that we might hear the voices of the dispossessed within the exodus story. For example, when Moses's purportedly biological father, Amram, laments that his wife might bear a son and that Pharaoh has outlawed sons, his fellow slave responds, "[Pharaoh] aims to keep us down so he'll always have somebody to wipe his feet on. He brags that him and the Egyptian nation is eating high on the hog now."[25] The language echoes the way nineteenth-century African American slaves might have discussed their white masters in America.

Rendering the narrative in this way, Hurston forces us to encounter ourselves in the story, as either protesting or upholding the royal consciousness. While Delbanco accuses Hurston of producing a "Blackface farce"[26] of the exodus story, she found African American dialect delightful and not denigrating. She invites readers to hear the Bible story no longer as belonging to the white church in 1930s America but as belonging to the same folk culture that invented Brer Rabbit tales. Writing *Moses, Man of the Mountain* in the way she did, Hurston frees this universal story from its false owners.

The story begins with the cry of the Hebrews: "Have mercy! Lord, have mercy on my poor soul!"[27] How can critics not read this as a protest novel? In echo of the Psalms, the novel opens with a cry to God on behalf of the dispossessed. Brueggemann points out that the "grieving of Israel . . . is the beginning of criticism. It is made clear that things are not as they should be, not as they were promised, and not as they must and will be."[28] The cries of the Hebrews initiate the dissent from the royal consciousness, and in Hurston's novel, these cries literally birth forth the possibility of a new reality. As Moses's mother, Jochebed, labors with him, she begs her husband not to let her scream, for fear the secret police will confiscate and kill her baby. Hurston describes the birth of Moses amid this fear; the mother and father and dissident midwife Puah must deliver the baby without being discovered. They risk their lives to bring this new life into the world. The scene may remind readers of American slaves who would hide births from their masters so their children would not be owned. Fifty years after Hurston's story, Toni Morrison would write in *Beloved* of a mother who kills her own child so that the baby may never know the denigration and misery of slavery.

Hurston depicts the fear of the Hebrews viscerally. Jochebed claws at her husband in pain, and he muffles her agony with his hand. During labor, Moses's brother Aaron runs into their home to report that the Egyptian soldiers just killed the neighbors nearby—including the baby, the father who tried to protect him, and the mother—for an illegal birth. At hearing this news, those in Moses's house "all swam in silence in the room. . . . Then suddenly Jochebed clenched her fists and groaned like the earth birthing mountains, and the body and feel of the sound threatened them like a sword until the cry of the newborn baby ended it all."[29] From silence to agony, Hurston charts the descent among the Hebrews from complacency with their plight to protest. This protest comes to fruition with the birth of Moses.

While Moses observes accurately the problem of Pharaoh's mistreatment of the Hebrews, his solution—killing an Egyptian (Exod. 2:11–15)—does little more than incite fear in the Hebrews.[30] As theologian Esau McCaulley points out, "Moses had properly diagnosed the problem of Israel's slavery, but this solution was ill conceived."[31] In the novel, Hurston writes this murder as a catalyst in Moses's new feelings toward the Hebrews: "He found a new sympathy for the oppressed of all mankind. He lost his taste for war," for "the fanfare and flattery of the court . . . had lost its glamor."[32] Previously Pharaoh assured Moses, "Egypt has no home problems that I can see."[33]

Following Moses's intervention to save the Hebrews from the overbearing foreman, he can no longer see with Pharaoh's eyes. Moses says "to the glory of struggle and victory, 'Go away, honey, you have lost your sweetness.'"[34] The royal consciousness no longer seduces Moses. Of his decision to abrogate his power, Moses confesses to his steward, "I feel the cursing thought of the law and power. I had always felt the beneficence of law and power and never stopped to consider that it had any other side. It is a sword with two edges."[35] Moses has been awakened to a wider perspective than the overriding narrative. To stay in power would be to accept the privileges of the unjust laws in Egypt.

Although God takes a back seat in Hurston's narrative (even underwhelming in her presentation), she seems unable to keep out the prefiguring of Jesus. When Hurston depicts God, he is hardly more than a bossy voice in a fiery bush. Yet after Aaron and the people forge the golden calf, Moses stands "like a crucifix," crying, "Who is on the Lord's side? Who is on the Lord's side?"[36] In the New Testament, Matthew evokes Moses's typology for writing his account of the life of Jesus. Of course, Matthew's audience is Jewish, so he is trying to show the fulfillment of the prophecies of Scripture. Like Moses, Jesus is born under the threat of death: Herod establishes a law to kill all infants under two years old in the hopes of slaying this alternate king. Similar to Moses, Jesus flees the ruling power. He fasts forty days, as did Moses. They both ascend mountains to bring the law to the people. Brueggemann describes the "Matthean presentation of [Jesus's] abrasive conflict with the powers that be," which points "to the emergence of an alternative consciousness."[37] If we gather the evidence from all the prophets and psalms and from Mary's Magnificat, we recognize how the Scriptures foretell a Messiah who would, as Moses did, free the enslaved from captivity. When Hurston lures us into the Moses account, she is pointing toward Jesus Christ, who will finally and forever liberate his people from unjust oppression.

Internal Liberation

Moses, Man of the Mountain concludes with a strange digression from the biblical story. Without an authoritative God in her novel, Hurston cannot concede to the account in Numbers 20:2–13, in which God forbids Moses from entering Canaan. So Moses must decide to leave the Israelites on his own, an unsatisfactory ending for readers that reinforces, by contrast, the aesthetic—not to mention theological—merits of the Torah. Moses sits atop a mountain overlooking the gathered people that he has attempted to lead to freedom. The scene adopts weightier significance if one imagines Hurston herself surveying her fellow African Americans: "He had meant to make a perfect people, free and just, noble and strong, that should be a light for all the world and for time and eternity. . . . He had found out that no man may make another free. Freedom was something internal. . . . All you could do was to give the opportunity for freedom and the man himself must make his own emancipation."[38] Although Moses freed the Hebrews from the chains of the Egyptians, the people still acted enslaved as they wandered in the desert. Hurston heard in the grumblings and complaints of the Israelites similar laments to those of her generation. Moses learns what his author learned about freedom, that it is an internal state.

In *Jesus and the Disinherited*, Howard Thurman stresses this internal liberation by examining the life and teachings of Jesus. "His words were directed to the House of Israel," Thurman writes, "a minority within the Greco-Roman world, smarting under the loss of status, freedom, and autonomy, haunted by the dream of restoration of a lost glory and a former greatness."[39] Thurman's description of the oppressed Jews parallels that of 1940s African Americans. He says as much explicitly: "The striking similarity between the social position of Jesus in Palestine and that of the vast majority of American Negroes is obvious to anyone who tarries long over the facts."[40] What does Jesus say to the oppressed from his position alongside them, suffering their same plight? "His message focused on the urgency of a radical change in the inner attitude of the people," Thurman writes. "He recognized that out of the heart are the issues of life and that no external force, however great and overwhelming, can at long last destroy a people if it does not first win the victory of the spirit against them." Thurman repeatedly underlines Jesus's message of internal liberation: "to the inner life of the individual" and "the inward center as the crucial arena."[41] Thurman's interpretation of Jesus's good news for the subjugated reiterates the wisdom of Hurston's Moses at the end of her novel, for both are speaking to the same readers— disinherited African Americans of the 1940s.

As a daughter of a Baptist preacher, Hurston grew up listening to the call and response characteristic of Black preaching. A common refrain was the question, "Can I get a witness?" Her novel asks such a question of its readers. Although twenty-first-century readers of Hurston's novel may interpret Moses as an Egyptian Hulk who parts the Red Sea with the strength of his oversized biceps, she envisions the strength of spirit within each person to be greater than what society renders them. She hopes readers witness a figure who defies the external restraints of the royal consciousness; she desires Moses to be an emblem of freedom for the dispossessed. While Hurston may have failed in her delivery of this hope, the biblical story of Moses does not, and her novel reacquaints us with that true word. In the Scriptures, Moses is empowered by the Spirit who comes and goes from his life, but for all of us born into this time after Pentecost, we have access always to the freedom of that same powerful and holy Spirit. And this truth sets us free to witness.

Waking Up and Woke

When Brueggemann explains how Jesus's ministry in the world fulfills the prophetic imagination that began with Moses, he describes how the Matthean Gospel emphasizes Jesus's confrontation with ruling powers and how the Lucan narrative highlights Jesus's compassion for the poor. As a Roman Catholic, Julia Alvarez writes *In the Time of the Butterflies* with that particular imagination of the world: the Mirabal sisters emblematize saints for readers in the way that they imitate Christ's prophetic example. In an interview with Alvarez, journalist Lauren LeBlanc ties the Mirabal sisters to Joan of Arc: "I saw Las Mariposas within a long line of women working against all odds to affect change. The struggle is universal; Alvarez links the history of Latin America to that larger narrative."[42] As these sisters fight against the unjust rule of General Trujillo (1930–61) so that the poor and disenfranchised in the Dominican Republic may live in freedom, they become examples of holy protest.

By experiencing their lives in this story, readers reflect on how they too might become Mirabals within their current times and places.

The starting place is awakening to the injustice around you. Before my husband married me, he had never before considered the ways women might suffer unequal treatment. However, after hearing my stories and witnessing how people treated me unfairly in several different jobs, my husband began to see the problem for himself. When a woman at his work was demoted because her subordinates did not think she smiled enough as their boss, my husband stepped in. He hired her to be a manager under him because he saw her skills as a leader. Instead of placing false expectations on her—to be always smiling and nurturing—my husband let her lead as she felt free to. In what ways might we need to wake up to envision more clearly the problems around us?

In the twenty-first century, the word "woke" refers to an awareness of injustice and its contagiousness within society. In his 1854 book *Walden*, Henry David Thoreau writes of waking up "to a poetic or divine life. To be awake is to be alive."[43] With humility, Thoreau admits he has never met someone so awake, but that waking up is a lifelong endeavor. In contrast to his depiction of waking up, which assumes there is always more to be awakened to, the word "woke" may assume a one-time waking that has occurred past tense. It sounds more like Plato's analogy of the cave: once a person awakens to the knowledge that the shadows on the walls are not the reality itself, she can never return to the darkness. Or like the film *The Matrix* (1999), which depicts a character waking up to all of reality being a technological hoax. One must wake up to the knowledge of what's real. Do we wake up once or many times over? Whichever is true, the awakening process means that you cannot return to former blindness and darkness. You cannot unknow what you have learned about the world.

In Plato, Thoreau, and these other stories of awakening, who reveals the truth? Who shows the person in the cave the way out? What draws Thoreau from being a laborer among many to living alone by a lake? Hurston's Moses transitions from Egyptian general acquiring power to the uplifter of the oppressed, without God as the source for his revelation. In the biblical story, God reveals his identity to Moses and calls him. Angels descend to Jacob or speak to the prophets or reveal the threat of Herod to Joseph and Mary. In Alvarez's novel, she pulls back the curtain to identify God as the one who reveals the needs of the disinherited to the Mirabal sisters. In contrast to Hurston's narrative, where Moses acts on his own power and authority, in Alvarez's novel God answers the people's prayers for liberation.

Patria is the oldest and most religious of the four Mirabal sisters. Although she does not enlist in the revolution as quickly as do Minerva and the youngest, María Teresa, her eyes are open to the distress in her country early in the novel. When the four sisters accompany their mother on a pilgrimage to a site where someone spotted the Virgin Mary, Patria arrives with a deep emptiness. She has recently undergone a stillbirth and has been disguising how this suffering has affected her faith. When the five women approach the Virgencita's image, Patria mocks the "locked case smudged with fingerprints from pilgrims touching the glass. . . . The whole thing looked gaudy and insincere." Then Patria turns around and sees "packed pews, hundreds of weary, upturned faces," and she says, "It was as if I'd been facing the wrong way all my life." Patria reflects, "My faith stirred. It kicked and somersaulted in my belly, coming alive."[44] The stirring in her gut acts like a new life to replace the one she has lost; something dead in her has come to life; something asleep has awakened.

Patria experiences compassion for these people in her very core. Her experience recalls the Greek word for compassion, *splanchnizomai*, which Brueggemann translates as letting "one's innards embrace the feeling or situation of another."[45] This rousing by the Spirit compels Patria to pray. She touches the dirty glass and challenges the Virgin to appear, as she supposedly had done previously in that spot. Patria asks, "Here I am, Virgencita. Where are you?" The answer comes not from the figurine within the glass but from "the coughs and cries and whispers of the crowd." The Virgin answers Patria, calling her by name: "*Here, Patria Mercedes, I'm here, all around you. I've already more than appeared.*"[46] In this moment where Patria hears the Virgin speak from the suffering of the pilgrims surrounding her, she awakens to seeing Christ in the disinherited.

The other three sisters wake up as they encounter knowledge of the president's misdeeds. Minerva will be the first "butterfly," the symbol of hope for the Dominican people. Both Minerva and Dedé befriend a man named Lío, who is soon revealed to be a revolutionary. Minerva says of the encounter, "When I met Lío, it was as if I woke up. The givens, all I'd been taught, fell away like so many covers when you sit up in bed."[47] Minerva had been taught to accept Trujillo as the equal authority with God; "El Jefe's" portrait hung equal with a picture of the Good Shepherd in her home, not from admiration but out of fear of the tyrant's power. For María Teresa, whose thoughts are conveyed by her diary entries, she learns from her older sister Minerva that they do not live in a "free country," as she had assumed. "It is so strange now I know something I'm not supposed to know. Everything looks a little different," María Teresa writes in her diary. "Before, I always thought our president was like God, watching over everything I did."[48] Like Minerva and María Teresa, Dedé realizes that the regime is unjust and irrational in its demands on the citizens: "The regime was going insane, issuing the most ludicrous regulations. A heavy fine was now imposed on anyone who wore khaki trousers and shirts of the same color. It was against the law to carry your suit jacket over your arm."[49] Similar to her sisters, she experiences a feeling of waking up—"How could she have missed so much before? But then a harder question followed: What was she going to do about it now that she did know?"[50] This is the question that the book asks readers: How will you choose to act once you have woken up?

Following a Crucified God

Patria becomes the most saintlike in her participation in the liberation movement. From the moment of her awakening, Patria must, she says, "get down on my knees to know my own mind."[51] She prays repeatedly throughout the novel. While at a church retreat, the site where Patria sits is bombed. This scene takes place on June 14, 1959, the day Trujillo squashed a cell of rebels in the mountains with his army and air force. As they flee to safety, Patria watches a young boy run toward her. She screams, "Get down, son! Get down," as though the boy is her child. Just as their eyes meet, a bullet hits him in the back. Patria cries as she recalls, "I saw wonder on his young face as the life drained out of him, and I thought, Oh my God, he's one of mine!"[52] In that instant, she becomes an avenging angel, as do many of the priests who had formerly hidden in the church in their attempt to refrain from politics.

Like many Christians who fear muddling the City of God with the City of Man, the Catholic Church in that province hesitates to join the revolution. Only after the priests witness the loss of innocent life do they declare defensive war against the regime: "The time was now, for the Lord had said, I come with a sword as well as the plow to set at liberty them that are bruised."[53] The Lord liberates the disinherited, and he calls on his saints to follow his charge. As a priest wipes clean his glasses during his meeting with Patria, she realizes they both now enjoy a clear vision of their vocation in the revolution. When Patria joins the underground resistance, she prays repeatedly, "God help us."[54] They all foresee that to enter the fight likely means they will lose their life. After all, God himself said that following Jesus meant going to the cross: "Whoever finds his life will lose it, and whoever loses his life for my sake will find it" (Matt. 10:39 ESV). These revolutionaries trusted their calling not to a worldly president nor to an earthly general but to a God crucified as a criminal.

Patria embodies this calling most strongly in her response to the liberation movement. Although the three sisters fight and suffer and die, Patria alone explicitly imagines her struggle as participation in the Lord's suffering. Patria speaks personally of her knowledge of the cross: "my cross became bearable," "my crown of thorns was woven of thoughts of my boy," who has been arrested and detained by the unmerciful dictator.[55] "The cross is the assurance that effective prophetic criticism is done not by an outsider but always by one who must embrace the grief, enter into the death, and know the pain of the criticized one," Brueggemann tells us.[56] As Patria attempts to endure the imprisonment of her husband, son, and sisters, she repeats five times to herself the refrain from the creed, "On the third day he rose again." She must keep before her not only the crucifixion but also the resurrection. Before the icons and with rosary in hand, Patria regularly prays. The crucified Jesus strengthens her and confers on her the spiritual resources to overcome the torture inflicted by Trujillo. When Patria begs for intercession from one of Trujillo's stooges, Captain Peña, she prays, "*Soften his devil's heart, Oh Lord.* And then I said the difficult thing, *For he too is one of your children.*"[57] Patria sees with the Lord's eyes that the Lord's children, such as the boy who was shot, are not the only victims; she imagines her enemies also as victims of the abuses of power.

María Teresa experiences a parallel revelation during her confinement in Trujillo's brutal prisons. Although she is carried screaming away from her daughter and suffers the worst possible indignities during her time there, María Teresa learns more about human nature in those few months of imprisonment than readers behold in her other years of diary entries. When she connects with the women incarcerated with her, those prostitutes and criminals and others in a lower class than herself, she wonders "about the real connection between people. Is it our religion, the color of our skin, the money in our pockets? . . . There *is* something deeper."[58] María Teresa discovers that "what matters is the quality of a person. What someone is inside themselves."[59] Not only suffering but also their shared revolt against the regime equalizes those women in the prison cell. As much as the regime tries to dehumanize her, María Teresa turns to courage, community, and charity. In her diary, María Teresa (Mate is her nickname) writes,

> You think you're going to crack any day, but the strange thing is that
> every day you surprise yourself by pulling it off, and suddenly you start

feeling stronger, like maybe you are going to make it through this hell with some dignity, some courage, and most important—never forget this Mate—with some love still in your heart for the men who have done this to you.[60]

She reminds herself to retain that love for the enemy, the same inexplicable, difficult love that Patria expressed to Captain Peña. It is the love that Jesus calls from his cross for his persecutors when he asks his Father to forgive those who are crucifying him (Luke 23:34).

Death Brings Forth Life

For suffering servants, as we will later see is the case with characters from Graham Greene's novels (chap. 7), death to self produces fruit in those who knew the saint. While Dedé (because of an abusive spouse) is prevented from joining her sisters, their sacrifice changes her. After Minerva is released from prison, she must travel to her former home and clean it out for the government to repossess it. On the way, Dedé and Minerva are stopped by guards who request their identity. Without hesitation, Dedé positions Minerva behind her and says, "My name is Minerva Mirabal."[61] No matter what repercussions may follow this lie, Dedé has learned courage from her sister. So, too, in prison, fear initially causes María Teresa to cower on the cell floor like a wounded animal. Yet when the guards force her sister Minerva into solitary confinement, the adjoining cells thunder, "*Viva la mariposa.*" As the shouts ring out, María Teresa recognizes, "Something big and powerful spread its wings inside me. Courage, I told myself. And this time, I felt it."[62] The sisters' courage inspires virtue in those around them.

After the three sisters are murdered by the government, Dedé must recover the bodies and transport them home for burial. As they pass through towns with Dedé sitting in the bed of the truck, clinging to their coffins, she watches as "men took off their hats, the women made

the sign of the cross . . . threw flowers into the bed [of the truck]."
Even their deaths inspire people to liberation. When they pass the
Servicio de Inteligencia Militar post, Dedé accuses the government
officials: "Assassins! Assassins!" Her husband Jaimito drowns out her
cries by gunning the motor. He reminds her, "This is *your* martyrdom,
Dedé, to be alive without them."[63] As the people mourn the sisters
and lift up their example, they persist more vigilantly in the cause
for liberation. Finally, one year after the martyrdom of the Mirabal
sisters, the people assassinate Trujillo.

Every time I read the novel, I weep with Dedé as she returns those
bodies—to imagine the children left without their mothers, the youth
of those murdered sisters, their fear in the face of death. The novel
also leaves out many questions that we may want answered after we
close the book: Was the June Fourteenth Movement justified in plan-
ning the death of their government leader? How can they pray and
love their enemies while also plotting their death? Howard Thurman
advocates violent resistance only as a last resort, but Dietrich Bonhoeffer died as a criminal after his failed attempt to assassinate Hitler.
Whose example do we imitate? While the Mirabal sisters followed
Jesus Christ by suffering martyrdom, in the Gospels, Jesus rejects the
Israelites' demand that he be the second Judas Maccabeus and lead
a revolt against Rome. Christians have wrestled with these dilem-
mas for centuries, and, in her novel, Alvarez does not attempt a pat
answer to the question. Rather, the story reminds us that following
the Gospels means reinterpreting the story and teaching of Jesus
within our own particular time and place. We worship a scandalously particular God.

The Call to Witness

After the girls are murdered by their government, their surviving sister, Dedé, questions their sacrifice, as any of us with personal losses
might. "What was it all for?" Dedé wonders, "the sacrifice of the

butterflies." She runs into a friend who knew the girls before the revolution, who credits their death with "free elections . . . our country beginning to prosper," but Dedé sees "bad presidents not put in power properly . . . the coast a clutter of clubs and resorts. We are now the playground of the Caribbean." The sisters protested Trujillo's bloody reign in the hope that their children would grow up in a free country, but Dedé frets that such freedom was only used for entertainment, "boy-businessmen with computerized watches" and "glamourous young wives with degrees they do not need."[64] Perhaps some Americans feel similarly on Memorial Day, when we remember the deaths of those who fought for this country's freedom. To what have we dedicated our freedom?

In a 1967 essay, Alice Walker asked a similar question about a revolution on American soil: "The Civil Rights Movement: What Good Was It?" She answers differently than the character Dedé but more aligned with how Alvarez might defend her reasons for writing the novel. Walker recalls watching Dr. King on television years before: "What Dr. King promised was not a ranch-style house and an acre of manicured lawn for every black man, but jail and finally freedom. He did not promise two cars for every family, but the courage one day for all families everywhere to walk without shame and unafraid on their own feet."[65] Prosperity was not the point. Material success means nothing if we are not free human beings. For Walker, cars and television are not signs of the civil rights movement's progress. Rather, the movement "awakened" her: "I fought harder for my life . . . than I had ever done in my life. . . . Now there was a chance at that other [bread] that Jesus meant when He said we could not live by bread alone."[66] Walker dismisses the life satisfied by bread that dissolves or is spent for the greater bread of freedom.

At the end of her essay, Walker repeats her question and answers it:

What good was the Civil Rights Movement? If it had just given this country Dr. King, a leader of conscience, for once in our lifetime, it would have been enough. If it had just taken black eyes off white television stories, it would have been enough. If it had fed one starving child, it would have been enough. . . . It gave us heroes, selfless men of courage and strength, for our little boys and girls to follow. It gave us hope for tomorrow. It called us to life.[67]

Similarly, Alvarez tells the story of the Mirabal sisters to show us heroes, selfless women of bravery and tenacity, for all of us to emulate. Their story reflects future hope. All of these great witnesses protest the cultural lies and awaken us to a freer existence.

In the 1970s in Argentina, during the "Dirty War" between the government and perceived subversives, Jorge Mario Bergoglio helped many people flee from the authorities to safety. Thirty years later, that revolutionary would be named pope of the Roman Catholic Church. On April 7, 2021, Pope Francis (formerly Jorge Mario Bergoglio) addressed the church about what it means to be a witness. "A saint is a witness," he said, one who has encountered Jesus and follows him. Witnesses need the examples of those who have completed the "human adventure" before them. Pope Francis describes how the prayers in the Bible show "traces of ancient stories, of prodigious liberations, of deportations and sad exiles, of emotional returns, of praise ringing out before the wonders of creation. . . . And thus, these voices are passed on from generation to generation, in a continual intertwining between personal experience and that of the people and the humanity to which we belong."[68] When Mary accepts the offering of God to bless her with Jesus, her Magnificat calls forth over a dozen lines from the voices of those saints who preceded her. Her response, "Here I am," echoes the examples of the faithful whose stories she knew by heart and remembered in that moment. The stories of those who prefigured and imitated Jesus—Moses, the prophets, Mary, the saints, and other heroes like the Mirabal sisters and Pope Francis—provide us with a company, a fellowship with whom to renew our imaginations. They furnish us with the courage we need to face injustice—and, against all earthly models, the saints remind us how to love our enemies.

"What is that thing that gringos say," Dedé Mirabal asks a friend, "if you don't study your history, you are going to repeat it?" Even thirty years after her sisters' deaths, she lives in the same home they shared surrounded by tangible memories of their lives, and she would rather die than move elsewhere and start over. "After the fighting was over," Dedé says, answering her own question, "we needed a story to understand what had happened to us."[69] Dedé's martyrdom was to survive her sisters' deaths, but her gift was to tell their story. And Alvarez's gift was to write it down. These authors are witnessing to those lives and stories that should never have been forgotten; our gift should be to pass it on—that those truths will not be lost. Our holiness depends on it.

Devotional

From *Moses, Man of the Mountain*: "'This freedom is a funny thing,' [Moses] told them. 'It ain't something permanent like rocks and hills. It's like manna; you just got to keep on gathering it fresh every day. If you don't, one day you're going to find you ain't got none no more.'"[70]

Scripture: "Then the King will say to those on his right, 'Come, you who are blessed by my Father; take your inheritance, the kingdom prepared for you since the creation of the world. For I was hungry and you gave me something to eat, I was thirsty and you gave me something to drink, I was a stranger and you invited me in, I needed clothes and you clothed me, I was sick and you looked after me, I was in prison and you came to visit me. . . . Truly I tell you, whatever you did for one of the least of these brothers and sisters of mine, you did for me'" (Matt. 25:34–36, 40).

Wisdom from the Saints: Fannie Lou Hamer: "The truth is the only thing going to free us. And you know this whole society is sick. . . . There's so much hypocrisy in this society and if we want America to be a free society we have to stop telling lies, that's all. Because we're not free and you know we're not free. . . . And it's time for every American citizen to wake up."[71]

Prayer: In your mercy, Lord, hear our prayer: for the disinherited, the dispossessed, and the disenfranchised. If we are among them, set us free; if we have contributed to the problem, enlighten us and change our hearts. Liberate us as you liberated the Hebrews from the Egyptians and all peoples from the power of sin. May we in turn participate in your liberation, having the courage to speak the truth with grace and authority, that all people everywhere may know your eternal freedom.

Discussion Questions

1. How has the Bible modeled for us the prophetic imagination that we need in order to be free from the influences of the world?

2. In these novels, what blind spots keep characters from seeing corrupt systems of power? How can we locate those blinders in our own culture?

3. Who are the disinherited in these novels? What features do they share? Where do we see the disinherited in our culture?

4. What spiritual practice thickened these saints against the corrupting influence of power?

5. What virtues are needed to act as prophets, witnesses, and revolutionaries on God's side within a particular culture?

Further Reading

Ray Bradbury, *Fahrenheit 451*
Octavia Butler, *Kindred*
Toni Morrison, *Beloved*
Aleksandr Solzhenitsyn, *The Gulag Archipelago*

5

Virgin, Bride, Mother

Women's bodies, heavy with children, dragged down by children, are a weight like a cross to be carried about. . . . This path of pain is woman's lot. It is her glory and her salvation.

—Dorothy Day, *On Pilgrimage*[1]

HAVING BEEN RAISED in an evangelical church, I was taught that motherhood was the fulfillment of my life. My biology determined my calling. I fought this imposition for decades. As much as I wanted to be a mother, I had other gifts that I felt God had granted me. From the time I could form letters, I could write well. When I spoke publicly at school and in Sunday school, I discovered I had the ability to capture audiences with what I learned about history or the Word of God. When I read about the Holy Spirit's distribution of spiritual gifts in 1 Corinthians 12, I recognized myself as a teacher. I attended college not to get the "MRS" degree that many evangelical women have been trained to desire, but to study great books, theology, and the craft of creative writing.

Over and over again, I heard from well-meaning Christians that my theology degree would prepare me to be a suitable pastor's wife. I cringed when young men—who had no spiritual gift for teaching—were compelled to practice preaching for the congregation: fixed gender roles proved to be as problematic for those males as it was for me. When my husband and I discovered during the ultrasound of our first child that she was a girl, I cried uncontrollably. I knew she faced a life in which people would tell her all the things she couldn't do. I feared she would suffer from eating disorders as I had, struggling to be the body that culture would reduce her to. I knew she would have to strive to show people she is more than an object. I wanted her to be known in her full humanity, as an embodied soul filled with the Holy Spirit.

The knowledge of my daughter's sex brought to the surface all the anger I had suppressed regarding the church's constraints on my calling, and I have spent nearly a decade reading books from all Christian traditions about women in leadership, women in the Bible, women in the history of the church. From medieval writers such as Julian of Norwich to modern ones such as Sigrid Undset, I have learned that the dichotomy between working and mothering is false. When we impose this false division, we force women to choose: either they can be a career woman who hands over the job of raising her children to others—or worse, who sacrifices her unborn to avoid the inconvenience it would cause in her work—or they can limit their world to the domestic sphere, dedicating all their time, energy, and emotion to their children while the other gifts and talents the Lord gave them lie fallow. In her 1912 reflections on the suffragette movement, Undset writes, "I have no doubt that women find fulfillment in their work . . . even if they have also been wives and mothers."[2] The false either/or neglects the fullness of a woman.

In Christian circles, we mistakenly view motherhood as the source of a woman's salvation. Paul's comment in his First Letter to Timothy, "She will be saved through childbearing" (1 Tim. 2:15 ESV), has been quoted out of context and pitted against his comments in his First Letter to the Corinthians where he argues that gifts will be distributed by the Holy Spirit and not limited by gender. These misinterpretations have compelled us to idealize the vocation of motherhood in a way that does not fit Scripture. Of the four potential interpretations of 1 Timothy 2:15, the most cogent one relates to the dangers that women in the ancient world faced in childbirth. In the context of the verse, Paul is discussing Genesis 3 and the curse: "A woman will be brought safely through childbirth," Paul assures his listeners, "if they [husband and wife] abide in faith and love and holiness with self-respect."[3] As Cynthia Westfall argues in *Paul and Gender*, "Paul understood the threat that childbirth posed for women, and he used it as a paradigm for people who needed to be rescued."[4] Read typologically, this claim about women as mothers refers more to God's rescue of the church than to any connection between childbearing and soteriology.

However, to reject the all-encompassing nature of motherhood as a woman's compulsory vocation should not reduce the beauty and uniqueness of the privilege of motherhood. Unfortunately, many of the writings on the beauty of motherhood romanticize it until the woman herself has faded away into an abstract ideal. These writers leave no room for the complexity of a woman, the various stages of her life, and the multiplicity of talents and desires she possesses. Just as a man will devote time to being a father while also giving himself to his work, so too might a mother dote on her children and rejoice in the gifts of pregnancy, delivery, and breastfeeding, while also creating art, teaching students, balancing budgets for organizations, running companies, or writing books.

Looking back on my days as a single woman, I devoted more time to being with God than I am always able to find in my days with small children. I used to be able to listen to worship music without being asked to turn on "Baby Shark" again. As a young bride, I relished in my husband's undivided attention. We could talk for hours without interruption, go on long runs together, and travel at a moment's impulse. As a mother, though, I have been grateful for the ways my kids renew my wonder for the world, their desire for me when I nursed them, their sweet prayers at night and soft voices when we sing good night to each other. Singleness, marriage, and motherhood have all been blessings, vocations as significant as any of my teaching, writing, or speaking has been.

More significantly—most significantly—a woman's primary call is not to be a mother but to be a Christian, come what may in her life. The Lord will call a woman to offer gifts as virgin, bride, and mother, so that we may learn more about what it means to follow Christ. In this sense, the uniqueness of a woman provides a fuller picture of who God is and what holiness may look like. In her novel *Kristin Lavransdatter*, Sigrid Undset, who was awarded the Nobel Prize in Literature, depicts a saint-in-progress whose role as mother reveals much about holiness and the character of God.

Women and Holiness

Sigrid Undset (1882–1949) is an underappreciated novelist who deserves a greater following, especially in Christian circles. While she has a steady readership with Christian pastors and academics, there is nothing about her fiction that demands an advanced degree. Her stories are readable and relatable. I read the *Kristin Lavransdatter* trilogy (1920–22) for the first time when I was twenty-one, and even though I had a poor translation of it, I could not put it down. I stayed up night after night over the Christmas holidays relishing the saga of her life. The story, set in fourteenth-century Norway, felt as close and real as my own. Undset had desired for decades to write a medieval story; her first attempt was rejected by publishers who recommended she write contemporary fiction. She wrote a handful of novels in this vein and became established as a novelist, but it was not until she returned to her love for the Middle Ages, with *Kristin Lavransdatter* and *The Master of Hestviken*, that she received the Nobel Prize.

For those of us who were miseducated about the Middle Ages, we might think it a strange setting for the exaltation of women. However, some of the most beautiful writings about God as a laboring woman, as a lactating nurse, and as our mother come from this period of church history. After Flannery O'Connor read *Kristin Lavransdatter*, she inquired of a friend, "Do you think she [Undset] could have done it without returning to the [fourteenth] century?"[5] Probably not, for the world of *Kristin Lavransdatter* is imbued with divine desire, the maternal imagery that saturated the medieval church, and a devotion to Mary long removed from the twentieth-century Lutheran Church in Norway. Undset was compelled to situate Kristin's story of sanctification in history because those feminine images of God have been largely erased from our contemporary imagination and may sound not only alien but heretical to American evangelicals. Theologian Natalie Carnes notes how, in the contemporary church, "women and children have remained largely absent from talk of divinity and humanity. But what if their lives were taken as significant sites for theological work?"[6] What might the lives of women teach us about holiness? To answer this question, Undset—once a wife but then divorced, a mother of three children, and adoptive mother of three others—decided to travel back in time. Perhaps by following her journey, we may find a way forward.

Catholic thinker Gertrud von Le Fort writes in 1934 that woman as differentiated from man should be considered symbolically as virgin, bride, and mother—three categories drawn from the example of Mary the mother of Jesus and that are used throughout Scripture to understand the relationship between God and his people, between Christ and the church. *Kristin Lavransdatter* is a trilogy whose three volumes align somewhat with those categories. The first volume, *The Wreath*, depicts Kristin's life as a virgin, for a wreath is worn by maidens and later replaced by a bridal wreath. By the end of this first volume, Kristin marries her chosen spouse, Erlend Nikulaussøn, with whom she has committed grievous sins and whose child she bears even on her wedding day. Volume 2 is called *The Wife* but could also be titled *The Mother*, for Kristin births eight children over the course of this second volume as she struggles with her tempestuous and unreliable husband. Finally, in the third volume, *The Cross*, Undset reimagines these roles as they participate in the cruciform life; we watch Kristin relinquish everything for Christ's sake, dedicating herself as a young widow to a convent and becoming a mother to the motherless in the world.

Over the course of her life—and for readers, from the beginning to the end of the novel—Kristin endures a divided will. She reflects, "Surely, she had never asked God for anything except that He should let her have her will. And every time she had been granted what she asked for . . . she was unhappy that she had been allowed to follow her will to the road's end."[7] Kristin experiences contrition when she realizes that she has brought herself to this place of unhappiness by insisting on her will against God's. As St. Paul writes in his Letter to the Romans: "For I do not do what I want, but I do the very thing I hate. . . . For I have the desire to do what is right, but not the ability to carry it out. For I do not do the good I want, but the evil I do not want is what I keep on doing" (Rom. 7:15, 18–19 ESV). We all struggle with the competing desires that Paul expresses. As the holiest character in the novel, Brother Edvin, explains to Kristin: "It's because our hearts are divided between love for God and fear of the Devil, and love for this world and this flesh, that we are miserable in love and death."[8] What we witness in Kristin is a life in the process of sanctification, in which, after years of stubborn insistence on her own way, Kristin finally subordinates her will to God. Although Kristin does not begin as a saint, she dies as one. With her, readers have the opportunity to learn how we might move from sin to holiness.

Sometimes Christians mistakenly despise the world and the flesh as a corrective to loving it too much, but Kristin shows us how the flesh might be a pathway to the love of God. The evocative portrayal of birth in its fleshiness offers us a visceral meditation on God as laboring for our salvation. Reading these passages closely, we may uncover why the Hebrew word for "mercy" stems from the word for "womb." As Kristin describes breastfeeding her infants, a practice usually delegated to a wet nurse, we may hunger for the milk of the Spirit. And although Kristin fails to surrender her virginity to God in the first part of the story, after Erlend's death she embraces the *via negativa* of the Virgin Mary, the ideal response. In the novel's rich descriptions of flesh, body, and blood, we may sense these truths more than merely think of them. The story trains our imaginations to become more sacramental, more attuned to the real connection between spirit and flesh.

The Opposite of the Virgin Mary

When I was a kid, I watched *Sister Act* and *The Sound of Music* on repeat. Those two films may not appear to have much in common, but for me, they contained my two competing dreams: to be a Broadway singer and to be a nun. Since this is a discussion on holiness, we'll focus on the latter dream. I would fall asleep praying and wake up to read the Bible before school. I would hold my own Sunday school classes while most of the kids played at the church playground. It bothered me that nuns had to wear black and white, but I convinced myself that I could sacrifice color for God. The dream was shattered when I discovered there were no evangelical convents. O'Connor once explained why she wrote about Protestant fanatics: "If you are Catholic and have this intensity of belief, you join the convent and are heard from no more; whereas if you are a Protestant and have it, there is no convent for you to join and you go about in the world, getting into all sorts of trouble and drawing the wrath of people who don't believe anything much at all."[9] O'Connor's view, that the call to holiness was special and led to a vocation as a priest or nun, prevailed in the pre–Vatican II Catholic Church. As a Protestant drawn to holiness, I have spent many years getting into lots of trouble with people who don't believe in much.

In *Kristin Lavransdatter*, set in the fourteenth century, a call to holiness meant that one left the world and joined a religious order.

While we can read Kristin's story and see the ways that God moved in her life outside of the convent, we need to assume this medieval perspective in order to understand the tension between becoming a wife and becoming a nun. In Kristin's time, joining the convent would have been a righteous dedication, but, as Brother Edvin points out, it had become a refuge for "daughters that are lame and blind and ugly and infirm." Or, he goes on, if parents "think He has given them too many children, they let Him take some of them back."[10] This explains why Kristin's parents dedicate her disabled sister, Ulvhild, to the cloisters but reserve Kristin for the honor of marriage.

In contrast to the prevailing worldview in fourteenth-century Norway, Brother Edvin recognizes that the call to join the convent is to return to God what he has given you. As he paints saints on glass windows, Brother Edvin inquires of Kristin, "How would you like to offer up those lovely curls of yours and serve Our Lady like these brides that I've painted here?"[11] For him, Kristin's beauty is a gift. All have recognized it. She is praised over the course of her life for exceptional good looks; in Norway, that meant hair like wheat and white skin. "Give beauty back," the poet Gerard Manley Hopkins writes, "back to God, beauty's self and beauty's giver."[12] Kristin's beauty is a glimpse of beauty's source, a reflection of the one who made her. In response to such a gift, she should give her beauty back to him. She refuses.

When Brother Edvin is painting saints in the windows of the church, he uplifts these models to Kristin, asking her to follow their example. There is the model of Saint Kristina, Kristin's namesake, with her "lovely pink and white" face and "golden hair" and "golden crown"— much like Kristin, though she dons a wreath and not a crown.[13] The legend of St. Kristina is that she was a twelve-year-old virgin from the fourth century who refused to worship the pagan gods of her parents, so she was tortured by beating, drowning, burning; even her breasts were removed, though they spilt milk instead of blood. Her example is fraught with implications for Kristin: On the one hand, the virgin submits her holy life to God and overcomes all suffering with prayer and devotion; on the other hand, like Kristin, she defies her father. Ultimately, St. Kristina has been sanctified by the ways she reflected the Virgin Mary, whom Brother Edvin has painted above her. When the angel Gabriel requests that Mary's virginity, her womb, be relinquished to the Holy Spirit for his purposes, she responds, "I am the Lord's servant. Let it be with me just as you have said" (Luke 1:38 CEB). The way she dedicates her virginity to the Lord becomes the example for the faithful.

Undset was not a Catholic when she wrote *Kristin Lavransdatter*. She had been raised by atheist parents in a predominantly Lutheran country, but she had been exposed to the Catholic writings of G. K. Chesterton, likely when she visited London in 1913, where she may have sat in on his talks. She also read and translated the writings of Catholic thinker Robert Hugh Benson, after whom she named her son. In 1924, Undset was received into the Catholic Church. For Chesterton, it was Mary who drew him to the faith "by being herself, that is by being beautiful."[14] This idea that Mary gives her beauty back to God influences Undset's depiction of Kristin. Even more influential was Benson's *The Friendship of Christ*, which Undset translated. He writes, "In the saints, therefore—through their individual characters and temperaments, as through prismatic glass—we see the All-holy Character of Christ, the white brilliancy of His Absolute Perfection, not distorted or diluted, but rather analyzed and dissected that we may understand it the better."[15] For Benson, Mary was the epitome of such a saint, who would reflect the character of Christ. Her "obedience and love of God was preliminary to the process by which the same race was redeemed."[16] Undset adopts this notion that Mary exemplifies virtue—not only for women but also for men—by returning her gifts to God for his purposes.

What we witness in Kristin is the opposite of such obedience; she defies her father (a representation of her heavenly Father) and surrenders herself to Erlend. Against propriety, Kristin has snuck away from the convent where she is to reside for a year until she marries her betrothed and instead meets with Erlend, a man with a reputation for seducing women. The loss of her virginity occurs against her wishes, for "she tried powerlessly to push him away."[17] While Erlend initially steals this gift from Kristin, she has invited his advances and continues to deliver herself over to him. Kristin looks at Erlend "as if she were afraid that he might be taken from her." Because Erlend is not her intended, Kristin views him as a transgression, an object of sin that might be kept from her, and she desires it. When Kristin describes embracing him "like having a child in her arms," she reveals her misapplied desire.[18]

In her essays on women, philosopher Edith Stein, who was a contemporary of Undset and an admirer of her fiction, writes, "The deepest feminine yearning is to achieve a loving union which, in its development, validates this maturation and simultaneously stimulates and furthers the desire for perfection in others; this yearning can express itself in the most diverse forms, and some of these forms may appear distorted."[19] While this yearning for loving union should be extended to include more than just the feminine, Stein rightly points to how such good motivations may become distorted. In the case of Kristin and Erlend, she should have relinquished herself to God, but she instead grants herself to Erlend as his "possession." Undset's description of their union—"Erlend had *done* this to her"[20]—underscores how Erlend's act perverts Mary's righteous prayer, "Let this be *done* to me" (Luke 1:38 AT). Their first union turns inside out all of the expectations for the sacrament. Kristin recalls in Erlend's eyes the look "of a man who had once been given food at the convent—he had kissed the bread they handed to him." As she connects her virginity with this memory of bread, a eucharistic image, Kristin should recognize the sacramental nature of the sexual act. Instead, "she sank back into the hay with open arms and let Erlend do as he liked."[21] By acquiescing to Erlend's desire, Kristin participates in the desacralizing of their union.

Whereas Mary's obedience opened the way for new life and salvation for all, Kristin's disobedience repeats the fall of Eve. Not only does she suffer, but Kristin causes shame for her parents, discord in their marriage, and worst of all, the death of Erlend's mistress. She confesses to Erlend's aunt, "I didn't realize then that the consequence of sin is that you have to trample on other people." Even when Kristin comprehends that sin causes destruction, she refuses to renounce Erlend. "I know I won't let go of Erlend," Kristin says with a "cold" smile, "even if I have to trample on my own father."[22] We feel the consequences of such sin as the warmth of her face and her heart turn cold.

The Mystical Bride of Christ

Kristin loves Erlend with a passion she should have reserved for God. Church tradition is filled with female saints—and the occasional male saint—depicting their union with Christ in erotic language. Rather than marrying a human man, these women envisioned themselves as Christ's bride. They had reserved their virginity for him, and as brides of Christ they participated in a spiritual union, borrowing imagery from the Song of Songs to express their relationship. Thérèse of Lisieux writes, "I think that the Heart of my Spouse is mine alone, just as mine is His alone." Teresa of Ávila describes her soul's longing for God in the vision of an angel with a hot spear thrust into her several times, penetrating her to her entrails. She moans in response, feels aflame with the "wondrous love of God," and desires more of this love.[23] If men and women alike are unable to dedicate themselves as Christ's spouse and feel they will be overtaken by the desires of the flesh, then the apostle Paul counsels them to marry (1 Cor. 7:8–9). But human marriage is second to a divine union.

Many in twenty-first-century America not only resist such intimate portrayals of the love of Christ but also downplay sexual misconduct as the sins of youth or the needs of the body. By setting *Kristin Lavransdatter* in the fourteenth century, Undset can avoid all the nonsense of the secular world regarding sexuality and remind readers of its sacred character. Alice von Hildebrand insists that we not categorize sex as an instinct like hunger or thirst. We should distinguish sex as different because the act requires another person and thus cannot be treated as lightly as we do hunger or thirst. Von Hildebrand asserts that sex is "at the service of the deepest human aspiration: love."[24] We desire to reveal ourselves to another person and to know them as they know us. In *Kristin Lavransdatter* what begins as sexual attraction is described as love, yet Erlend and Kristin must see their marriage as a foretaste of divine love, which is selfless and sacrificial.

Kristin struggles in her marriage because she views her passion for Erlend as lust and not a glimpse of holy love. Like those raised in purity culture who feel guilty engaging in sex even with their spouse, Kristin cannot connect her relationship with Erlend to Jesus Christ. Her husband should be reflecting this love to her, and she should be responding to him as though she is the church. Erlend's brother Gunnulf, a priest, reminds Kristin of the relationship between marriage and divine love:

> You cannot settle for anything less than the love that is between God and the soul. All other love is merely a reflection of the heavens in the puddles of a muddy road, but if you always remember that it's a reflection of the light from that other home, then you will rejoice at its beauty and take good care that you do not destroy it by churning up the mire at the bottom.[25]

This metaphor depicts how God's love for our souls is manifest through our relationships with people here on earth. Their love should lead us to God.

I hear a lot of people advise newlyweds not to find fulfillment in their spouse but to always look to Christ. While these words are wise, we practice our love for God in *how* we love our spouse. As a married woman, I love my husband as though he is Christ, but not in substitution of Christ. I should see in him a divine reflection. Those who are single love Christ mystically without a surrogate, and this love for the divine pours outward into every person made in the image of God. Only at the conclusion of the story does Kristin learn how to be wedded to Christ in this way.

God as Laboring, Merciful Mother

Women love to share birth stories like they are tales of victories in battle. The blood, the sweat, the tears, and the glory of that tiny gift pulled from your flesh, beginning her own life in the world. I remember each of my children's births with a clarity preserved for moments of exultation and crisis. The birth of a child is synchronously both joy-filled and painful. Mothers viscerally recall the moment they first met their children.

For Kristin, her first son's birth instructed her in God's mercy. She fights within herself over whether she even wants this child to be born. "Conceived in sin. Carried under her hard, evil heart," this baby represents to Kristin her antagonistic will.[26] Providentially presiding over her difficult labor, Erlend's priest brother reprimands Kristin for not wanting this child. "Are you so arrogant," Gunnulf asks her as she screams in labor, "that you think yourself capable of sinning so badly that God's mercy is not great enough?"[27] In Hebrew, the word "mercy," *rachamim*, comes from the word *rechem*, which means "womb." God's mercy breaks forth from his inner core, from his metaphorical womb. Mothers who have given birth understand this etymology, for we know in our flesh what it means to suffer from within our wombs for another's good.

While still true that Kristin's baby was "conceived in sin" and "carried under her hard, evil heart," the newborn is "pulled out of her sin-tainted body, so pure, so healthy, so inexpressibly lovely and fresh and innocent. This undeserved beneficence broke her heart in two; crushed with remorse, she lay there with tears welling up out of her soul like blood from a mortal wound."[28] After Kristin delivers the baby, she completes her thoughts not with sin and evil but with mercy. Undset describes the sin in three phrases, then uses five phrases to describe the infant's purity as though overturning the negative and finding nearly twofold redemption. She draws on the language of pain to tie this experience of mercy to compassion and to suffering: *broke, crushed, tears, blood, wound.*

The baby is delivered on the morning of the Feast of the Annunciation. The humble acquiescence of Mary to Gabriel's request overthrows Kristin's sin, as written in 1 Timothy 2:15: "She will save through childbearing." One interpretation of that enigmatic verse is that we are saved through Mary's childbearing of Jesus. Throughout Kristin's delivery, Mary's image hovers everywhere, reminding us of this salvation. During labor, Kristin begs, "Blessed Virgin Mary—will it be long before you help me? Oh how it hurts, it hurts, it hurts."[29] Then she screams. As Erlend listens to his wife's pain from an adjoining house, he recalls "a heifer shrieking in the grip of a bear." The thought of this agony induces him to pray, "My Kristin, oh, my Kristin. Lord, for the sake of Your blessed Mother, have mercy."[30] Tradition considers Mary's delivery of Jesus to have been painless,[31] but the pain and prayers of this scene resonate with women who have given birth. When we think of Mary's delivery of Jesus or of God as a laboring mother, these images of suffering remind us of the vastness of his mercy.

The prophets, the psalmists, Jesus himself, and the church's writers throughout history have all drawn on the imagery of God as a laboring mother. In labor, Kristin tries "to hold out a little longer, before she gave in and screamed."[32] Her labor echoes how the Lord describes himself: "I have been quiet and held myself back. But now, like a woman in childbirth, I cry out, I gasp and pant" (Isa. 42:14). The prophet Isaiah dictates God's image of himself as a panting woman in labor, that we might feel how deeply God desires to deliver us from our sin. Similarly, the psalmist writes, in reference to the coming of the Messiah, "Out of my womb before the morning star I bore you."[33] Jesus is birthed from the womb of the Father; in God's mercy, he delivers Christ to us. When Jesus explains salvation to Nicodemus, he relies on the image of birth: "No one can enter the kingdom of God unless they are born of water and the spirit" (John 3:5). There is the first birth from a woman, followed by the second birth through the Holy Spirit.

As opposed to our biological mothers, who "bring us into the world to suffer and die," as Julian of Norwich writes, Jesus as our spiritual mother "bears us into joy and eternal life; blessed may he be! So he sustains within himself in love and was in labor for the full time until he suffered the sharpest pangs and the most grievous sufferings that ever were or shall be, and at the last he died. And when it was finished, he had born us to bliss, even this could not fully satisfy his marvelous love."[34] Julian is one example of a medieval writer who contemplated God as our spiritual mother. Drawing from the words of Jesus that we be born again, early churches designed their baptismal fonts in the shapes of vaginas. They did not see the image as sexually charged but as maternal. This yonic imagery in the church symbolizes anti-autonomy, our dependence on another being to bring us forth and raise us in his image.[35]

In his commentary on Isaiah, John Calvin explains that the image of God as laborer underscores God's love and affection. By comparing "himself to a mother who singularly loves her child, though she brought him forth with extreme pain," God emphasizes the suffering he will endure in saving us.[36] In imitation of Christ, Paul describes his relationship to the Galatian churches with this metaphor: "My little children, for whom I am again in the pain of childbirth until Christ is formed in you . . ." (Gal. 4:19 NRSV). Pope Saint John Paul II extends this birthing metaphor to all of creation. He writes in *Theology of the Body*, "Just as labor pains are united with the desire for birth, with the hope of a new child, so too, the whole of creation 'waits with eager longing for the revealing of the sons [and daughters] of God' and cherishes the hope to 'be set free from its bondage to decay and obtain the glorious liberty of the children of God' (Rom. 8:19–21)."[37]

We need not substitute a mothering image of God for our understanding of God as Father, but we should not limit our knowledge to God as *only* our Father. Early Christian writers saw no problems with God as both Mother *and* Father. Tenth-century theologian Gregory of Narek writes, "The Father I called Mother, Christ's mother and our mother as well. The Father, consequently, was in labor through the message of the Law and the Prophets. . . . Thus, there is indeed only one Mother, our Birther, the Father Almighty."[38] One image does not replace another. After all, God created male and female from his one nature: the female is not other to him. One reason God chose primarily masculine grammar to figure himself as Father and Son is because the "image of a suffering female would not challenge the powers of this world because she would merely be one more victim."[39] The problem there is with the world's categories, not with God's image. This neglected image of God might increase our knowledge of him who is both Mother and Father to us.

God as Nursing Mother

Nursing in Undset's novel becomes Kristin's way of participating in spiritual renewal. She acts against the customs of her class and chooses to nurse her infants. The first description of her nursing occurs while she is pilgrimaging to Nidaros Cathedral, where the remains of St. Olav are interred. She is journeying to be absolved of her sins, carrying the child no longer within her but in a wrap on her back. She pauses in a field to feed the baby. "It felt good to hold him to her breast," Kristin reflects. "A blessed warmth coursed through her whole body as she felt her stone-hard breasts bursting with milk empty out as he nursed."[40] Although the suffering of the pilgrimage is purgatorial, the baby's "little mouth at her breast warmed her heart so well that it was like soft wax, easy for the heavenly love to shape."[41] In nursing, Kristin, who has been so selfish for most of the story, relinquishes her will for the life of another. She will nurse half a dozen children through the story, giving birth to eight sons (one of whom is given to a nurse and another who refuses to nurse and dies of starvation).

The novel does not dwell on the frustrations around nursing—the infant who rejects the nipple or prefers the bottle, the baby who requires hourly feeding, the vexation of having nothing to show for your day but a fridge full of pumped milk. For some women, the time to do nothing but nurse an infant is a welcome reprieve from a busy life. For others, hours alone in a chair with a speechless baby who takes and takes and takes is isolating and exhausting. Nursing presses the human bounds of love. It demands self-sacrifice. It demands that you surrender all your plans for the day to the needs of another person. Like a monk who prays the hours, lowering himself to his knees, keeping God before him regularly and submitting himself in supplication, a nursing mother remembers her infant every two to three hours, physically engorged in pain if she does not cater to her child's needs.

Not to say there are not personal benefits for the nursing mother. The bond created with my infants was pleasurable. I felt their need for me, enjoyed the look in their eyes as they suckled, and held their limp bodies as I watched dribbles of milk flow over their chins. Research proves that nursing increases a connection between mother and child. Not to mention, when I nursed my babies, with all the energy it took from me, I could devour three to four waffles with butter and cups of syrup and half a package of bacon. Mothers bond to the vulnerable one who needs them, and the baby is aware of the difference between the parent who smells like food and the one who doesn't. My children all said "dada" first, but at least for a short season, they wanted their mama more.

The way Undset depicts Kristin nursing should bring to mind God as our lactating mother. In Isaiah, the Lord asks rhetorically, "Can a woman forget her nursing child, or show no compassion for the child of her womb?" His answer emphasizes how much he will remember us. Like a nursing mother who yearns to place her suckling babe at her breast, the Lord says, "Even these may forget, yet I will not forget you" (Isa. 49:15 NRSV). In his First Letter to the Thessalonians, Paul compares his nurturing of the church to a wet nurse or lactating mother: "But we were gentle among you, like a nurse tenderly caring for her own children. So deeply do we care for you" (1 Thess. 2:7–8 NRSV). Similar to how God expresses his compassion for his children, Paul declares his gentle care for the church. Medieval artists depicted icons of Mary nursing Jesus to emphasize his humanity and her charity. Throughout the Middle Ages, theologians drew on this image to stress the sacrificial nature of God's love. As a priest reminds Kristin, "God will find you. . . . Stay calm and do not flee from Him who has been seeking you before you even existed in your mother's womb."[42] Knowing how a mother loves her nursing child may reassure Kristin of God's devotion to her despite her sinfulness.

Holy Tears

While many Christians will never experience motherhood or nursing, holy tears are a spiritual practice available to all followers, and one that Kristin exemplifies. Erlend reflects with one of his sons about his wife's ability to cry: "I remember back when your mother was young, and she wept as readily as the dew drips from goat willow reeds along the creek."[43] He recalls her ability to weep as evidence of her gentleness, a characteristic that he corroded in her through his misdeeds, causing her to harden as she aged. Tears signify a tender spirit and reflect supernatural intercession as we feel with others, lament over the fall, mourn over death. "Although tears are such an ordinary phenomenon," writes Simone Weil, they are not merely psychophysical: "The tears of a saint in a state of genuine contemplation are supernatural."[44]

When we shed tears for those in pain, we imitate Jesus, who weeps at the tomb of Lazarus (John 11:35). The shortest sentence in Scripture, "Jesus wept," describes a mysterious moment in which the God-man—who knows he is about to raise Lazarus from the dead—mourns with holy tears over the death of his friend. Jesus does not hurry to the grave to act, but he pauses purposefully in lamentation. He spends the time to grieve. In 2013, when a boat full of migrants wrecked at Lampedusa, Italy, Pope Francis delivered a homily in response to the tragedy in which he asked, "Has any one of us wept because of this situation and others like it?"[45] We may worry that such tears are pointless—what do they achieve? Yet our ability to mourn over loss and suffer with those who are not us is central to our humanity. By responding with tears at the death of his friend, Jesus reveals the fullness of his humanity, and we can fulfill his calling to follow him when we weep for others.

In imitation of her son, Mary also empathizes with sufferers. She is called the *mater dolorosa* (mother of sorrow), and it is to Mary that Kristin looks as she travels for the final time away from her home and toward the convent. Staring at a flowing river, she experiences an inner vision. The moving water seems to reflect her life, a restless rushing through the wilderness. The narrator refers to Kristin as "the mother" in this scene, and Kristin prays to the epitome of mothers, Mary. With "her sorrows" Kristin seeks comfort under the cloak of the "Mother of God": "With her grief over the children she had lost, with the heavier sorrows over all the fateful blows that had struck her sons . . ." Mourning the sins she has caused as well as the pain she and her children have endured, Kristin finds solace in Mary as the sorrowful mother who feels with her. For Mary "had grieved more than any other mother, and her mercy would see the weak and pale glimmer in a sinful woman's heart." Despite all her sins, all her misdirected passion and disobedience to her father, Kristin believes that Mary will see that her heart "was still a mother's heart."[46] She buries her face in her hands in tears. As Kristin feels overwhelmed by the pain of separation from her sons, her confession, prayer, and weeping commence her transition from a mother who has caused her own sorrows to a mother who, like Mary, will comfort others in their suffering.

Mother to All

Because of the protagonist's many imperfections, readers of *Kristin Lavransdatter* struggle to see her as a saint. Hagiographies are filled with the recollection of perfect acts by holy figures. Yet Sigrid Undset's hagiographies—and she wrote many—are unique in their dedication to the sins that vexed the saint in the process of sanctification. Of Undset, Evelyn Birge Vitz writes, "She knew how hard it is to be, not just 'pious' in some superficial sense, but truly holy; how hard it is to want God's will, not our own."[47] Desiring to be a saint herself, a longing the faithful should all share, Undset writes of real human beings who move from transgression to perfection. This is the beauty of the story of Kristin Lavransdatter; we see this obstinate, proud sinner become a saint by the end of the story.

In the final scenes of the third volume, *The Cross*, Kristin, like Christ, dies to herself. She appears in these episodes to be both herself and a new version of herself. When Kristin enters the city Nidaros, a pack of boys harangues her, but the way she bears their insults changes them. They fall silent before her, grow shamefaced, and stare in awe. They do not stare at Kristin's beauty as people did when she was young, but they look into her "big, clear, calm eyes" and notice her "secretive smile." In spite of her wrinkles, "she didn't look particularly old."[48] Kristin has a youth of spirit now. Saintliness transfigures a person so that people cannot tell their age—recall the neither-young-nor-old look of Ransom and of Laurus. The boys trail behind Kristin, reminding her of her sons. Now her motherhood extends toward those not born of her flesh but of the spirit. When a mother pilgrim hands Kristin her screaming child, Kristin consoles the child as a spiritual mother of the infant. Later, the priest Gunnulf comes across Kristin's kneeling form and finds not a penitent but a spiritually wise sister. Their roles have reversed: when he speaks harshly about his brother Erlend's memory, Kristin speaks graciously of him. No longer does she doubt God's mercy. Kristin herself has become a vessel for it.

The novel ends in the midst of the Black Death. As in *Laurus*, people are dying everywhere in grotesque, uncomfortable, horrifying ways. Kristin watches holy sisters who do not die well, begging for extended life. Kristin fears that the approach of death will become the test of what she has truly believed. Thankfully, the end of Kristin's life is more filled with grace than any other moment in her life, and it reveals the enduring love of God.

As the townspeople fret over the seemingly endless suffering of the plague, they revert to pagan practices. When Kristin herself intervened to save her nephew, earlier in the novel, she too committed the sin of pagan superstition. In this later episode, Kristin knows that such pagan rituals will damage their souls and rushes to save these citizens from themselves. Caring more about their souls than her own life, she accompanies the abbess and a cohort of sisters to a graveyard where a group of men is burying a boy alive as a sacrifice to a pagan goddess. The poor child complains because they are dirtying his bread as they toss soil on his head. Kristin pulls the child from the grave. The men protest: "Isn't it better to sacrifice *one* than for all of us to perish? This boy here, who belongs to no one—" Kristin interrupts, "He belongs to Christ."[49] She speaks truth, functioning according to a spiritual logic that trumps their worldly reason. A man threatens Kristin with a knife and calls on the name of Satan. Kristin refutes him with a fiery sermon about the holy sacrifice of these wedded brides who now stand before him, risking their lives for this boy.

The man assumes that Kristin too is a wedded bride, but in a demonstration of great humility, she claims to be more like him than like a holy sister. He compares her to the boy's mother, a prostitute who has died and not been buried. In horror, Kristin responds, "And no one has had enough mercy to put her into consecrated ground?" Her look shames the men standing there as they fully recognize their sins. Only one obstinate fool dares Kristin to go and bury the "whore" if Kristin is "all full of holiness and virtue."[50] Not to prove her goodness but out of an overwhelming mercy for the dead woman, Kristin runs to the hovel. Her old servant Ulf appears bearing the news that two of Kristin's sons have died of plague. The crushing personal loss does not distract her from her holy task, a moment that illustrates hating one's family for the sake of Christ (Luke 14:26). As Ulf helps Kristin cart the corpse to the cemetery, the plague reveals itself in Kristin's flesh. She vomits blood that covers her body. Before Ulf carries Kristin to the convent to die, Kristin kisses the dead woman's shoe and prays on her behalf. "You will have found Christ," Flannery O'Connor writes, "when you are concerned with other people's sufferings and not your own."[51] Although she herself is suffering from the plague, Kristin extends charity to the destitute one who has died.

Thrashing against the sickness, Kristin remembers that she has promised to pay for the burial and Mass for the dead woman. Since she relinquished all of her earthly possessions when she came to retire at the convent, Kristin only retains two items, her father's cross and her wedding ring. The choice between the two is the final decision between obedience to her father and devotion to her husband. Spiritually, it is a choice between God and her earthly lover. Kristin cries in torrents, comprehending the significance of the choice. Yet, as she surrenders the ring, she regrets neither the good nor the bad in all the days of her life. She understands it has all led to this moment. Beneath her ring, like a scar, is an indention in her finger, the letter "M" for Mary, which had been engraved inside the ring. Kristin's last clear thought is happiness that this mark will not fade before she dies:

> It seemed to her a mystery she could not comprehend, but she was certain that God had held her firmly in a pact which had been made for her, without her knowing it, from a love that had been poured over her—and in spite of her willfulness, in spite of her melancholy, earthbound heart, some of that love had *stayed* inside her, had worked on her like sun on the earth, had driven forth a crop that neither the fiercest fire of passion nor its stormiest anger could completely destroy. She had been a servant of God—a stubborn, defiant maid, most often an eye-servant in her prayers and unfaithful in her heart. . . . And yet He had held her firmly in His service, and under the glittering gold ring a mark had been secretly impressed

upon her, showing that she was His servant, owned by the Lord and King who would now come.[52]

Kristin's final acts are selfless, sacrificial, and full of mercy. Like a martyr, Kristin dies covered in blood and tears, and with happiness.

The Conversion of the Author

Two years after finishing *Kristin Lavransdatter*, Sigrid Undset was baptized into the Catholic Church. It was 1924. After a marriage to an unreliable man and losing two of her own children, Undset wrote the novel *Kristin Lavransdatter* as a confession, a purgation, and a hope. Whereas before writing this novel, Undset had reflected that she "would personally prefer anything to marriage and motherhood as an occupation," she uplifts the marriage and motherhood of Kristin Lavransdatter as a path to the woman's holiness.[53] What changed the novelist from her worldly feminism to her Catholic feminism?

For Undset, the move to Catholicism made sense only after she spent so many years with God's friends, the saints. She writes, "By degrees my knowledge of history convinced me that the only thoroughly sane people, of our civilization at least, seemed to be those queer men and women which the Catholic Church calls the Saints. . . . They seemed to know the true explanation of man's undying hunger for happiness."[54] Studying the saints led Undset to faith. They were her apologetic for the truth of the church and all its teaching. This is why she dedicated much of her later life to writing hagiographies, to lead people to the faith as she herself was led. But Undset had already done so much in writing a fictional saint in Kristin Lavransdatter, in giving us a woman we could relate to, whose sins turned her gradually away from the world and toward Christ, and whose sanctification was an undeserved gift by his providence. May we be, as Kristin was and as Undset herself seemed to be, purged of our desire for our own ways and be turned toward his will.

Devotional

From _Kristin Lavransdatter_: "Surely she had never asked God for any-thing except that He should let her have her will. And every time she had been granted what she asked for—for the most part. Now here she sat with a contrite heart—not because she had sinned against God but because she was unhappy that she had been allowed to follow her will to the road's end."[55]

Scripture: "Not my will but yours be done" (Luke 22:42 NRSV).

Wisdom from the Saints: Julian of Norwich: "The mother can give her child to suck of her milk, but our precious Mother Jesus can feed us with himself."[56]

Prayer: Father God, Mother Jesus, and Holy Spirit, may we not limit our-selves in our knowledge of you by conforming to our time and culture, but may we always be reexamining your Word to know more about who you are and who you have called us to be. May we look to the virgins, mothers, and those childless brides who you made and who all show us more about who you are. May we relinquish our will to follow your road to the highest end.

Discussion Questions

1. What might we learn about holiness from examining the lives of women?

2. When you consider Kristin's life, do you think she would have arrived at a holy death had she obeyed her father, married her betrothed, and so forth? What would her life have looked like?

3. As we remember our own lives, where do we see those cross-roads, those moments where we chose our own way over God's?

Where has it led to now? How might we repent and learn from those moments without regret?

4. In what areas in our life (singleness, motherhood, tears) might we see God that we currently have not seen as pathways to holiness?

5. Where do you see sacraments in the novel? How does the novel emphasize the sacramental nature of reality?

Further Reading

Louisa May Alcott, *Little Women*
P. D. James, *Children of Men*
Julian of Norwich, *Revelations of Divine Love*
Gertrud von Le Fort, *The Wife of Pilate*

6

Contemplative and Active Life

Our corpselike world needs the scandal of poetry, just as it needs the scandal of truth.

—Georges Bernanos, letter to Jorge de Lima, January 1942[1]

QUARANTINE WAS MISERABLE FOR EXTROVERTS. I never realized how much I depended on friendship for my sanity until I was spending days without human interaction beyond my family. At first, the silence and stillness of my schedule brought relief. I had overcommitted myself to projects, speaking engagements, committee work. Suddenly, my calendar cleared, and I could turn off my alarm clock, eat muffins with my kids, and play Chutes and Ladders all morning. We went on hikes and bike rides, picked tomatoes from our garden, and baked bread, like everyone else did. Because we were moving homes, we only barely held back from getting chickens.

As time went on, the retreat from my hectic schedule became a perpetual reality. My kids could not return to school. I had to leave

my job. My friends sequestered themselves at home, fearful of infecting their aging parents with Covid-19. This relative isolation and restricted activity carried on for over a year, and it began to wear on me. I missed church. We attended occasionally on the church lawn, separated six feet apart with masks, in camping chairs. But where were the smiles, the hugs, the passing of peace? Where was the body and the blood that I had taken for granted? I missed the communal service with the taste of the sacraments and passing the peace by touch, and how it all shaped my weeks.

To quell the loneliness, I spent more time on social media. Only, that distraction was a false sense of community. Not that relationships cannot be formed through that medium, but those people are so far away. They cannot hold my hand. They can like me, but not really love me. They can applaud my work, but I needed appreciation of my personhood. I longed for presence. To overcome the sense of unworthiness, I sent out emails that made me feel as though I were accomplishing tasks. I scheduled future appointments. I folded laundry, washed dishes, made beds, organized toys. But nothing fixed the sinking emptiness. Because nothing could.

In February 2021, the South, especially Texas, but also where I live in Arkansas, was blanketed by more snow than we had seen in a century. None of the infrastructure was prepared for such a hit, and we became further isolated from one another. Even Zoom was no longer an option during that week because of restricted electricity usage. There were no people, no normal routines, no work, not even sunshine. I discovered the limits to my optimism. The joy that had persevered in my heart for a year grew as cold as the weather outside. I began to know what others called depression. We watched the TV show *WandaVision*, in which the main character describes her grief as an experience of drowning. She keeps trying to lift her head, but the waves persist in coming over her. I felt that, and it scared me. I had never known despair before. Sadness, yes. Pain and suffering, yes. But despair was new. After facing waves of despair for days, I lifted my head. Or rather, God lifted my head. The answer to my despair came over me—prayer.

I had spent the previous weeks rereading Georges Bernanos's 1936 novel *The Diary of a Country Priest*, which once upon a time had first shown me how to pray. Here I was in the midst of this empty spiritual season, not listening to the very book about which I was trying to write. I was reading Thomas Merton's books on contemplation and contemplative prayer. I had just finished reading Tish Harrison Warren's *Prayer in the Night*. As a teacher, I had been reading all of these books to discover paths for others to follow, but I had forgotten the necessity of prayer in my own life. "When we are in danger of drowning upon the open sea," Hans Urs von Balthasar writes, then prayer, as a conversation with God's initiating word, "is the rope ladder thrown down to us so that we can climb up into the rescuing vessel."[2]

Learning to Pray

When I first read *The Diary of a Country Priest*, I started weeping when, about midway through, the priest reflects, "Oh miracle—thus to be able to give what we ourselves do not possess, sweet miracle of empty hands!"[3] "Yes!" I wanted to exclaim—but I held back because I was reading on an airplane with a few dozen travelers. I wanted to cry out because I understood what he meant: to live in Jesus Christ is to experience the miracle of giving what we do not have. The story of *The Diary of a Country Priest* is rather mundane if you tell it by plot points: a young priest in the countryside of France keeps a diary; his parishioners misunderstand him; he suffers from what he thinks is indigestion, but (spoiler alert) he dies of stomach cancer. But this axiom of giving what we do not have becomes crucial for understanding what you are reading—you have to see what isn't there. You have to attend to the unseen reality at work in the novel so that you might comprehend the gift of empty hands.

In the story, the unnamed priest struggles to serve his parish. They all mistrust his youth, his poverty, his selflessness; ultimately, they distrust his holiness. He does not consider himself holy but continually reflects on his ineptitude. Several times the priest laments that he speaks clumsily. When I have taught this novel in the past, students believe what the priest says about himself. They think him ignorant, foolish, and clumsy, as he professes to be in his diary. I have to point out his humility. We should never believe truly humble people when they list their faults. Not that they lie. Rather, their humility guards their words and thoughts from too highly estimating their place and their function in God's kingdom. For those of us who suffer from pride, reading this priest's diary becomes an exercise in humility.

In the pages of this diary, readers hear the honest and authentic confessions of this priest. He begins writing the diary as an exercise in concentration: "I had thought it might become a kind of communion between God and myself, an extension of prayer, a way of easing the difficulties of verbal expression."[4] As the priest scribbles in his empty journal, alone in his room, with only the lamp to light up his words, he experiences the sense of another's presence, "which surely could not be God," he protests.[5] But why not God? The reader seems more in tune with the priest's sanctification than he is. We can feel the presence of God at work in the priest's diary. The diary genre of the novel not only becomes a model for us as readers to imitate for our own prayer journey but also invites us into the inner life of the priest, which is where we witness contemplation, prayer, and the saint's very inscape. Without the diary, we could only know the priest by his external words and deeds. Because of the diary, we see one who has "admitted once and for all into each moment of our puny lives the terrifying presence of God."[6]

While the mode of the diary may appear at first to be a monologue—one voice narrating the story—it creates an intimacy with the reader in which we become the other dialogue partner. In this way, we as readers both experience the priest's inner life from his perspective and receive the gift of distance as a reader, by which we can assess how truthfully he perceives reality. We are the priest *and* his listener, his silent conversation partner. The very form of the book, then, trains us in the disciplines we need to pray well. The novel as a prayer journal provides us an example of how to dialogue with God while simultaneously requiring us to listen to the priest's words, just as we need to listen for God to speak. We experience that prayer must be a practice of listening more than speaking.

After all, what have we to give God that he has not given to us? What have we to tell God that he does not already know? The miraculous gift from empty hands occurs when we are willing to assent to his generosity. "I am certain, that many men never give out the whole of themselves, their deepest truth," the priest reflects. "How many men will never have the least idea of what is meant by supernatural heroism, without which there can be no inner life!"[7] The path to spiritual heroism is surrender of the whole self. We discover our deepest truth, our inner life, through this self-emptying form of prayer. This priest, through his daily examen and the spiritual practice of writing this diary, reveals his interior self to readers. He exhibits his own emptiness, through which we see God reaping a beautiful harvest in his small, rural community. What we learn through his recorded prayers is how much prayer is not about delivering anything to God, not even our meager words. Rather, our spiritual heroism depends on receiving from God the riches of inner life, which springs from our prayers.

The Dark Night of the Soul and the Failure of Saints

Ten years after Mother Teresa's death, her letters were published, revealing that for fifty years of her ministry, this saint had felt abandoned by God. Since the sixteenth century, when St. John of the Cross penned a poem with this theme, Christians have referred to such experiences of God's absence as "the dark night of the soul." Too often in contemporary American churches, we fear admitting the darkness. When I was teaching George Herbert's poetry one term, a student protested that we should not be focusing on sin and suffering because of Jesus Christ's resurrection. The New Testament compels us to be joyful always, she asserted; therefore, we have no right as Christians to dwell in the darkness. With patience, I kindly rebuked her: joy and darkness are not incompatible. The mystical paradox unveiled in the dark night of the soul—and that all Christians must remember about the life of faith—is that the Lord experienced crucifixion before his resurrection. Because the crucifixion was Christ's sacrifice for us, we call the memory of that day *Good* Friday. The darkness, doubt, dryness of a Christian's walk is a reality that cannot be dispelled. But we do not go there alone. God is with us, even when we cannot feel his presence. Mother Teresa knew this truth, which is how she continued to serve the suffering in Calcutta. She prayed without ceasing to a God who gave her no sign that he was listening.

We may feel that our prayers are unanswered, but we must not stop praying. To pray is not a task only for the elite holy ones. Just as we are all called to be saints, we are all called to pray. Saints, such as Mother Teresa and Bernanos's priest, show us how to pray in the darkness. Bernanos's priest persists "almost desperately," as he admits. He fears that he prays badly because of how difficult such prayer is for him. Despite receiving no response from God that he can understand, the priest reflects in his diary, "I know, of course, that the wish to pray is a prayer in itself, that God can ask no more than that of us."[8] Although the priest cognitively knows this truth, he admits his desire: "I needed prayer as much as I needed air to draw my breath or oxygen to fill my blood. . . . A void was behind me. And in front a wall, a wall of darkness."[9] This saint-in-process experiences the night entering into him, a dull solitude of lovelessness. Yet he takes comfort, for the "saints experienced those hours of failure and loss."[10] With their example and in their company, the young priest continues praying in the void.

In his Letter to the Romans, St. Paul reminds us that the Spirit will pray for us when we feel as though we cannot pray. "In certain ways we are weak, but the Spirit is here to help us. . . . When we don't know what to pray for, the Spirit prays for us in ways that cannot be put into words" (Rom. 8:26 CEV). The priest does not rely on his own ability to pray, nor does he limit his prayers to his own words. Our vocabulary is so weak when it comes to expressing our fears, needs, desires to God. The church tradition offers countless prayers that have aided the saints that we may draw on to overcome our shortcomings when we pray. The priest recalls how he used to pray with his whole being "riveted on a passage in the breviary," which is the collection of psalms, Bible verses, hymns, and of course prayers of other saints.[11] A young soldier compares the priest's face to a "very old missal," as though he has become the prayers themselves.[12] When the priest's mentor, the Curé de Torcy, reminds the priest to pray, he points the younger father to the angels—"The world is full of angels"—and to Our Lady—"the mother of all flesh, a new Eve."[13] When we experience those dark nights of the soul or even external weariness, we may invoke strength from heavenly resources to help us pray.

The church has known all kinds—the blood of martyrs and the fear of thousands of sinners—and the Lord provides ways for us to pray as the mystical body of Christ, for one another and with one another in our need. Who has not experienced that place where we fear we cannot pray? After one of my miscarriages, I begged others to pray for me because I didn't want to pray and could not seem to do it myself. Another time in my life, I felt so scared of the grief I was experiencing, I merely penned the word "HELP" on my palm and hoped God would read it. In the novel, when the young soldier describes the priest's face also as "one of those half-rubbed-away engravings on ancient tombstones," he is recalling the tradition of Christians to touch saints' names as they reach out to another for help, especially one who may be experiencing paradise and already seeing God as Moses did, face to face. The priest's very face reflects his "habit of prayer" so that he appears as one from whom others may receive prayer when they long for it most.[14] He explains, "My inner quiet—blessed by God—has never really isolated me. I feel all humankind can enter, and I receive them thus only at the threshold of my home."[15] Reading the priest's prayer diary shows us, ironically, that prayer is not a solo endeavor but very much relies on the whole church. As the priest reflects, "We never pray alone."[16]

Vita Activa and *Vita Contemplativa*

We've been talking about prayer in the novel because praying is the practice most of us associate with the contemplative life. To some, the very phrase "contemplative life" may be unfamiliar. *The Diary of a Country Priest* exemplifies the symbiotic relationship between the active and contemplative life. Bernanos thought that "the contemplative and the active life should be intertwined or, as other Christian mystics expressed the same thought, that 'Martha and Mary must work together' in a cooperative effort for the benefit of all."[17] We must learn to see the two ways of being in the world in harmony to understand God's call.

For the past few centuries, the church, especially the Protestant arm, has been enamored more of the active life than the life of prayer and contemplation. Books such as *Made Like Martha: Good News for the Woman Who Gets Things Done* prioritize Martha-ness, the life of doing, over the life of Mary, the contemplative exemplar in the Gospels. Our predilection for action may even set up a hurdle against our enjoyment of the novel: this priest doesn't seem to *do* anything. He fails in his attempts to change teenagers in his pastorate; his best friend foregoes his ordination; the doctor under his supervision commits suicide. What exactly does the priest *do*? Not to mention, the genre of the novel does not permit much dramatic action. Unlike a superhero movie or a Western, this novel has no big explosions or climactic romances. This novel doesn't even have the humor of Charles Portis or the violence of Flannery O'Connor's work that might hook a reader. We must read differently to understand the story. We must become contemplative in the process of reading, slowing down in our attention, and meditating on these scenes to see beneath their externals. Reading *The Diary of a Country Priest* redirects us toward contemplation.

In the Gospels, Jesus calls contemplation the higher end. While Martha frets over preparing the house for the disciples to visit, Mary sits at the Lord's feet and listens to his teaching. Jesus speaks about both women: "Martha, Martha! You are worried and upset about so many things, but only one thing is necessary. Mary has chosen what is best, and it will not be taken away from her" (Luke 10:41–42 CEV). Thomas Aquinas expounds upon this passage, offering several reasons why the contemplative life supersedes the active life, including its internal nature, capacity for delight, leisure, rest, and direction toward the divine and eternal.[18] Yet the Lord's words are sufficient reason: contemplation is best.

Throughout the church's history, theologians have struggled to understand the relationship between the active and contemplative life of the believer. The terms are ancient in origin, pointing back to Aristotle, who prized the life of the mind over the actions of a worker. For Aristotle, contemplation was the highest good because of its sufficiency as an end; it could not be *used* for anything else. In the church, we've baptized contemplation as the contemplation of God, the enjoyment of him who cannot be used for anything else. As I love to tell my students, "God is useless." God is the end of all other useful things. In contrast to Aristotle, however, theologians in the church have recognized how such contemplation, although high above the active life, might actually invigorate the active life.

In the contemporary church, we fallaciously separate the two: we have our Marthas versus our Marys, our doers versus our thinkers, our social justice workers versus our lovers of mercy. Instead of viewing the two in opposition or as separate paths, the saints of the church historically have shown how the active and contemplative life relate to one another. Gregory the Great, in the sixth century, writes, "Breadth pertains to charity for the neighbor; height to the understanding of the Maker. While [the soul] enlarges itself in width through love, it lifts itself in height through knowledge, and it is as high above itself as it extends outside itself in love of neighbor."[19] We reach up toward God and out toward one another. We contemplate the source of love, then we exhibit that love toward our neighbor. In the Lucan narrative, before the Gospel writer shares the Lord's commendation of Mary's contemplative posture, he relates Jesus's parable of the good Samaritan, which expresses the Lord's praise for the active life.

In the novel, we witness the confused division between action and contemplation. The Curé de Torcy knows the priest to be a contemplative, but he misunderstands what that means. "I've got nothing against your contemplatives," the Curé tells him. "Each man to his job. They provide us with bunches of flowers beside the music." From the Curé's modern perspective, contemplatives add music and flowers after the active ones have "done the housework, washed up, peeled the spuds and laid the table."[20] Following centuries of conditioning toward action, we resemble the Curé more than we do the priest. What would the world look like if Christians curled themselves up "all snug and safe," in the Curé's words, "in Abraham's bosom"? We all love the so-called Christian high of getting swept up by God, but as the Curé de Torcy observes, "the real snag is to stick there, and know how to get down again."[21] Although the Curé de Torcy is more experienced in pastoring than the young priest, the latter is further along on his sanctification journey. He recognizes the fallacy in the Curé's words—the "real snag" is to see the active life as flowing from the contemplation of God. Instead of envisioning the contemplative life as decorative to existence, the young priest shows us how it is the origination and culmination of the active life.

In meditating on this relationship between the two, I thought of the verse in Haggai when the prophet laments how the exiles who have returned to Judah have neglected to rebuild the temple. Haggai speaks on behalf of the Lord Almighty: "You have planted much, but harvested little. You eat, but never have enough. You drink, but never have your fill" (Hag. 1:6). We may stir ourselves into a frenzy of activity on behalf of God, but none of it will bear fruit without contemplation. The exiles needed to rebuild the temple not because God is a created being who required housing but so that they would place worship at the center of their lives. Without contemplation of the source of life, what is the point of the active life? Such an active life will be frenetic, fruitless, and unsatisfying, for contemplation is the act of knowing the Maker of all meaning. It is how I felt after a year of quarantine when I had neglected prayer. Without God, all seemed meaningless.

In *The Diary of a Country Priest*, we perceive in the life of the priest a cyclical relationship between his contemplation of God, as practiced through his prayers, and his action in the community. In contrast to the priest, we watch characters who are active in the community but do not reflect any contemplative life. When the priest visits the great Madame in town, she protests, "I've never failed in a single duty. Sometimes I've even found happiness."[22] What more can God ask for than for us to do the right things—go to church, give alms, raise our families, keep our reputations above suspicion? However, the priest confronts the Madame's righteousness as despair, and her actions as meaningless apart from love. When she refers to her home as a "Christian household," he rebukes her: "You may bid Christ welcome, but what do you do to Him when He comes? He was also welcomed by Caiaphas."[23] As an aristocrat in the town, the woman is unaccustomed to hearing truth spoken so harshly—the priest implies she's a murderer of Christ. Although others in town allow the Madame her charade of faith, the priest defames her pious standing as little more than "a silk shroud on a rotting corpse."[24]

As the two of them converse privately in her home, the priest plays the role of both father and child before her, loving her with authority and humility. He discovers, as she confesses, that the Madame lost a son when he was not yet two years old. Since his death, she has refused to love God. Although she has perpetuated the *acts* required of a "good Christian," she has not loved, enjoyed, or prayed to God since the boy died. Josef Pieper defines contemplation as "a knowing which is inspired by love. Without love there would be no contemplation."[25] Because the Madame has fostered hatred within herself, she has not been able to contemplate this source of love.

Although this wound was known only to God, the priest, because of his prayer life, is able to see through her dissembling. The priest credits God with his ability to speak honestly to her, to know her heart, and to move her to return to her faith:

> While I struggled with all my might against doubt and terror, a spirit of prayer came back to my heart. Let me put it quite clearly: from the very start of this strange interview I never once had ceased to "pray" in the sense which shallow Christians give to the word. A wretched creature into which air is being pumped may look exactly as though it were breathing. That is nothing. Then air suddenly whistles through the lungs, inflates each separate delicate tissue already shriveled, the arteries throb to the first violent influx of new blood—the whole being is like a ship creaking under swollen sails.[26]

The priest's habit of prayer has prepared him for a crucial spiritual battle. In this moment, his action would not have sufficed to save this soul from hating God. The priest is only able to act as he does because of the years prior that he has spent contemplating God.

When St. Augustine writes about our longing for God as increasing our capacity for God, he means that our prayers have reformed us. Praying acts on us like weightlifting on a muscle—the fight and the strain prepare the muscle to lift more in the future. The priest acknowledges the mystical nature of this encounter with the Madame: "Words seemed so trivial at that moment. I felt as though a mysterious hand had struck a breach in who knows what invisible rampart, so that peace flowed in from every side."[27] Knowing his weakness, the priest relies on the Lord's strength, on his words, on his knowledge of the Madame.

Several times in the encounter, the Madame displays shock. For the priest's words speak to her very soul in a way that she cannot imagine this young man's having the ability to do. She questions whether the priest is quoting from a book, for surely, she thinks, he does not possess the wisdom that he shares. When I read this section,

I remember moments when I unwittingly have said something that another person needed to hear, when I said more than I knew or meant by my words. These are moments when we recognize that the Holy Spirit is alive and active. Just imagine if we gave so much of ourselves to prayer and contemplation that the Lord could regularly move through us in this way. When we neglect the practices of prayer and contemplation, we limit God's ability to act.

By the end of this scene, the priest urges the Madame to pray the "Our Father" in imitation of Jesus Christ's prayer. She admits that she has not said these words since the Lord took her son from her. Yet, for the love that she hopes will return, that her son may know her in the next life, she prays, "Thy kingdom come, Thy will be done." This prayer frees her from her sin. That same evening, the Madame writes a confidential note to the priest celebrating that she again is experiencing—for the first time in decades—God's peace and hope. It is in his peace that she passes away that very evening. As the priest stands over her corpse the next morning, he laments, "With God's help at last I managed to pray."[28] This story reminds us that every moment should be seen in light of eternity. "Sweet miracle of empty hands," the priest writes after her passing, "to be able to give what we ourselves do not possess."[29] Their shared prayer returned her to God's peace.

Habits of Preparation

The priest could not have intentionally prepared for that moment when the Lord permitted him to participate in the Madame's salvation, for he could not have known what was in her heart. However, his habits of prayer readied him for any encounter, that he might act as God's instrument whenever needed. Because we Protestants may fear emphasizing works in our faith, we hastily marginalize right practices. Sometimes we disapprove of spiritual practices such as poverty, chastity, and fasting out of concern that we may mistakenly claim our righteousness by these acts. However, N. T. Wright, in *After You Believe*, walks through the necessity of habits toward the cultivation of virtue, what we moderns call "character."[30] To flourish fully as a human being, one must practice the habits of faith that lead to virtuous action at the right moment. Looked at in this light, the regular habits of the contemplative increase his or her potency of action. The novel itself is a testimony that contemplation cannot be considered in the abstract: we know what it means when we witness a *life* of prayer.

What practices till the soil, so to speak, for the life of contemplation? The twelfth-century monk St. Aelred of Rievaulx claims that the contemplative life requires an exercise of virtue: "The discipline of virtue consists in a certain way of life, in fasting, in vigils, in manual work, in reading, in prayer, in poverty, and other such things."[31] Because of the priest's illness, he can only manage a diet of bread and wine. In light of this meager fare, churchgoers in his parish abuse the priest as a drunk, an insult that the Pharisees also hurled at Jesus in the Gospels. Yet, with the insight provided by the priest's diary, readers behold a saint subsisting on the Eucharist for his survival. We also witness his vigils, his care of the parish, and his poverty. He visits his parishioners so regularly that other priests call him excessive. In the home of the Curé de Torcy, the priest is uncomfortable because of its luxury: "a massive mahogany bedstead, a wardrobe with three heavily carved doors, armchairs upholstered in plush, and a big bronze statue of Joan of Arc on the mantelpiece."[32] Although he's embarrassed by his poverty (so much so that when a cleaning woman comes to help, he buys underwear and shirts to seem less poor), the priest registers indulgence as incompatible with the contemplative life. His state of temperance cultivates his soul for the contemplative life.

In Dante's paradise, the contemplatives are associated with the virtue of temperance. Revolving around Saturn, these saints reside in the seventh sphere. The Curé de Torcy implies that the priest is destined to be among them when he quotes the advice to "descend again from your seventh heaven."[33] We associate temperance with

restraint—dining less often on gourmet fare, abstaining from sex, sur-
rendering worldly goods. In the Old Testament, the prophet Daniel
was the exemplar of this virtue, for he rejected the Babylonian diet to
prepare to receive the Lord's visions. In the New Testament, Mary of
Bethany pours out her costly perfume at the Lord's feet, showing her
love for God over material things. However, theologians also consider
virtues such as humility, forgiveness, hospitality, and mercy to be signs
of temperance. Each of these positive virtues exhibits the restraining
of an impulse. As St. Edith Stein writes of temperance, "Only the
person who renounces self-importance, who no longer struggles to
defend or assert himself, can be large enough for God's boundless
actions."[34] One surrenders pride to be humble, relinquishes a grudge
to forgive, and so on. The contemplative foregoes earthly pleasures
for satisfaction in the divine, in the love of God. In turn, this love of
God becomes the love of neighbor, which often means having less so
that another might have more.

Contemplation and Self-Knowledge

The idea of self-knowledge has been a perennial interest at least since
Socrates, though he used the phrase "Know thyself" as a reminder
to recognize one's humble position in the universe. We Americans
think of self-knowledge as an exaltation of our greatness. We've been
inundated with commands such as "Love yourself," as though the
self is worthy of great exaltation. Oprah, Deepak Chopra, and Justin
Bieber participate in an industry that makes such sacrilege palatable.
However, Flannery O'Connor thought the opposite: "The first prod-
uct of self-knowledge is humility . . . for to know oneself is, above
all, to know what one lacks."[35] We must judge ourselves against the
God who is so high above us and see our smallness in comparison.
But how to acquire such a vision of oneself?

   If we on earth possess limited vision with which to examine ourselves, we cannot see ourselves clearly as we are. To look into our

selves would be to see what we want to see or are capable of seeing, which is not accurate. "We are unknown to ourselves, we knowers," Friedrich Nietzsche famously asserts, but he stops there.[36] Christians grant that premise but add that thus we must know ourselves through the God who knows us best. Hence, churches are not filled with mirrors but with stained glass. The light of God shines through the image of a saint, showing us who we are called to be. As the poet George Herbert reflects on his vocation as a preacher, he asks,

> Lord, how can man preach thy eternal word?
>   He is a brittle crazy glass;
> Yet in thy temple thou dost him afford
>   . . . .
> To be a window, through thy grace.[37]

We are but broken pieces of glass. Yet by God's light, by his grace, we become what we were meant to be. The Christian life requires that we begin with a vision of ourselves as sinners (broken glass) and then recognize our call to be saints (as portrayed in cathedral windows). We must comprehend the paradox of both our lack of goodness and our power to become great by the grace of God.

The Diary of a Country Priest reflects both realities of that paradox. As the priest tries to understand himself as a weak sinner and show others their smallness before God, he must simultaneously trust his authority in the parish, granted to him by God. The priest recognizes this vision of sinfulness as the necessary precursor to the end as spiritual hero—what he calls "supernatural heroism." When the Madame, who has set store by her external acts of righteousness, confesses that she feels no shame, the priest responds, "God grant you may despise yourself."[38] In order to confess our sin, we have to experience guilt. If we are to know the vast grace of God, we must see ourselves in need of it. The priest imagines everyone in his parish as diseased, enduring cancer without discomfort, harboring inner wounds that ooze spiritual puss. In his diary, he worries that after death "they will find themselves as they really are, as they were without knowing it—horrible undeveloped monsters, the stumps of men."[39] O'Connor, who read Bernanos in graduate school, later called us goods "under construction."[40] We would look freakish if a person's external appearance matched their spiritual reality. This vision of our distorted nature, our broken and wounded self, must precede any knowledge of ourselves as supernatural agents of grace.

In superhero films, you often have a moment when the ordinary person becomes aware of their extraordinary gifts, and this self-knowledge frees them to be more powerful than they ever imagined. These characters then assert proudly that they know who they are. In *Black Panther*, the soon-to-be-king is fighting a challenger to his throne, and his mother encourages him from the sidelines: "Show him who you are." He then fights more fiercely, claiming his identity: "I am Prince T'Challa." When Wanda Maximoff in *WandaVision* confronts Agatha Harkness, she insists, "I don't need you to tell me who I am." She embraces her powers when she acknowledges her identity. Similarly, Captain Marvel registers the extent of her powers and claims her name: "My name is Carol." These films are playing off our modern existential crisis that we do not know who we are. But when we figure that out, such knowledge of our self is accompanied by power. There is a glimmer of truth in these stories that we feel and celebrate.

Where the superhero narratives differ from the Christian story is in the source of the power and what it means. To claim *my* name means very little, and I would access no greater power to stand up and shout, "I am Jessica Hooten Wilson." For Bernanos, the human person was called to be a knight of faith, like Joan of Arc, an undersized farmgirl who led an army. That particular saint is referenced three or four times in *The Diary of a Country Priest* as a model. As Balthasar writes, Bernanos saw that "sanctity is an adventure . . . the terror of a superhuman hope."[41] But what does such supernatural heroism look like in his world? Sanctity is often more anonymous than venerated. We don't always know the holy superheroes in our midst.

Our power comes when we assert our true identity as those called to be saints. We may exclaim, "I am a child of the living God." The Lord establishes a new identity for us by calling us his own. Throughout the Scriptures, the Lord renames those he has called: Abram and Sarai become Abraham and Sarah, Jacob becomes Israel, Simon becomes Peter, Saul becomes Paul. In the Orthodox and Catholic Church, you receive a saint's name at baptism or confirmation; you surrender your identity and receive his or hers as a reminder of your calling and your telos. We have a redeemed name that reminds us of the source of our power, the "superhuman dignity of our calling," in the priest's words.[42] We are called to achieve tasks beyond our competence, but as the priest tells his doctor, prayer confers "strength."[43]

By contemplating the love of God, we come to know ourselves as we truly are, as both less and more important. Throughout the Scriptures, we are called to be "his handiwork" (Eph. 2:10). When St. Peter describes us as the "living stones" of God's church (1 Pet. 2:5), such a vision is humbling. For those of us who worry that life is meaningless, we are part of a grander vision than we could achieve by ourselves. Isaiah calls us the clay and God the potter (Isa. 64:8). To see ourselves as mud might sober our ambitions, but to recognize that the Creator of every atom, star, galaxy, and wave is molding me into a designed piece of art is also exhilarating. When we submit to God's calling and design for our lives, we can do more than we ever could apart from it. The priest tries to explain this to the Madame: "That poker there is only an instrument in your hands. Had God endowed it with just enough consciousness to put itself into your hands whensoever you needed it, that would be more or less what I am for all of you—what I wish to be."[44] The reality of our place tempers any grand ambitions we have for charting our own course or filling our schedules with unnecessary action. In her *Prayer Journal*, Flannery O'Connor prays to God, "Please give me some place, no matter how small, but let me know it and keep it. If I am the one to wash the second step every day, let me know it and let me wash it and let my heart overflow with love washing it."[45] The priest seems to have prayed this prayer regularly in his parish: "Am I where Our Lord would have me be? Twenty times a day I ask this question."[46] Our power comes from knowing our place, knowing who God called us to be.

As a man, the priest is weak. As a priest, nameless to readers but named by God, he has unlimited strength and authority. Several times in the novel, the priest is surprised that parishioners heed his commands. He speaks as one with authority, and they are shocked to hear the confidence of his words. Everyone obeys him, whether or not they despise every moment of surrender. He himself is often surprised that they listen, and he wonders why. For Walker Percy (who borrows this idea from Kierkegaard), such authority explains the difference between a genius and an apostle, between one who speaks on behalf of himself and one who speaks on behalf of another. An apostle is merely a messenger of God, and as such, his authority comes from a higher source. In the novel, the parishioners recognize this other-worldly authority of the priest. They obey the weak figure before them because they believe in the source of his power. In conversation with his doctor, the priest humbly explains, "I only know God has given me all that is needed so I may return it, someday, to Him."[47] The priest's words are a model for us to repeat. Without God, our hands remain empty. Without him, not only are we not superhuman, we are less than human.

Enjoyment of God

For those of us who grew up at church camp singing "Jesus, Lover of My Soul," we feel comfortable discussing the enjoyment of God. Evangelicals refer to such occasions as "God moments," "spiritual highs," or "asking Jesus into our hearts." As someone who feels things deeply, I've always longed for these moments. I love teaching on the mystics who share their contemplative experiences—women like Julian of Norwich, Teresa of Ávila, Margery Kempe. Initially,

Protestant students find them off-putting and weird for their sensual descriptions of the love of God until I connect these accounts to moments in their own lives when they have experienced ecstasy they could not put into words, ineffable moments of energy or power or elation. Karl Rahner writes, "The devout Christian of the future will either be a 'mystic,' one who has experienced 'something,' or he will cease to be anything at all."[48] Our knowledge of God depends on the joy and love found in contemplation. We are called to be mystics.

If such otherworldly contemplation feels beyond you, consider the contemplative life as a ladder with many rungs. This image has been used by theologians throughout church history, drawing from Jacob's vision in Genesis: "He dreamed that there was a ladder set up on the earth, the top of it reaching to heaven; and the angels of God were ascending and descending on it. And the LORD stood beside him and said, 'I am the LORD'" (Gen. 28:12–13 NRSV). God reveals himself to us at the height of the ladder, the rung of contemplation. A twelfth-century Carthusian monk, Guigo II, outlines three previous rungs: *lectio*, reading the Word; then *meditatio*, which seeks to interpret the meaning; followed by *oratio*, prayer.

While I have spent most of this chapter fleshing out prayer and aiming toward contemplation, we need to step back a moment to understand the two preceding steps on the ladder. Rather than look inward with our own limited appraisal, we turn our eyes first to the Word, the revelation not only of God's character but of his creation and his people. It's why the country priest relies on a breviary for his regular devotion, why churchgoers hold the Book of Common Prayer in such esteem, and why *sola scriptura* is still a popular slogan after five hundred years of use. My former colleague Robbie Castleman always reminds students that, unless they are regularly getting to know the One revealed in the Word, they are only worshiping a God of their own image. In his book *Prayer*, Balthasar reminds us that prayer is a dialogue, and God speaks primarily through his Word: "Contemplation's ladder, reaching up to heaven, begins with the word of scripture, and whatever rung we are on, we are never beyond the hearing of this word."[49] The practice of praying with Scripture is called *lectio divina*; it is essentially self-emptying attention to the Word of God. From there, one may then interpret, pray, and contemplate.

The priest fights to pray throughout most of the novel. We might imagine that his journey toward the enjoyment of God began at seminary, where he learned to interpret the Word. Over many pages, readers witness how he has endeavored to pray. A few times, God has intervened and met him where he was in prayer. The priest writes, I "could feel my soul in touch with God."[50] In another instance, after sharing his concerns with God, the priest wakes "full of courage and hope. Providence has answered my jeremiads, a very gentle reproof." In his imagination, God seems to be "like a watchful mother shrugging her shoulders at the first clumsy steps of her little child."[51] Near the end of his life, the contemplation of God becomes both "painful" and "happy." He rises in the dark and prays "till daylight." The priest describes contemplation "like a great murmuring of the spirit. It made me think of all the rustling leaves which herald the dawn. What morning can be breaking in me? Will God's grace shine on me?"[52] Such moments do not come easily, nor does the priest take them lightly. He has paid dearly for them, suffering humiliation, feeling God's absence, sharing in what he describes as the Lord's agony in the garden. Through the priest's journey toward contemplation, readers understand the cost of the joy of the Lord.

The final pages of his journal are desperate prayers to come to terms with death. Although I missed signs of his impending death on my first read, with knowledge of how the book ends, you can find all the hints that the Lord grants the priest to forewarn him. The Lord has shared this journey with him. Even in his last moments, the priest expends his energy sharing the love of God. He looks around him at the street flooded with sunshine. Cocks are crowing, and he recalls the joy of the previous day when he rode on the back of a motorcycle. "With fearful speed the visible world seemed to slip away from me in a maze of pictures; they were . . . so full of light and dazzling beauty. How is this? Can I have loved it all so much?"[53] Contemplation, the priest's story shows us, not only converts our vision of ourselves, so that we may see rightly, but also increases our love of God, of our neighbors, and of the world around us. Through the knowledge of God, we see ourselves as stumps of human beings called to be superheroes or knights of faith. By contemplating the God who is love, who created, sustains, and redeems all things, we may share the imagination of the priest. In his final words, the priest whispers the true vision that he's been granted by contemplation: "Grace is everywhere."[54]

Conclusion

Throughout 2020, I had been praying. My husband and I pray each evening. I pray with my kids before school. We prayed each Sunday the prayers of the church and the Lord's Prayer. But not until February 2021 did I realize that I had not been praying without ceasing, the kind of prayer that transfigures every activity into a way of glorifying God, of listening to God, of attending to the most sustaining relationship in existence. I had not been praying in the way that the early Christian and medieval writers called contemplation, the full attention on God. If I had been praying, I was talking more than listening. My prayer life had become a monologue of praises, complaints, requests—but not a conversation. Not a space for the joy of the Lord to flow into me and from me.

When the snow lifted that February, so did my spirits . . . a bit. My husband sent me on a bike ride while he cared for the kids. As I rode my bike, with each movement of my body, each gust of wind, each trill of a bird, I felt more like myself again. I prayed, not with words as much as with attention. I emptied myself of plans. I focused on the rocks and roots on the path. I watched the trail for when it would turn, when I should brake, when I should accelerate. I thought about how similar bike riding was to prayer. Self-emptying attention, what in Greek is called *kenōsis*, frees one to see the path ahead more clearly. As I climbed, pushing the bike upward, I prayed. My body was asking

God to do hard things through my weak form. In the silence of the ride, I prayed. I thanked God for the coolness of his air. I recognized his breath in me as a gift.

With such attention to the sights and sounds around me, I realized suddenly that there were deer up ahead moving through the trees. I stopped my bike to watch them. I could see their slow, stealthy movements in flashes between dried brambles and leafless limbs. One doe stopped, turned her head, and stared at me. We were yards away from one another, but she faced me as though determining my risk for her family. Her fawns passed behind her. Being a good twenty-first-century American, I tried to capture the moment with my iPhone, but the camera did not pick up the three-dimensional deer. They remained in full view to me, but for the phone, they were hidden in the trees. I reflected again on how much prayer is a way of seeing. When we pray, no matter the exact words, the Spirit is groaning for God to show us his hiddenness. Technology failed in the moment; it became a symbol of how I had filtered my vision of things through the world's eyes. I had kept myself active, but I had neglected the purpose and power behind that action.

Prayer is the link between our life of action and the highest end of life, the contemplation of God. Without it, whether amid blessings or clouded days, we will not know the meaning of existence. Although the adventure of sanctity may appear mundane to the world, we know the reality of who we are and who we are called to be. Through an imagination cultivated by stories such as that of the country priest, through his prayers and our own, through the example of contemplation and our pursuit of it, we will return to God. Our hands will no longer be empty, but they will be filled with miracles.

Devotional

From *The Diary of a Country Priest*: "For those who have the habit of prayer, thought is too often a mere alibi, a sly way of deciding to do what one wants to do. Reason will always obscure what we wish to keep in the shadows. A worldling can think out the pros and cons and sum up his chances. No doubt. But what are our chances worth? We who have admitted once and for all into each moment of our puny lives the terrifying presence of God? . . . What is the use of working out chances? There are no chances against God."[55]

Scripture: "And then he told me, 'My grace is enough; it's all you need. My strength comes into its own in your weakness.' Once I heard that, I was glad to let it happen. I quit focusing on the handicap and began appreciating the gift. It was a case of Christ's strength moving in on my weakness" (2 Cor. 12:9 MSG).

Wisdom from the Saints: St. Aelred of Rievaulx: "The love of God requires two things: love in the heart and productive virtue. So we must work in the exercise of virtue and love in the sweetness of spiritual experience. The discipline of virtue consists in a certain way of life, in fasting, in vigils, in manual work, in reading, in prayer, in poverty and other such things. Our love is nourished on salutary meditation. And in order that this sweet love of Jesus may grow in your heart, you must practice a threefold meditation: in memory of the past, then awareness of present things, concern for future things."[56]

Prayer: *Shema.* Listen. Be still. Behold. May we see with your eyes the needs of those around us and grant us the grace to pursue the joint adventure of sanctity and adventure of eternity.

Discussion Questions

1. What are the greatest impediments to the contemplative life?
2. What should be the relationship between contemplation and action?

3. In *The Diary of a Country Priest*, how does the young priest fail in the eyes of the world but succeed in holiness?

4. How does the priest's prayer life inspire you to pray differently? In what ways would you want to imitate his contemplative practice?

5. Do you agree with the priest's last words, "Grace is everywhere"?

Further Reading

Italo Calvino, *Mr. Palomar*
Leif Enger, *Peace like a River*
Diane Glancy, *Island of the Innocent*
J. F. Powers, *Morte d'Urban*

7

Sharing in His Suffering

I must not attempt to control God's action; I must not count the
stages in the journey He would have me make. I must not desire
a clear perception of my advance upon the road, must not know
precisely where I am upon the way of holiness. I must ask Him to
make a saint of me, yet I must leave to Him the choice of saintliness itself and still more the means that lead to it.

–Mother Teresa, *No Greater Love*[1]

BEFORE AUGUSTINE CONVERTED to Christianity, he prayed, "Lord,
make me chaste—but not yet."[2] Am I the only one who has prayed
similar prayers: "Lord, make me a saint—but not yet"? What do
we fear? Am I afraid that if I pray for humility, the Lord is going to
embarrass me in public? Or, if I pray for patience, that he'll strike
me with an incurable disease? We are so accustomed to our comfort
that we are afraid of the trials that would purge of us our worldly
desires and sanctify us for eternal life. Yet God is not a devious genie
who twists our prayers to grant us the bad instead of the good. At the
same time, God moves through our suffering to cast us into saints.

Because suffering is unavoidable, our only choice is how to respond to it—with pride and protest or with humility and openness to what God may be accomplishing through it.

A few years ago, I sat on a Q&A panel on suffering with Eleonore Stump, the acclaimed professor of philosophy who literally wrote the book on suffering—*Wandering in Darkness: Narrative and the Problem of Suffering*. She was the keynote, and I the lucky young professor there to answer the softball questions. After a dozen or so hands had shot up and people had their five minutes before the microphone asking about how a good God could allow pain and evil in the world, Dr. Stump paused and asked, "Can any of you name a hero who has not gone through trials of many kinds?" We all sat there in stunned silence as we realized the profundity of her question. Although we know that suffering produces perseverance and then character, hope, and so on, we all want it to happen to other people and not ourselves. We would like to somehow become heroes or saints without suffering. Stump enlightened us to the reality that this ambition is an impossibility in a fallen world. If we long to be saints, we must be conditioned for suffering.

Suffering as Purgatorial

In 1946, Flannery O'Connor prayed, "It is hard to want to suffer; I presume Grace is necessary for the want."[3] O'Connor's prayer sounds nothing like the way I pray. Perhaps we could shrug off her prayer as the zealous imagination of a twenty-year-old girl and put little stock in it. On the other hand, that young girl would become one of America's most gifted writers—some have argued the only great Christian writer that America has ever produced.[4] So, what do we do with the troubling assertion of this prayer?

O'Connor is not alone in her investigation into the instrumental good of suffering. Contemporary with these prayers, British novelist and fellow Catholic Graham Greene wrote *The Power and the Glory* and *The End of the Affair* about characters who receive sanctification through suffering. Of his desire to tell these stories, Greene says he "suffered . . . obsessions."[5] He shares in his autobiography that, as he was writing *The Power and the Glory*, he was also whittling away at a hopeful bestseller to earn his keep—a story about "the man who has learned to love justice by suffering injustice."[6] The word "suffering" is a constant in Greene's writing, always on his mind and integral to our existence. When Greene converted to Catholicism, some part of him may have expected "an untroubled sea," as he writes, only to discover "faith was a tempest in which the lucky were engulfed and lost, but the unfortunate survived to be flung battered and bleeding on the shore. . . . What was the Church for but to aid these sufferers?"[7] Through his stories, Greene attempts not only to aid those suffering but also to answer for himself how God works through suffering for sanctification.

O'Connor began her prayer journal from a desire to love God more, to know him more through personal prayers rather than the ones she memorized during her catechesis. She confesses, "I do not mean to deny the traditional prayers that I have said all my life; but I have been saying them and not feeling them."[8] Instead, O'Connor prays to overcome her "mediocre" faith, as she repeatedly calls it, to become more like a saint. At the time she wrote these prayers, she was reading the Catholic thinker Léon Bloy, who wrote, "The only real sadness, the only real failure, the only great tragedy in life, is not to become a saint."[9] For O'Connor, sainthood became a lifelong ambition, and the path of sainthood—suggested by Bloy, by other theologians whose texts O'Connor studied and reviewed, and by the memoirs and biographies of saints she read—is a call to suffering.

Bloy was extreme in his views on this. For Bloy, suffering was the *only* road to redemption. Because God became a human in order to suffer, the consequence was a necessary vocation of suffering. He took phrases such as "The first will be last" as imperatives that Christians should strive to be last, to be on the bottom, to be poor not only in spirit but also in life. For Bloy, we should seek suffering because it redeems our guilt and allows us to participate in Jesus's suffering. What O'Connor found attractive in this thinking was Bloy's disgust at all lukewarmness.[10] Here was a route to overcoming her mediocrity of faith and increasing it to greatness. O'Connor prayed in her youth, "I am afraid of pain and I suppose that is what we have to have to get grace. Give me the courage to stand the pain to get the grace, Oh Lord."[11] Presumably, O'Connor was not praying for the power to withstand cauldrons of boiling pitch or arenas of lions. Rather, she indicates an undefined pain that acts as the conduit for grace.

Bloy was not proposing masochism when he asserted the need for Christians to suffer. Rather, he reminds us of Paul's words to the Romans that "we are children . . . of God . . . if indeed we share in his sufferings" (8:17) and of Christ's instruction to his disciples that if they are to follow him, they must take up their cross (Mark 8:34). In the epigraph for *The End of the Affair*, Greene chooses a line attributed to Bloy: "Man has places in his heart which do not yet exist, and into them enter suffering in order that they may have existence." Mysteriously, suffering evacuates the self from overstuffing the heart and opens room for deeper participation with Christ. In his final words before his execution, Greene's whiskey priest in *The Power and the Glory* echoes Bloy: "It would have been quite easy to have been a saint. It would have only needed a little self-restraint and a little courage. . . . He knew now that at the end there was only one thing that counted—to be a saint."[12] Although the "saints" in Greene's stories die in the narratives, readers see the fruit borne from their sacrifice; they are the grains of wheat that have fallen to the ground (John 12:24).

A few years after O'Connor drafted these prayers, the dreadful disease that would ultimately kill her began to show its symptoms. She was diagnosed with lupus at twenty-five and suffered for fourteen years, during the whole of her writing career. O'Connor disapproved of any attempt to connect her disease with her writing life. When one interviewer asked whether her lupus affected her fiction, she quipped— "No, since for my writing I use my head and not my feet."[13] However, the suffering in her own life does appear to affect her stories. "It has always seemed necessary to me to throw the weight of circumstances against the character I favor. The friends of God suffer, etc.," she writes.[14] Not only does O'Connor assume the axiomatic truth that God's friends suffer, but she herself, when imitating God in her fiction, places the heaviest suffering on her favorites. The way to sainthood, in O'Connor's world, is more than narrow; it is harrowing and painful.

If you ask a reader of O'Connor about her stories, they will remember freaks, sinners, and violence; readers of Greene find his work shocking and overly sexual. And these are Catholic writers? Yet there are saints in these narratives—that's why these novels are imaginatively persuasive, the realism of sin and grit through which God works extraordinarily to propel humans into holiness. The challenge in seeing the light within the dark stems from our own skewed vision. Christian readers especially are guilty of succumbing to a vision of the Christian life that is all rainbows above Noah's ark, Christ high-fiving people out of the grave, and gleeful Christians donning "Light of the World" T-shirts. O'Connor knew this: "What people don't realize is how much religion costs. They think faith is a big electric blanket, when of course it is the cross."[15] The holiness in these narratives might be hard for us to see or hear in the same way it was hard for those in the Gospels to see or hear the reality of Christ. Remember, for thousands of years, God had warned his people that their eyes would have trouble seeing and their ears would be hard of hearing when truth arrived. So it is in O'Connor's and Greene's novels. The Christians there will look foolish, dirty, small; they will use words like "burn" and "pierce"; they want whiskey and sex; they may even yell or be violent. But, over the course of their lives, through their suffering, they show readers that sainthood comes at a cost.

Suffering Persecution

Greene's *The Power and the Glory* is set in Mexico during the Cristero War (1926–29), the persecution of the Catholic Church by the

Mexican government. Before and after the official "war," around forty priests were executed and thousands exiled from the country. In *The Power and the Glory*, a priest who is grappling with his saintly calling flees for his life from the police who are seeking to execute him. Greene visited Mexico in the 1930s with the intention of writing a nonfiction book about the atrocities committed by the government against the Catholic Church, but God had other plans for him. Although condemned by the Vatican, *The Power and the Glory* was named by *Time* magazine as one of the top one hundred novels of the twentieth century.[16] When my Well-Read Moms book club read and discussed the novel, I had not read it for a decade, and the story struck a new chord with me after all those years.

The book shows how this persecuted priest fails at being a saint. Never named but only referred to as "Father," the whiskey priest may be identified by readers as ourselves. While the priest never recants his faith at any point in the story, he does not appear to live as a Christian. He is a compulsive drinker, a coward, and, in a moment of weakness, has produced a child with one of his parishioners. When the story begins, the priest is attempting to escape the state on a boat. But a young boy approaches him and begs for his services for his dying mother. Grudgingly, the priest does his duty, certain that missing this boat means that he will eventually be executed. Although the priest is disgraceful, he believes, to the point of death, that heaven exists, that God is judge, and that the sacraments of Christ's body and blood are offered to even the worst of sinners who repent.

Midway through the narrative, the priest is arrested and thrown into prison for carrying whiskey; the officers do not know that he is a priest, the one they have been hunting for months. In the prison, readers discover that the priest has been transformed because of suffering persecution; he has moved from an arrogant position in society as an exalted agent of righteousness to a criminal, like Jesus Christ on trial before the Roman rulers. He refers to himself as a "criminal [who] ought only to talk to criminals." A pious woman, a fellow prisoner, accosts him and begs him to hear her confession. Unable to see herself as a criminal, the woman scorns those around her. She considers only the priest worthy of her conversation. He reflects that "in the old days" when he was a fat and happy priest, when he did not bear persecution and would have shared her disdain for the criminals surrounding them, "he would have known what to say to her . . . feeling no pity at all, speaking with half a mind a platitude or two."[17] His new status as a criminal reveals his feebleness. The priest acknowledges his unholiness: "We are not saints, you and I."[18] Ironically, this humility and identification of his sinfulness and former pretense are part of his sanctification. The priest has offered this woman more truth than any platitude about faith he could have devised.

In America, most of us consider ourselves free from persecution because we do not fear the removal of our property or public stoning in the city. Yet, as early church father St. Jerome writes to a young Christian, "What a terrible mistake, my brother, if you imagine there is ever a time when the Christian does not suffer persecution. One is attacked most powerfully when he fails to realize he is being attacked at all."[19] Jerome references the unseen attacks, the invisible anguish of our souls being drawn away from God's image without fathoming it. He suggests that the world is assaulting us most when we are being conformed to it yet are physically free from its external attacks. To me, this is a most fearful state if it is true. It is the lukewarm and mediocre place that O'Connor prayed against, and for which she believed affliction was an antidote.

At the start of O'Connor's second novel, *The Violent Bear It Away* (1960), Mason Tarwater appears to be a crazy person, claiming persecution and calling himself a prophet. The primary plot regards the choice between following Jesus and following the self; its protagonist is a fourteen-year-old boy named Francis Marion Tarwater. His great-uncle Mason has raised him to be a prophet, but Mason dies at the start of the story. Thus, Francis envisions himself as free to choose whether to obey the plans God laid out for him or to chart his own way in the world. The title of the book is drawn from Matthew 11:12, a passage O'Connor had underlined in her Douay-Rheims Bible, in which Jesus proclaims, "The kingdom of heaven suffereth violence, and the violent bear it away." The Scripture indicates two connected forms of trials to be borne by those who follow Jesus and submit to the kingdom of heaven: one is persecution and the other is asceticism, neither of which sounds appealing to the teenage Tarwater.

Mason has already warned Tarwater about the torment that prophets face. When Mason's nephew Rayber, a psychologist, writes about Mason's delusion as a prophet who has called himself into ministry, Mason spits and yells, "Called myself! I, Mason Tarwater, called myself! Called myself to be beaten and tied up. Called myself to be spit on and snickered at. Called myself to be struck down in my pride. Called myself to be torn by the Lord's eye."[20] Because the world does not want to hear his prophetic word, Mason suffers like a twentieth-century John the Baptist. Where did we get the idea that those who are in misery have fallen out of favor with God? Not only does God correct this error of thinking in the ancient book of Job, but the Lord allows the persecution and execution of his own Son. When Mason lists all the ways he has suffered, he is producing evidence that God has called him to this vocation.

Suffering Asceticism: Voluntary or Involuntary

The second type of suffering related to the call to be a priest or prophet who may be persecuted by the culture is a vocation of asceticism, denying oneself the luxuries of the world. In a letter, O'Connor refers to St. Thomas Aquinas's gloss on Matthew 11:12: "The violent Christ is here talking about represent those ascetics who strain against mere nature."[21] O'Connor names the prophets of the Old Testament or the apostles or the early church fathers or saints like Francis and Dominic as "the violent" because they forego the feasts of Babylon or live nomadically without roofs and sofas. They suffer as a vocation.

By the end of *The Violent Bear It Away*, young Tarwater receives this call. He feels hungry, but "no longer as a pain but as a tide," the narrative says—it is a hunger for the bread of life. "He felt it rising in himself through time and darkness, rising through the centuries, and he knew that it rose in a line of men whose lives were chosen to sustain it, who would wander in the world, strangers from that violent country where the silence is never broken except to shout the truth."[22] Here, Tarwater understands himself as "chosen" to endure violence; he is a part of the "violent country," the kingdom of heaven, and must "wander" like Elijah and Paul and Francis, for whom he has been named. Tarwater also lists Daniel and Moses as his predecessors, as well as Abel, implying that his call may be martyrdom. As he strides toward the city to initiate his ministry, Tarwater has "singed eyes, black in their deep sockets . . . ready to envision the fate that awaited him."[23] This once-resistant teenage boy has been burned by the Word of God, purged of his former pride and selfishness. Only after a harrowing experience of causing violence and experiencing agony himself is Tarwater ready to bear not only persecution for the kingdom but also the self-denial needed to withstand it.

Readers often wrestle against the violence of O'Connor's narrative, not to mention the force of her dramatic imagination. For those readers, Greene provides a realistic story with the same theme—the necessity of asceticism in resisting temptation to worldliness. *The End of the Affair* is set in London during the time of the bombings; two characters, Sarah and Bendrix, engage in adultery. The novel shifts between their two viewpoints. We begin with Bendrix's version of the story, but the narrative switches when Bendrix reads Sarah's diary. After the affair is over, from Bendrix's perspective, Sarah appears to be an unfaithful flirt who quit their romance presumably to chase after other men. However, from the diary, Bendrix learns a shocking revelation.

When their hotel was bombed during one of their liaisons, Sarah discovered Bendrix supposedly dead under the stairs. She touched his cold hand and begged God for a miracle. In her diary, Sarah records the deal she enters with the God whom she did not then believe in.

As she stands naked on the stairs, she recalls, "I pressed my nails into the palm of my hand until I could feel nothing but the pain, and I said, I will believe. Let him be alive, and I *will* believe. . . . I'll give him up forever, only let him be alive with a chance, and I pressed and pressed and I could feel the skin break."[24] Sarah inflicts pain on herself, breaking her skin, shedding her own blood to seal this pact with God. The moment resembles earlier saints who trained their bodies into submission by inviting pain on their flesh. Not only does Sarah mete out this small pain on herself, more significantly, she has promised the agony of denying herself a relationship with Bendrix, whom God resuscitates miraculously. God delivers this miracle for Sarah, and she fulfills her end of the bargain by renouncing her affair.

As with *The Diary of a Country Priest*, in these sections of *The End of the Affair*, readers are privy to the innermost thoughts of the sanctified hero. After her promise, Sarah struggles to live without Bendrix; she compares this ascetic life to that of a monk in the desert. Her entire existence feels barren and dry without him. She confesses in her diary to how much she desires Bendrix, how much she covets her life before she committed herself to God, how much she craves the illicit sexual pleasure of their union instead of this empty self-denial. In the hopes of foregoing her vow, Sarah visits a deformed young man who stands on street corners blaspheming God. She hopes that this atheist named Richard will convince her that God does not exist so that she can return to Bendrix. Instead, the combination of her ascetic practice, the renouncement of her lover, and Richard's blasphemy drives her to a complete embrace of God.

While the whiskey priest of *The Power and the Glory* is not an ascetic by choice, we see that the involuntary asceticism purged him of his sins as much as if it had been voluntary. Greene's priest discovers how dreamlike his love for his congregants had been before his persecution. Loving them cost him nothing. In fact, his priestly duties earned the priest money when he married or baptized fellow Catholics. They revered him as though he were famous. And he indulged in all of his desires, including those from which his vows called him to abstain. Counseling the pious woman in prison, the priest says, "Saints talk about the beauty of suffering, [but] suffering to us is just ugly. . . . It needs a lot of learning to see things with a saint's eye."[25] His misery has wrought a change in him.

As the police approach the city where the priest is leading a church service illegally, he preaches a sermon quickly that would have been meaningless to him in any other circumstance: "We deny ourselves so that we can enjoy. . . . Pray that you will suffer more and more and more. Never get tired of suffering. . . . Perhaps without [suffering]—who can tell?—you wouldn't enjoy heaven as much."[26] His words are untrue in the way that he means them and yet true in another way. It may not be necessary to know suffering on earth in order to enjoy God's goodness, yet without suffering, this priest would not enjoy heaven; he would have found all his joy on earth. He would have loved earthly things over heavenly things. Only when all the earthly pleasures have been stripped from him does this priest seek the heavenly goods that he was meant to love. Whether suffering is volitional, a by-product of Christian virtues, or happenstance of this fallen world, God works through it to transform his wayward creatures into saints.

It may be tricky for us to transfer onto our own context the world of 1940s bombed-out London or that of the persecuted priest in 1930s Mexico, but there are ways of practicing or accepting asceticism in our twenty-first-century American setting. Dorothy Day, who forwent luxury regularly in New York, observed, on a visit to her daughter's home, that "families with small children [lead] ascetic lives. There are vigils, involuntary ones, fasting—due to nausea of pregnancy, for instance—but St. Angela of Foligno said that penances voluntarily undertaken are not half so meritorious as those imposed on us by the circumstances of our lives and cheerfully borne."[27] We need not seek out ways of resigning all worldly goods, but we might reimagine our current struggles as possessing the potential to sanctify us.

I have a friend who often says, "I'm tired of being sanctified." She's referring to her task as homemaker, where, as Day describes it, motherhood "leaves her no time for thought of self, for consolation, for prayer, for reading, for what she might consider development."[28] Yet the world of a mother is much like the desert of a monk, where our senses are mortified by our surroundings—dirty diapers, oatmeal on the table, grapes squished beneath our feet, unflushed toilets, a husband's socks in every conceivable place—and our interior world is mortified by adapting our interests to our children. Day notes the joys but also the "thorns . . . of night watches, of illnesses, of infant perversities and contrariness. There are glimpses of heaven and hell."[29] When we read novels like *The Violent Bear It Away* or *The End of the Affair*, we can reimagine our travails less as frustrations, inconveniences, or unnecessary hardships, and more as ascetic realities. Just as those characters become sanctified through their voluntary or involuntary denials, so we might see our pains as training grounds for the Lord's work in us.

Suffering: Vicarious Substitution

Whether or not we believe in mystical substitution, in which one suffers on behalf of another, it seems true that sharing another's burden eases the pain. I think of Dietrich Bonhoeffer, who returned to Nazi-occupied Germany to suffer alongside his brothers and sisters because he believed that this was "a physical sign of the gracious presence of the triune God."[30] He advises his fellow theologians to read the psalms each day for one another: for when you read a psalm of joy, perhaps you are not in a joyous state but you celebrate a brother or sister who may be; and likewise, when you read a psalm of lament when you yourself are not grieving, you grieve in prayer on behalf of those who are hurting in Christ's body. It may be that the only response to affliction in the world is to share in it, to take it on and thus perhaps lessen it for others. O'Connor writes, "Remember that these things are mysteries and that if they were such that we could understand them, they wouldn't be worth understanding. A God you understood would be less than yourself."[31]

In O'Connor's short story "Greenleaf," Mrs. Greenleaf is a saint who attempts vicarious suffering on behalf of others. Although the story revolves around the arrogant Mrs. May, Mrs. Greenleaf stands out as the title character. In the eyes of Mrs. May, who is "a good Christian woman with a large respect for religion, though she did not, of course, believe any of it was true," Mrs. Greenleaf appears foolish. While ordering around her field hand Mr. Greenleaf, Mrs. May is stopped short by a "guttural agonized voice [that] groaned, 'Jesus! Jesus!'" The screaming persists. Mrs. May calls it "piercing" and "violent." Fearing that someone has been hurt, she rushes toward the sound only to find "Mrs. Greenleaf sprawled on her hands and knees off the side of the road, her head down." When Mrs. May shrilly demands to know what is going on, Mrs. Greenleaf raises her head, her face "a patchwork of dirt and tears" and her small eyes "red-rimmed and swollen" with an expression "as composed as a bull-dog's." Rather than answer her, Mrs. Greenleaf continues, "Oh Jesus, stab me in the heart!"[32] She shrieks and falls to the ground with "her legs and arms spread out as if she were trying to wrap them around the earth."[33] Like St. Teresa of Ávila, pierced through the heart by the love of God, Mrs. Greenleaf asks for suffering, that by vicariously taking on others' pain she may know God's "piercing" love.

Mrs. Greenleaf deems this daily practice "prayer healing." "Every day she cut all the morbid stories out of the newspaper—the accounts of women who had been raped and criminals who had escaped and children who had been burned and of train wrecks and plane crashes and the divorces of movie stars. She took these to the woods and dug a hole and buried them and then fell on the ground over them."[34] And then she prays. When my students read this, they express as much disgust as Mrs. May. "Jesus . . . would be *ashamed* of you," Mrs. May responds. "He would tell you to get up from there this instant and go wash your children's clothes!"[35] Yet perhaps Mrs. Greenleaf's actions accord better with reality—*with the unseen reality*. Why are we not as horrified at the headlines? Do we pray for all of these losses around us, all the sin and death and suffering? Are the people who express sorrow publicly for all to see on social media also interceding in prayer in a closet before the One who can actually heal the hurt and remove the tears?

In *The End of the Affair*, Sarah progresses from her initial resistance to pain to a place where she hopes to adopt others' suffering. Writing in her diary about her husband Henry, she wonders in complete honesty why some pains are easier to bear: "If I could love a leper's sores, couldn't I love the boringness of Henry?"[36] Similarly, I have found myself washing dishes and hearing "Mom" on repeat and wondering how I have so little strength to bear this easy cross and from where I might draw the power to withstand a thousand demons. But the practice of bearing another's suffering is what increases Sarah's ability. Not only does she become patient with her husband's dullness, but she's compelled to kiss the deformity on the atheist Richard's face, with whom she's developed a friendship. As she does so, Sarah prays to God, "I am kissing pain and pain belongs to You as happiness never does. I love You in Your pain. . . . You might have killed us with happiness, but You let us be with You in pain."[37] While Sarah mistakenly attributes to God pain more than happiness, she means the temporal happiness of happenstance and contrasts those pleasures with God's eternality. Only in the life to come will we saints withstand the power of God's eternal blessedness.

Sarah journeys toward belief along a road of suffering until her own agony becomes negligible. "It's their pain I can't stand," she prays to God. "Let my pain go on and on but stop theirs. Dear God, if only you could come down from your Cross for a while and let me get up there instead. If I could suffer like you, I could heal like you."[38] What a beautiful meditation! Sarah dwells on how Christ's suffering exhibits his healing. She longs to suffer that she might remove the burden from others.

Suffering according to the World

From a worldly perspective, suffering should be feared, and those who suffer intentionally should be diagnosed with a mental disorder. By allowing the weakest to survive, to paraphrase Nietzsche, we undermine "the vitality of the race," and by saying no to our desires, we "corrode our will to live."[39] This antagonism to Christianity's ascetical nature is reflected in Greene's lieutenant, a police officer who arrests and executes the priest. This figure was based on a real person, Governor Tomás Garrido Canabal, a socialist (who named his son Lenin) who believed that Christianity is nihilistic, that it asks us to deny ourselves and thus holds us back from becoming excellent. When the lieutenant argues with the priest, he accuses him, "You say—perhaps pain's a good thing, perhaps [the poor]'ll be good for it one day. I want to let my heart speak." The priest counters, "At the end of a gun," to which the lieutenant agrees, "Yes. At the end of a gun."[40] And therein lies the problem. The lieutenant is willing to kill so that humanity excels, whereas the priest is willing to be killed so that God is glorified.

In his investigation into the "value of saintliness," William James writes, "The whole feud [between the Nietzschean worldview and that of Christianity] revolves essentially upon two pivots: Shall the seen world or the unseen world be our chief sphere of adaptation?"[41] For the lieutenant, the poor here and now must be saved from their poverty, and he will do so by exterminating all the priests from his state with the force of his gun. He believes in his own strength to save them and justifies his actions as "love" for humanity, a love as theoretical as the ideals for which superheroes fight in the comic book world. Flannery O'Connor calls this "love" tenderness, "which, long cut off from the person of Christ, is wrapped in theory. When tenderness is detached from the source of tenderness, its logical outcome is terror. It ends in forced-labor camps and in the fumes of the gas chamber."[42] O'Connor asserts this claim from a standpoint that in hindsight recalls the Jewish Holocaust, whereas Greene looking forward predicts such atrocities. When the lieutenant concurs that his love will be brought forth at the end of a gun, the priest mutters, "And a girl puts her head under water or a child's strangled, and the heart all the time says, love, love."[43] In response, the lieutenant is silent.

The love that the world manifests apart from Christ is not love. For the lieutenant, for Nietzsche, for the Communists who exiled Aleksandr Solzhenitsyn, for any of those who disconnect love from the incarnation, from the cross, and from the God who is love, heroic acts of love will be no more than steps toward violence. The priest describes God's love as unrecognizable here on earth, scary even: "It set fire to a bush in the desert, didn't it, and smashed open graves and set the dead walking in the dark? Oh, a man like me would run a mile to get away if he felt that love around."[44] God's love should cast in us fear and trembling, and stories of his love in action should scandalize and discomfit us. As we've seen, God's love might hurt.

In *The Violent Bear It Away*, a young girl named Lucette Carmody is the daughter of missionaries; she preaches to a congregation about the "Word of God" that burns one clean. Her name is likely drawn from St. Lucy, the saint of vision, who is also Dante's saintly visitor who helps him through purgatory. Lucette begins her sermon, "Jesus is love. . . . If you don't know what love is you won't know Jesus when He comes."[45] Then she tells the story of how God sent his Word Jesus to be king for the world, yet the world did not recognize him. When Jesus was born, he "came on cold straw . . . warmed by the breath of an ox," and the world asked, "Who is this? Who is this blue-cold child and this woman [Mary] plain as the winter?" The world could not see how the Word of God could be as cold as wind or his mother plain as winter. "Where is the summer will of God?" the world demands. "Where are the green seasons of God's will? Where is the spring and summer of God's will?" *Where, the world may ask, is the electric blanket?* Rejecting this Word of God, the world "nailed Him to a cross and run a spear through His side."[46]

But, Lucette reminds her listeners, he will come again. "Will you know the Lord Jesus then?" she asks. "Listen," she repeats again and again. "The Holy Word is in my mouth!"[47] "Are you deaf to the Lord's Word? The Word of God is a burning Word to burn you clean, burns man and child. . . . Be saved by the Lord's fire or perish in your own!" she shouts.[48] And there is the ultimate choice always offered in O'Connor's fiction: Will you suffer beneath the Lord's flames that he might remove from you all your unholiness? Or will you destroy yourself by rejecting his Word, his will, his suffering?

Bearing Fruit

"Unless a kernel of wheat falls to the ground and dies, it remains only a single seed. But if it dies, it produces many seeds. Anyone who loves their life will lose it, while anyone who hates their life in this world will keep it for eternal life," Jesus tells his disciples (John 12:24–25). Perhaps to those listening to these words, the meaning was lost. Only after they saw Jesus crucified on the cross would this teaching become comprehensible. Russian novelist Fyodor Dostoevsky chose this verse from John 12:24 as the epigraph for *The Brothers Karamazov*. In the novel, after a young boy dies from sickness and poverty, a group of friends gather around his burial mound lamenting his death. Alyosha, a novice at the local monastery, speaks encouraging words to them about the resurrection and the salvific effect of remembering the departed. We listen to his response to the unjust suffering of this boy, and we recall how Alyosha arrived at this place of understanding. When Alyosha's mentor, Father Zosima, dies, the young novice writes down Zosima's story as a hagiography. In retelling the life of this saint, Alyosha hears how Zosima lost his own brother at a young age, became a wayward soldier engaging in duels, remembered his brother's death, and returned to the faith. In the story Alyosha writes, readers witness how Zosima becomes a saint by the practice of loving regardless of whether others slap your cheek, threaten your death, or humiliate your faith. After the young boy dies, Alyosha imitates his hero,

Zosima. The saint's story has borne fruit in Alyosha's life. He then passes on the seeds of instruction to the young boys congregated with him in the cemetery. We should see Dostoevsky's story as instructive for how these stories from O'Connor and Greene are meant to teach us.

In *The Power and the Glory*, the whiskey priest fears he is going to God "empty-handed, with nothing done at all."[49] Yet, like Bernanos's country priest who pronounced the miracle of empty hands, God has worked through this unfaithful priest. As Mr. and Mrs. Fellows discuss the priest's execution, readers discern through their dialogue that he converted their daughter Coral to the faith before her death: "the way she went on afterwards—as if he'd told her things."[50] The dentist who once sheltered the priest is reuniting with his wife, who has found religion. A young boy who formerly rejected stories of holy ones realizes that the priest is a martyr, and the revelation opens him to the church. In *The End of the Affair*, following Sarah's death, Richard's face miraculously heals, and she cures a poor boy suffering from appendicitis.

Even after Sarah's supposed miracles, her former lover Bendrix refuses to believe in God because of Sarah's sinfulness. He speaks to her (though she is dead!):

> For if this God exists . . . and if even you—with your lusts and your adulteries and the timid lies you used to tell—can change like this, we could all be saints by leaping as you leapt, by shutting the eyes and leaping once and for all: if *you* are a saint, it's not so difficult to be a saint. It's something He can demand of any of us, leap.[51]

While Bendrix expresses disgust at the notion that we could all be saints, this is exactly Greene's point. The sinfulness of the whiskey priest and Sarah allows us to relate to them, which means we also can hope that God may work miraculously through our empty hands. These testaments that follow the saints' deaths are an invitation to the reader, that we may ask God to use our suffering to bear his fruit.

When O'Connor prayed for suffering at twenty years old, she could not have imagined her battle with lupus. As the disease debilitated her, she confessed two truths: "I'm sick of being sick"[52] *and* "I can with one eye squinted take it all as blessing."[53] Her honest frustration with sickness reveals her human limits to seeing suffering; yet there was another vision granted her. Through her other eye, she saw the potential blessing of her sickness. Sickness, she writes, "is more instructive than a long trip to Europe . . . [it is] one of God's mercies."[54] If suffering is a grace, then perhaps it is to be prayed for. If it cleanses us of impurity, opens us up to a vocation of sainthood, and lessens the burden of others, then O'Connor's and Greene's stories make more sense. "It is hard to want to suffer," as O'Connor writes. But if these stories are true, then may the Lord grant us all the grace and courage we need to ask for it.

Devotional

From *The Power and the Glory*: "One of the fathers has told us that joy always depends on pain. Pain is part of joy. We are hungry then think how we enjoy our food at last. We are thirsty. . . . We deny ourselves so that we can enjoy. . . . That is why I tell you that heaven is here: this is a part of heaven just as pain is a part of pleasure. . . . Pray that you will suffer more and more and more. Never get tired of suffering. The police watching you, the soldiers gathering taxes, the beating you always get from the jefe because you are too poor to pay, small pox and fever, hunger . . . that is all part of heaven— the preparation. Perhaps without them—who can tell?—you wouldn't enjoy heaven so much."[55]

Scripture: "We continue to shout our praise even when we're hemmed in with troubles, because we know how troubles can develop passionate patience in us, and how that patience in turn forges the tempered steel of virtue, keeping us alert for whatever God will do next. . . . We go through exactly what Christ goes through. If we go through the hard times with him, then we're certainly going to go through the good times with him!" (Rom. 5:3–4; 8:17 MSG).

Wisdom from the Saints: Miguel de Unamuno (1864–1936): "Suffering tells us we exist; suffering tells us those who love exist; suffering tells us the world we live in exists, and suffering tells us that God exists and suffers; and this is the suffering of anguish, the anguish to survive and be eternal."[56]

Prayer: Suffering Servant, Crucified God, we pray for suffering, not that it is good but so that we may not fear the evil things that you have overcome. We pray to know how to suffer well, how to look to you, our suffering Lord, and patiently await the good things you are doing through our suffering and the pain endured by those we love. We pray to think of others' suffering more often than our own, and that you give us eyes to see how to help those who are suffering. May we be less the cause of suffering of others and more a part of your instrumental goodness in the world.

Discussion Questions

1. Based on these novels, what types of suffering should specifically Christians expect or seek to endure?
2. What's the difference between asceticism and masochism?
3. What's the difference between internal purgation and external persecution?
4. Where do we see, in our contemporary culture, people who believe, as the lieutenant in Greene's novel does, that suffering should be eradicated by removing the sufferers?
5. How might Christians respond in holiness to the sufferers near us?

Further Reading

Léon Bloy, *The Woman Who Was Poor*
Randy Boyagoda, *Beggar's Feast*
Shūsaku Endō, *Silence*
Ron Hansen, *Exiles*

8

Ars Moriendi

Tell me, what is it you plan to do
With your one wild and precious life?

—Mary Oliver, "The Summer Day"[1]

THE SEDLEC OSSUARY in Kutná Hora outside of Prague boasts a chandelier composed entirely of human bones. Pelvises, femurs, and skulls artistically connect to create a rather foreboding light fixture. But it does not stand apart from the rest of the décor. Skulls are strung across the ceiling like celebratory banners, and fibulas outline the doorways. Over forty thousand human skeletons adorn the walls of the ossuary. My husband and I visited there with our six-month-old daughter when we lived in Prague. She was unfazed by the spectacle of human remains, the thousands of bones piled high in a vast receptacle or assorted into macabre sculptures. My husband was more perturbed. Each eyeless, skinless skull haunted him, and he wanted out of there as quickly as we entered.

As a teenager, I had visited the Capuchin Crypt in Rome, so Sedlec Ossuary was not my first bone church. The bones reminded me, as

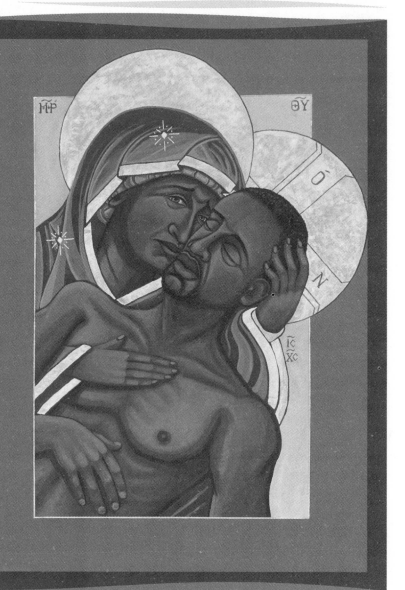

they are intended to, of my own mortality. Here were the skeletons of those who used to be enfleshed souls. They had once walked the narrow streets of Sedlec, or had come from farther off in Bohemia, with the desire to be buried in this holy earth. It was rumored that the thirteenth-century abbot of Sedlec Abbey had returned from his pilgrimage to Jerusalem with a jar of soil from Golgotha, the crucifixion site of Jesus. Hence the requests from thousands upon thousands of believers that this destination be the eternal resting place of their remains. As you tread slowly through the ossuary, you can wonder: In hundreds of years, who will be visiting your grave or staring at your fleshless skull?

"Remember you must die," a voice informs an octogenarian at the start of Muriel Spark's 1959 novel *Memento Mori*.[2] Spark was only forty when she wrote the novel, but the story revolves around a group of elderly folks who all live as though death is not near at hand but a distant unreality. There are no real heroes or saints in the novel. Yet Spark, recently converted to the Roman Catholic Church, narrativized the practice of *memento mori*, a staple of the Christian faith since the early church. As the psalmist sings, "Teach us to number our days, that we may apply our hearts unto wisdom" (Ps. 90:12 KJV). Our family has this psalm as a *memento mori* written in blue marker on our family calendar. If we are to plan out all our days rightly, we must keep in mind our unavoidable death.

Avoiding the Subject: Death

When we imagine our life as a story being written, how does it end? Many twenty-first-century Americans fear meditating on death. Like my husband, who practically fled the Sedlec Ossuary, contemporary evangelicals tend to sideline discussions of death. As an internal medicine primary care doctor, Lydia Dugdale has witnessed hundreds of deaths. Too many people dread its approach, not answering questions about the end of life as they know it. They choose resuscitation at all costs, despite how it tortures their bodies and affords them only minutes or hours more. Instead of adhering to the traditional practice of dying at home among friends, they isolate themselves in hospitals or advocate for physician-assisted suicide; they do not want to burden their family and friends. "In failing to die well," Dugdale observes, "we fail to live well. By avoiding questions of the meaning of death, we avoid questions of the meaning of life. By avoiding finitude, we ignore infinitude."[3] How we end our story completes the picture: it either exposes the lie of a self-determined existence or points beyond itself to an infinite good. As my father's pastor used to joke when people would ask how he was doing, "I don't know. I haven't finished yet." A good end marks a good life.

What Makes a Good Death?

There's more than one way to die well. If we look at the history of the church—even just at the book of Acts—we see a multiplicity of holy deaths. Dugdale reminds us of the *oughts* of a good death—community, virtuous disposition, and how those after the loss remember the dead. By community, Dugdale means the necessity of dying among friends and family. If you can prepare for death, you should surround yourself with people so that you may ask for their pardon, express your love for them, and become, for others, a *memento mori*. Think of Jacob in Genesis gathering all of his sons to his bedside and speaking blessings (some of which sound like curses) on each of the twelve tribes to be. I pray each night over my children that they may die as old men and women surrounded by their loved ones, and that I might be on the other side, welcoming them to the presence of God. The end of our life reminds us that we never belonged to ourselves.

Like the fifteenth-century manuscript on dying, *Ars moriendi*, Dugdale updates the art of dying for contemporary readers, encouraging virtue in the face of death. We all fear death, the fear of the unknown. What does it mean to die? When a friend of mine was dying in hospice, he could no longer open his eyes or speak. He had grown so perilously thin, and he was gasping for air. We all knew he was in his last days, yet he seemed to be holding on to life. I bent over and kissed his forehead. Not sure whether he could hear me, I assured him that he could go on. We loved him and would miss him, but there was nothing left for him to do here on earth.

Only saints, by God's provision, triumph over this universal terror of death. When Jesus faced his death at Golgotha, he was fearless. Jesus Christ exemplifies for all of us how to confront our death, which is one reason that Catholics hang his crucifix on the walls of their homes. Christ is before them on the cross as they draw near their end. In contrast, Protestants perhaps have focused so much on the resurrection that they've overlooked the example set by Good Friday. "What exactly is it about Jesus' way of dying that is to be imitated?" theologian Christopher Vogt asks. His answer is patience, compassion, and hope.[4] In three novels—Ernest Gaines's *A Lesson before Dying*, Walker Percy's *The Last Gentleman*, and Willa Cather's *Death Comes for the Archbishop*—we see imitations of Christ in the way that characters die. From these imagined holy ends may we learn how to die well.

The Blood of Martyrs

A good number of saints in the Catholic Church are martyrs. I bought an illustrated book on saints' lives for my daughter, who took it upon herself to count the few that did not die violent deaths. When we witness martyrdom today, we mourn the loss of time for that person or the torture they endured. However, the early church celebrated such deaths as increasing the kingdom—oh, to suffer as Christ did! What a gift! "The blood of the martyrs is the seed of the church," second-century theologian Tertullian said. In Flannery O'Connor's short story "A Temple of the Holy Ghost," the child narrator reflects on becoming a saint. Because of her great pride, the little girl fears sanctity is too far out of reach for her, "but she thought she could be a martyr if they killed her quick."[5] This story points to the mystery of martyrdom. In spite of a person's sins, to die for Christ redeems previous wrongs. Sanctity is received as an immediate gift by a sinner's righteous death.

Although not uncommon in the global church, martyrdom may seem distant for Americans, and only remotely can we imagine how such a calling relates to those of us practicing our faith in the land of freedom. If we look back at the martyrs of the Middle Ages or the early church, we may gain a sense of the virtues to imitate and see how these ennobling traits play out in our current stories. The premier medieval story for illustrating saintly virtue is Dante's *The Divine Comedy*. When the pilgrim ventures into heaven, we encounter many saints who are all reflecting themselves down from their thrones near God to converse with Dante and educate him about sanctification. The fifth circle of paradise, the realm of Mars, reflects the souls of martyrs, those who exemplified the virtue of courage. The souls dance together to create a cross, showing Dante the pilgrim that the epitome of virtue is the cruciform life. From this gathering of martyrs, Dante is greeted by his ancestor Cacciaguida, who died in the Second Crusade as a warrior for Christ.

Rather than encourage Dante to follow his example by becoming a crusader, Cacciaguida explains how affliction will be cast on Dante. He prophesies,

> You'll leave behind you everything you love
> most dearly: this will be the arrow shot
> first from the bow of exile.[6]

Dante will be undeservedly exiled from Florence. The arrows that strike him will not be literal but figurative. To fulfill his calling as a warrior of Christ, then, Dante must pick up not the sword but the pen. He must counteract this injustice by writing honestly, no matter how it offends the church. Dante understands this is the courage being demanded of him:

> But if I'm a too timid friend of truth,
> with those who'll call these days the days of old
> I fear I'll lose the fame that lengthens youth. (3.17.118–20)

His "martyrdom" will be to act bravely in response to an unjust punishment, what we call "speaking truth to power."

Contemporary Martyrdom: *A Lesson before Dying*

The Black church in America has consistently cast the victims of slavery, lynching, civil rights antagonism, and the executed innocent as martyrs. Countee Cullen describes the crucified Jesus as "the first leaf in a line / of trees on which a Man should swing."[7] Because they followed Jesus in their innocence, in suffering violent deaths, and in the way their deaths lived on in communal memory, these victims of racism became transformed in the imagination of African Americans into martyrs.[8] If we are to consider examples of those who faced unjust death heroically in contemporary America, we need to look no further than to our neighbors.

Ernest Gaines published *A Lesson before Dying* in 1994, but he sets the story in the 1940s, before the Civil Rights Act was signed. In this novel, an innocent man is convicted of murder and executed. How he goes to his death teaches us about what it looks like to die as a martyr. The novel starts with the convicted man's version of the story. Twenty-one-year-old Jefferson is an African American in the wrong place at the wrong time. He hitches a ride with two men who plan to rob a bar for a pint, but the plan ends with both them and the white store owner dead. After the shoot-out, Jefferson is left standing, neither victim nor criminal. But in 1940s Louisiana, a white man has been shot, and someone has to die for it—Jefferson becomes the scapegoat. The story could easily be reduced to another tragedy in a long list of unjust deaths of African Americans at the hands of a prejudiced legal system, but in the way that Gaines tells the story, Jefferson is transformed into a hero.

The narrator is Grant Wiggins, who grew up on the same plantation as Jefferson, but through education became a schoolteacher with an ambition to live a better life than those he serves in the quarter. In the first lines of the novel, speaking about the trial where Jefferson was convicted, Wiggins says, "I was not there, yet I was there. No, I did not go to the trial, I did not hear the verdict, because I knew all the time what it would be. Still, I was there. I was there as much as anyone else was there."[9] He invites us to experience the intimate connection between his life and those of his people, the Black workers who are treated so inhumanely in that segregated community. They share a fate of suffering that feels inevitable. These opening lines also may be read mysteriously—Wiggins was "there as much as anyone else was there." The Black attendants in the courtroom are not really there either, feeling as though they barely exist because of how little they can control what is happening.

Only when the defense attorney dehumanizes Jefferson before the white jury does the Black audience become invigorated. "Do you see a man sitting here?" the white lawyer asks facetiously of the room full of mostly white people. He calls Jefferson a "cornered animal," an empty "skull," a "thing to hold the handle of a plow, a thing to load your bales of cotton." Worst of all, the lawyer refutes that justice would be done by his execution: "Why, I would just as soon put a hog in the electric chair as this."[10] The insult becomes the catalyst for the rest of the story. Jefferson's grandmother decides that he must prove all the white people wrong. She asks Wiggins to educate Jefferson before his execution, to "change him from a hog to a man in the little time he's got left."[11] If Jefferson must die, his grandmother insists that he die a human being in the eyes of everyone.

Wiggins resists this obligation because he does not know what it means to be a person. He confesses to his fiancée his doubts and questions: "What do I say to him? Do I know what a man is? Do I know how a man is supposed to die? I'm still trying to find out how a man should live. Am I supposed to tell someone how to die who has never lived?"[12] These are the questions that Dugdale says every person must face at the end of their life, and Gaines is forcing readers to confront these questions in this novel. While we don't know how we are going to die, we become more prepared for our death through Wiggins's and Jefferson's experiences confronting their mortality. Dugdale argues that contemporary Americans suffer a "deficit in imagination" that prevents us from contemplating our own finitude.[13] Yet, here, with Wiggins and Jefferson, readers tackle the ultimate question: What does it mean to die well?

Against his desire, recognizing his own inadequacy, but for the sake of his community, Wiggins undertakes the schooling of Jefferson. While Wiggins, like many of us, does not know how to die, he encourages Jefferson to act courageously in accepting his death. The two men stride in circles around the prison's cafeteria. Choking back tears and wiping his face on the shoulder of his prison suit, Jefferson shuffles in chains alongside Wiggins. They're whispering to not be overheard by Jefferson's grandmother and the local reverend, who sit at a table with bowls of homemade gumbo that is getting cold as the two men repeatedly circle the room. "I want you to show them [white people] the difference between what they think you are and what you can be," Wiggins says.[14] Wiggins grows increasingly passionate during his pep talk. "To them you're nothing but another n——," Wiggins says. "—no dignity, no heart, no love for your people. You can prove them wrong."[15] He elevates Jefferson as the hero in the story of the Black community in Bayonne. "A hero does for others," Wiggins tells him. "I'm no hero. . . . You—you can be bigger than anyone you have ever met."[16] The chance to be a hero has been thrust on Jefferson because of his conviction and looming execution. His death is inevitable, but Jefferson may choose to die in such a way that demonstrates to the whole town that he is more than a hog; he is a hero.

To explain to Jefferson how a person without dignity may be converted into a model for others, Wiggins reminds Jefferson of how a local man, Mr. Farrell, crafts slingshots out of driftwood:

> You have the chance of being bigger than anyone who has ever lived on that plantation or come from this little town. . . . You have seen how Mr. Farrell makes a slingshot handle. He starts with just a little piece of rough wood—any little scrap wood—then he starts cutting. Cutting and cutting and cutting, then shaving. Shaves it down clean and smooth till it's not what it was before, but something new and pretty.[17]

The passage should remind Christians of how the Lord describes himself as the potter who shapes us out of clay (Isa. 29:16; 64:8; Jer. 18:1–9; Rom. 9:14–24). To be shaped by the potter is painful. The Lord will cut and shave away all that does not fit until we are what he wants us to be. As someone who does not believe that our God is the Lord, Wiggins places on Jefferson the burden of being craftsman, that he may form himself into something other than scrap wood. But the reality is more mysterious. Wiggins is right: "That's all we are . . . all of us on this earth, a piece of drifting wood."[18] But God carves us into something greater. In this story, the Lord is reshaping Jefferson, through this persecution before death, into a hero in the mold of Christ.

How are we to die, and what does this have to do with how we live? For the reverend in the story, the answer is a belief in Jesus Christ. But both Wiggins and Jefferson understand that such belief may be merely words or lies. A century ago, George MacDonald preached, "Instead of asking yourself whether you believe or not, ask yourself whether you have this day done one thing because He said, Do it."[19] What matters is one's actions, not that these deeds may earn reward, but that they may exhibit faith. When Wiggins and Jefferson discuss their beliefs in God, Wiggins says, "I think it's God that makes people care for people, Jefferson. I think it's God makes children play and people sing." For Jefferson, there is no more time for playing and singing and loving. Instead, Jefferson decides to imitate Jesus in the way that he dies: "And He never said a mumbling word. . . . That's how I want to go, Mr. Wiggins. Not mumbling a word."[20] Of Christ's death, the prophet Isaiah writes,

> He was oppressed and afflicted,
>   yet he did not open his mouth;
> he was led like a lamb to the slaughter,
>   and as a sheep before its shearers is silent,
>   so he did not open his mouth. (53:7)

To face death with courage is to follow Jesus Christ not merely with words but in action.

Jefferson dies in a way that witnesses to the whole town of Jesus Christ's sacrifice. In his last conversation with Wiggins, Jefferson protests, "Me to take the cross. Your cross, nannan's cross, my own cross. . . . Y'all axe a lot."[21] But Jefferson does take up the cross. He writes a diary, which reads like the prayer from the Garden of Gethsemane: "i been shakin an shakin but im gon stay strong."[22] His final words are addressed to Wiggins for the whole town to hear. It reads like a testimony: "tell them im strong tell them im a man."[23] Gaines writes the final chapter in a way that imitates the Gospel narrative. As we see in the biblical story how the disciples act when the Lord is led to be crucified, so Gaines shows us what the townspeople are up to during Jefferson's execution. Some are kneeling and praying. Some closing their shops and hiding. From a distance (because he lacks the courage to witness the execution), Wiggins asks for Jefferson's forgiveness. What we see in all of these accounts is that Jefferson's death is bearing fruit in the community.

The most notable testimony is that of Paul, the white guard who leads Jefferson to the electric chair. Jefferson entrusts his diary to him to be delivered to Wiggins. Paul relays all of the action that Wiggins missed. He tells how Jefferson walked like a man to the chair: "Straight he walked. I'm a witness. Straight he walked."[24] Like a man who has been converted, Paul cannot stop talking about what he has witnessed at Jefferson's death. After watching Jefferson die, Paul is ready to live a new life. Because he "saw the transformation" in Jefferson, he asks to be friends with Wiggins—a rare friendship across color lines in the 1940s South. Jefferson's death changes those in the community from people divided to those with the potential for friendship. Paul declares, "I don't want to forget this day. I don't ever want to forget him." It is not coincidental that this prison guard shares the name of the persecutor who turned apostle in Acts. Paul's testimony is that Jefferson "was the bravest man in the room."[25] By his exhibition of bravery and strength that seemed to come not from his own resources but from the aid of God, Jefferson dies as a martyr.

The story of Jefferson is not real (we don't even receive a last name), but stories like his defile this country's history—thousands of African Americans wrongly convicted and unjustly executed. Not to mention the millions who perished in the slave trade, died in bondage, or were lynched in our streets. We cannot change the past, but we can remember their stories. We can lament their deaths. We learn from Jefferson about bravery in response to injustice and from Wiggins about the small role we play in creating change. And we learn to repent of complicity in racism and model Paul in attempts at friendship. With him, we should declare, "I don't want to ever forget." As we approach our death, we all must face the question, Did I contribute to the problem, or did I do all that I could to fight against it? Like Dante, we must not be "a too timid friend of truth." And, like Jefferson, we must take up the cross.

Time for Preparation

We have never been promised eighty or a hundred years on this earth. The Lord himself, whose life we are to imitate, received thirty-three years and suffered unjust execution. Why then do we assume that good people deserve old age and a peaceful death? A few years ago, I attended a friend's fortieth birthday party where there was a trivia game that no one seemed to be playing except me. One question had four names listed: Flannery O'Connor, Dietrich Bonhoeffer, George Herbert, and Blaise Pascal. What did they all have in common? I answered correctly, "They all died at thirty-nine." Four prodigious Christians, four great saints of church history, all dead before their fortieth birthdays. Although one was martyred, the other three died of illness. None of them lamented that they would die young. None of them accepted as true the twenty-first-century fallacy that the most blessed life is the longest life. For O'Connor, quite the opposite. She once wrote a friend, "Sickness before death is a very appropriate thing and I think those who don't have it miss one of God's mercies."[26] Our imaginations about dying young or from illness have been infected by the world's expectations, not by our faith.

Even more precarious is our inability to deal with decaying flesh and to handle the reality of sickness and its fatality. We spread false optimism. We run away from the sick. We give thanks that someone else carries that burden and not us. Walker Percy writes of sickness before death in *The Last Gentleman*, a novel that Percy intended to be "an ass-kicking for Jesus." Percy had converted to Christianity after nearly dying of tuberculosis; novels brought him to believe in Christ and his church. Because reading fiction while facing his mortality guided him to faith, Percy hoped to write novels that would accomplish the same conversion in others. "This life is too much trouble, far too strange," Percy realized, "to arrive at the end of it and then to be asked what you make of it and have to answer 'Scientific humanism.' That won't do. A poor show."[27] Percy wanted to offend readers with his fiction so they would realize the impotence of any professed beliefs in scientific humanism before the reality of their death. In *The Last Gentleman*, Percy offers vicariously to readers what O'Connor calls God's mercies to the sick. He provides the chance to raise the significant questions about the meaning of life before we pass from it.

While *The Last Gentleman* follows the travails of a Southern wayfarer named Williston Barrett, his journey gets tangled up with the Vaught family, especially with their youngest son, Jamie, who is sixteen and has only months to live. Barrett meets the family in New York, where Jamie has been seen by specialists ad nauseam to find ways to extend his young life. Unfortunately, all attempts have failed, and everyone in the family expresses their own ideas about how best to spend the time Jamie has left to live. The novel is about life and its purpose as much as it is about death.

In Jamie's siblings, we see conflicting views on the purpose of life and therefore how to die. Jamie's sister-in-law Rita continues to hope for new drugs and treatments. She insists, "I desire for Jamie that he achieve as much self-fulfillment as he can in the little time he has. I desire for him beauty and joy, not death."[28] Rita is convinced that a fight for life, in spite of how it diminishes the quality of that time, is the best course of action. Motivated by a worldview that admits no resurrection, Rita considers all other options deranged. For example, Jamie's sister Val, a Catholic nun, cares that Jamie not "die an unprovided death." She tells Barrett, "I don't want him to die without knowing why he came here, what he is doing here, and why he is leaving."[29] The novel submits to the reader the choice of which viewpoint coheres best with reality. As we experience Jamie's death in the fiction, do we imagine it tragically or ultimately as a comedy that concludes in an unwitnessed resurrection?

In sickness, the body deteriorates to the point of humiliation. We return to our infant state, in many cases, where others must help us eat or sleep or clean up our messes. Barrett must observe Jamie's death, and the experience haunts him:

> It was the shame of it, the bare-faced embarrassment of getting worse and dying which took him by surprise and caught his breath in his throat. How is this matter to be set right? Were there no officials to deal with the shame of dying, to make suitable recompense? It was like getting badly beat in a fight. To *lose*. Oh, to lose so badly.[30]

All the ways that we have been fashioned by the world—by our education, by government, by the marketplace, by dominant culture—have taught us that we are in control of our destiny. That we can make the choice of which cereal to buy, of whether to get in shape, of applying for that degree online, of voting for our choice candidate. We get to decide everything, the world tells us. But then death comes, and we realize that we can no more choose our exit from life than we chose when and how we entered.

The end of *The Last Gentleman* haunts and entrances me every time for its juxtaposition of the sacred rite of new birth with the profane indignity of Jamie's death. Barrett has requested that a hospital priest administer Jamie's baptism because Val has charged him with this duty to her dying brother. As Jamie exits this life, he has a brief moment of consciousness. He rises to empty his bowels away from the bedpan, filling the room with stench, which Barrett describes as "the dread ultimate rot of the molecules themselves, an abject surrender. It was the body's disgorgement of its most secret shame."[31] In a sterile hospital room that stinks of death, a priest, while staring at a brown stain on an opposite wall, professes the truths of the Christian faith. By rote, the priest asks Jamie,

> Do you accept the truth that God exists and that He made you and loves you and that He made the world so that you may enjoy its beauty and that He himself is your final end and happiness, that He loved you so much that He sent his only Son to die for you and to found His Holy Catholic Church so that you may enter heaven and there see God face to face and be happy with Him forever?[32]

Percy gets away with stating so baldly and boldly the claims of the faith by inserting them into the mouth of this robotic-sounding priest. He states these realities in the course of business; it's his job to administer sacraments to the sick and dying on a regular basis. Death is part of his everyday life.

In its mixture of profound spiritual mystery and unsettling earthliness, this episode recalls the incarnation. Jesus Christ, Son of God, born into a manger, surrounded by animals and their dung, wrapped

in the poor cloths of a young girl and her fiancé. As the priest pours
water over Jamie's bruised forehead, a bread truck passes under a
streetlight outside. A soul has been saved, and bread is being delivered. The spiritual and the mundane act on the same plane, but only
for those who have eyes to see. The priest, "in the same flat mercantile
voice" in which he described the doctrines of faith, promises Jamie
that today "you will be with our Blessed Lord and Savior and that
you will see him face to face and see his mother, Our Lady, see them
as you are seeing me."[33] Like the criminal who received Jesus's assurance of his resurrection at the crucifixion, Jamie accepts this promise
at his death. He clutches the priest's hand until he passes from this
life into the next.

In *The Last Gentleman*, Barrett detects an interesting phenomenon: he feels best when death is near. Before this moment, he has
felt most alive when close to death: a chandelier once fell in an art
museum and nearly killed him; a hurricane came close but let him
go unscathed. "I felt better in the hospital than anywhere else," Barrett says.[34] In proximity to death, we remember what matters most
in life. Jamie's salvation at death is not important for him—he's
fictional. It matters for the reader. That we live with knowledge of
the nearness of death and that we know what we believe about the
end. Do we think, as Rita did, that we are meant to live for as much
self-fulfillment as possible with the longest amount of time here
on earth as we can get? Or do we accept the truth of the priest's
words, that death is merely the undesirable entrance into the presence of God?

Death Comes for the Archbishop

The sixteenth-century Protestant artist Hans Holbein created thirty-
nine woodcarvings called *The Dance of Death*, in which a skeleton,
personifying Death, leads people away from their daily worlds. Antagonistic to the Catholic Church because of the recent Reformation,

Holbein depicts monks, nuns, and a bishop with fearful countenances fleeing Death's grip. In addition to being intrigued by the life of Father Lamy, a missionary to New Mexico in the nineteenth century, Willa Cather was inspired, in part, by these illustrations, from which she drew her book title *Death Comes for the Archbishop*. As Death comes for each person in the woodcut, the state of their souls is revealed in their response. The bishop grimaces at the skeleton clutching his hand, but for the fictional Father Latour, based on the legendary missionary, death is God's will, the gracious end of his good life.

Despite her agnostic stance toward Christianity, Cather found saints alluring. I'm always astounded when non-Christians are attracted to the saints. One of my teachers used to say that the greatest witness of the church was its saints; no other faith has such a legacy of those who lived selflessly for other people. She was impressed that these "countless fanciful figures of the saints, no two of them alike, seemed a direct expression of some very real and lively human feeling."[35] A Christian would explain that this "real and lively human feeling" being expressed by the saints is the incarnation. Jesus Christ is the most human of us all, so imitating him fulfills our design. In other words, reflecting the likeness of Jesus Christ, saints are those who excelled at being human.

In preparation for writing a holy life, Cather read the saints' stories. She was surprised that "all human experiences, measured against one supreme spiritual experience, were of about the same importance." These human episodes would be colored differently when read in light of the saint's death, their moment of spiritual ascent. Written in the past tense, the novel reads like an elegy for the main character. *Death Comes for the Archbishop* becomes the premier novel on *ars moriendi* by showing "the trivial incidents" of Father Latour's life that led to his faithful death.[36] While Cather hoped to create through words the aesthetic of Puvis de Chavannes's painting *The Pastoral Life of Saint Genevieve*, she led every event in the novel toward a seemingly darker end, the saint's death.

Before readers experience Latour's death, we observe other deaths with which to compare and contrast his end. Early in Latour's ministry to New Mexico, a priest who preceded him in that region, Father Lucero (a name that should make readers think of Lucifer), dies. He is a hypocritical priest with a large following. People attend his deathbed as though it is a privilege. Latour administers the last sacrament, though with some reservations, for Lucero perpetually meditates not on heaven but on the fortune that he leaves behind. From another wayward priest, the late Father Martinez, Lucero has stolen money and buried it under his floor. As he passes from this life, Lucero fears someone will rob him. His last words are, "'Comete tu cola, Martinez, comete tu cola' (Eat your tail, Martinez, eat your tail)."[37] Those who overhear him become convinced that Lucero has not gone on to a heavenly reward but instead has joined Father Martinez in eternal torment.

In opposition to these hypocritical priests who die potentially damned, Father Latour and his closest ally, Father Valliant, display good deaths. The priests have inspired strong devotion from those around them, an attraction that usually characterizes saints. One of Valliant's colleagues, Father Revardy, is dying in a hospital in Chicago, but he rallies to attend the priest's funeral and leans his head against his Christian brother's coffin, only to die a few days later himself. When Latour sees Valliant's body at the funeral, he distances himself from the corpse: "The shriveled little old man in the coffin, scarcely larger than a monkey—that had nothing to do with Father Valliant."[38] Unfortunately, in this sentiment Cather betrays her agnosticism. She sounds more Platonic than Christian, seeing the flesh as a shell that has been departed by the soul. For a Catholic priest, the body would retain its holiness even in death. This is why Catholics keep locks of hair, fingers, and even preserve the entire body of saints as relics. But Latour does express his faith in the resurrection in his letter to Valliant's sister Philomène: "'Since your brother was called to his rewards,' he wrote, 'I feel nearer to him than before. For many years Duty separated us, but death has brought us together.'"[39] Many

Christians express similar sentiments. They feel the closeness of the departed more after death than they did in life.

The death of Latour's friend makes it easier for him to depart this life. He writes to Philomène, "The time is not far distant when I shall join him. Meanwhile, I am enjoying to the full that period of reflection which is the happiest conclusion to a life of action."[40] With contentment and peace, Latour awaits death as a desirable end. All of the primary characters in the novel have died before Latour, leaving very little for him to want to hold on to in this life. "During those last weeks of the Bishop's life he thought very little about death; it was the Past he was leaving. The future would take care of itself."[41] Unlike Father Lucero, who feared what would happen to his money when his body turned cold, Latour cares little about how the world will carry on. In dying, Latour exhibits trust in God's sovereignty, just as he did in life. As he told Valliant the last time they saw one another, "Whenever God wills. I am ready."[42] Latour has already accomplished what has been asked of him, as readers have witnessed throughout the previous few hundred pages. Knowing his good life has granted readers the assurance of his good death. As Father Latour tells the young man who cares for him in his final days, "I shall die of having lived."[43]

Because so much about death is unknown and unknowable, witnesses used to gather at a loved one's deathbed to learn more about what to expect at their own end. Cather's narrator reminds readers,

> In those days, even in European countries, death had a solemn social importance. It was not regarded as a moment when certain bodily organs ceased to function, but as a dramatic climax, a moment when the soul made its entrance into the next world, passing in full consciousness through a lowly door to an unimaginable scene. Among the watchers there was always hope that the dying man might reveal something of what he alone could see.[44]

Unlike our current empirical approach to death—the single beep on a heart monitor that signifies the end—for thousands of years, people considered death a spiritual experience. Although she herself did not believe in the same hereafter as the archbishop, Cather invites readers to reconsider Father Latour's death in its spiritual reality. We gather at his deathbed so that we may know more about what to imagine when we lie on our own.

Just as holiness is always a reflection of God at work within a human life, we see holiness in death when the dying one imitates Jesus Christ. When Jefferson walked to the electric chair, he was as silent as the Son of Man bravely approaching his execution. At Jamie's death, his circumstances recalled the incarnation. The conflation of his baptism with his literal death should remind us of our figurative death in Christ as we await our death and resurrection. And the peaceful end for Father Latour calls to mind Jesus in Luke's Gospel, where the Obedient Servant shows us how to relinquish the gift of life: "Father, into your hands I commit my spirit" (Luke 23:46). From these fictional predecessors we may learn about the art of dying well. We practice through these imaginative experiences that we might be ready to act faithfully when death comes for us.

Memento Mori

On Ash Wednesday each year, in preparation for Lenten observance, I attend a church service in which the pastor reminds me, "From dust you came and to dust you shall return." Then he wipes a smudge of dust on my forehead in the shape of a cross. We are dust, called to live a cruciform life, reflecting the cross in all we do, and returning to the dust that we may be resurrected with Christ. Never has the Ash Wednesday service moved me as it did the first time that I brought my children up the aisle. It is one thing to remember that you must die. It is another to imagine that the babies you have been given are not yours to keep. They too will return to dust. As the pastor pressed the dust against my one-year-old daughter's soft brow, I struggled not to weep aloud lest the cries echo against the high ceiling. I nearly choked on my tears as my heart acknowledged the truth of his words. My daughter came from dust. I did not form her, and I cannot control how long she lives or when she dies. She belongs to God. If we are to treasure rightly the gifts of this life, we must remember that all—our world, our loved ones, ourselves—will die.

Several years ago, a friend delivered the graduation speech at the college where I taught. She was retiring, so it was her final address to the university. She stunned the young graduates with her words: "Only one generation after you, or at most two, will know you, for you will be forgotten when you die." Many of us know very little about our great-grandparents, and few can even recall the names of their great-great-grandparents. Life is not about making a name for yourself. Remember that sinners tried such blasphemy at the Tower of Babel. But your life has unseen effects on those around you. How you practice virtue when blessed with abundance or when deprived to the point of despair. How you love others more than yourself. How you face death when it comes. Though my daughter may be dust, she has the breath of God in her. She lives and moves and has her being in him. No one may remember her, but I love her. And she will learn from that love how to love. This is the perpetual witness of the church, not in names or in fame, but in love.

Devotional

From "The Death of Ivan Ilyich": "'What if my entire life, my entire conscious life, simply was not the real thing?' It occurred to him that what had seemed utterly inconceivable before—that he had not lived the kind of life he should have—might in fact be true. It occurred to him that those scarcely perceptible impulses of his to protest what people of high rank considered good, vague impulses which he had always suppressed, might have been precisely what mattered, and all the rest not been the real thing."[45]

Scripture:

> Because God knows how we're made,
>   God remembers we're just dust.
> The days of a human life are like grass:
>   they bloom like a wildflower;
>   but when the wind blows through it, it's gone;
>   even the ground where it stood doesn't remember it.
> But the LORD's faithful love is from forever ago to forever from now
>   for those who honor him.
>   And God's righteousness reaches to the grandchildren
>   of those who keep his covenant
>   and remember to keep his commands.
> The LORD has established his throne in heaven,
>   and his kingdom rules over all. (Ps. 103:14–19 CEB)

Prayer from the Saints: Cardinal John Henry Newman's "Prayer for a Happy Death":

> *Oh, my Lord and Savior, support me in that hour in the strong arms of Thy Sacraments, and by the fresh fragrance of Thy consolations . . . breathe on me, and my Angel whisper peace to me, and my glorious saints . . . smile upon me; that in them all and through them all, I may receive the gift of perseverance, and die, as I desire to live, in Thy faith, in Thy Church, in Thy service, and in Thy love. Amen.*

Discussion Questions

1. Why does American culture seem afraid to deal with death? Where do you find examples in culture (film, books, music) that long for endless life on earth rather than death?

2. How would you answer the questions that these novels raise about death? What does it mean to die well?

3. What biblical precedents do these fictional stories recall for you? What might we learn about a good death from these biblical stories?

4. How do these characters balance the tension between our solace in resurrection and our lament over death?

5. How would you write the end of your story, if you could?

Further Reading

Robert Bolt, *A Man for All Seasons*
François Mauriac, *Viper's Tangle*
Muriel Spark, *Memento Mori*
Leo Tolstoy, "The Death of Ivan Ilyich"

Conclusion

In a letter dated July 9, 1939, C. S. Lewis recommends the novels of George MacDonald to a nun because they are full of holiness. He worries that such holy characters are rare because "to imagine a man worse than yourself you've only got to stop doing something, while to imagine one better you've got to do something."[1] Lewis identifies a reality that feels daunting. We all have so much to do—how can we possibly add a holy to-do list?

When I told a friend that I was writing this book, she cringed. She didn't want more reasons to feel guilty for all the ways she is not living like she should. But this book should not make anyone feel guilty. Quite the opposite, for here we meditate on the heroes of our faith and increase in our love for them and thus for God. The two greatest commandments are so intimately connected: to love the Lord increases our love for our neighbor and vice versa. Holiness is not about what we are to do but about who he is. The more we see his work in the lives of saints who have gone before us, even fictional ones, the more we come to know and love him. And the practice of loving these neighbors intensifies our love for God. From this great upsurge in love, the Lord blesses us with his holiness. That is so much of what holiness is: increasing the capacity to love.

We examine closely each of these saints to consider what about them looked so similar to God's holiness, but in reality, all their gifts are connected and rooted in his love. When a saint meditates on death, the things of this world and its luxuries matter less. Prayer and contemplation dominate her time, and she becomes a natural ascetic. Foregoing the comforts of the world leads to a suffering that purges one's soul of inordinate desires. In place of those passions grows greater love for the earth and those around her. Out of love for the mistreated creatures of the world, the saint grows strong in her devotion to speak truth against illicit powers. And the threat of death means nothing to one who began this journey of holiness by considering her life in light of its highest end. She may die a holy fool, eager to return to God, leaving behind those who, like little children, want to follow her example.

Although this book considers various novels and highlights particular saintly virtues in each one, readers should notice how these saints are not merely mothers but also prophets; not only ascetics but also holy fools; not only lovers of the earth but also contemplatives. While Christ plays in ten thousand places, as Gerard Manley Hopkins puts it, the dynamic Holy Spirit does not act as a surgeon, operating on one piece of anatomy at a time. Rather, as an inflowing of water or fire, the Spirit removes all grit and grime so that holiness flows out from the whole saint.

When Lewis recommended reading MacDonald's novels, he did not intend to give this nun more holy tasks, but he knew that reading the book itself would be an experience that magnified holiness within her. And what a joyful experience! Novels introduce us to ways of imagining God already at work in our hearts, present in the world, transforming and sanctifying his creation all the time. By reading these stories about those who pursued his holiness, our desire for sanctity strengthens, and we share the burdens of our lives with a company of those who, like us, have been purged of their distractions and temptations. We join the company of saints who have been set free to become scandalously holy.

Acknowledgments

I began this book after I taught a graduate course on holy figures in American literature at Charles University in Prague on a Fulbright Fellowship, so I must acknowledge that phenomenal opportunity. Following my initial inquiry into the question of holiness in literature, I have since taught these novels to various classes, and I am thankful for the feedback of students and colleagues from John Brown University, as well as from Biola University, where I spent my 2017 sabbatical discussing suffering in Flannery O'Connor. I shared chapters in progress during presentations at the CiRCE Institute, University of Dallas, Oklahoma Baptist University, Redeemer College, and Grove City College; I thank these schools for the privilege of speaking at their institutions.

There have been many people who have helped craft these ideas into their current form. My editor Bob Hosack spent hours with me on perfecting the introduction so that I could communicate well my intentions for this book; I'm grateful that he saw the potential in this book. My agent Keely Boeving showed me how to craft these pages to be as inviting as I hope that they are. Jeff Reimer is my reliable copyeditor, a voice of reason when I write a wayward sentence. As well as the copyeditor at Brazos Press, Eric Salo, who refined this manuscript.

In the weeks before diving into writing the book, I spent a week in retreat, hosted by the Collegeville Institute, where we workshopped this book idea, and I received substantial feedback from other writers, but especially from Lauren Winner. I've looked up to Lauren for almost twenty years; she was a writer who I hoped to imitate. It is with much awe and immense gratitude that I thank her for writing the foreword to this book.

Finally, I am so thankful for the readers of this book. If you're reading well, you are beginning, as C. S. Lewis advises, by assuming that I have something to say worth listening to, and I hope that I deserve such a compliment. Without readers trusting me to write what is worthy, admirable, and scandalously good, this book only exists as dead letters on unturned pages. Thank you so much for your time. May the Lord bear fruit through your reading.

Notes

Foreword

1. Augustine, *Confessions* 1.13, trans. Carolyn J. B. Hammond, Loeb Classical Library 26 (Cambridge, MA: Harvard University Press, 2014), vol. 1.

2. Benjamin Rush, quoted in Carrie N. Knight, "Reading Themselves Sick: Consumption and Women's Reading in the Early Republic, 1780–1860," *Book History* 24, no. 1 (Spring 2021): 42.

3. Quoted in Cathy N. Davidson, *Revolution and the Word: The Rise of the Novel in America* (New York: Oxford University Press, 1986), 43.

Introduction

Portions of this introduction were published previously in Jessica Hooten Wilson, "The Power of Imitation on the Path to Holiness," *Angelus News*, June 2, 2020, https://angelusnews.com/faith/the-power-of-imitation-on-the-path-to-holiness; "Willing to Suffer: How One of America's Greatest Christian Authors Viewed the Thing We All Fear," *Fathom Magazine*, October 16, 2017, https://www.fathommag.com/stories/willing-to-suffer; and "C. S. Lewis's Mixed Bag of Tangents and Asides," *Church Life Journal*, October 28, 2019, https://churchlifejournal.nd.edu/articles/c-s-lewiss-mixed-bag-of-tangents-and-asides.

1. Thomas Cahill, *How the Irish Saved Civilization: The Untold Story of Ireland's Heroic Role from the Fall of Rome to the Rise of Medieval Europe* (New York: Doubleday, 1995), 218.

2. Dostoevsky relates this story to his wife Anna in a letter dated June 7, 1880. The response followed his speech in honor of Alexander Pushkin. Fyodor Dostoevsky, *Selected Letters*, ed. Joseph Frank and David I. Goldstein (Rutgers, NJ: Rutgers University Press, 1987), 504.

3. C. S. Lewis, *Surprised by Joy: The Shape of My Early Life* (New York: Harcourt Brace, 1955), vii.

4. Lewis, *Surprised by Joy*, 237.

5. C. S. Lewis, *An Experiment in Criticism* (Cambridge: Cambridge University Press, 1961), 103.

6. Lewis, *Surprised by Joy*, 18.

7. Lewis, *Surprised by Joy*, 167.

8. Gerard Manley Hopkins, "As Kingfishers Catch Fire, Dragonflies Draw Flame," available at https://hopkinspoetry.com/poem/as-kingfishers-catch-fire.

9. Lewis, *Surprised by Joy*, 170.

10. Lewis, *Surprised by Joy*, 174.

11. Lewis, *Surprised by Joy*, 181.

12. C. S. Lewis, *The Voyage of the Dawn Treader* (New York: HarperTrophy, 1952), 270.

13. Alasdair MacIntyre, *After Virtue*, 2nd ed. (Notre Dame, IN: Notre Dame University Press, 1984), 216.

14. C. S. Lewis, "Learning in War-Time," in *The Weight of Glory and Other Addresses*, ed. Walter Hooper (1949; repr., San Francisco: HarperOne, 2001), 52.

15. American Academy of the Arts and Sciences, "New Evidence on Waning Reading Habits," July 15, 2019, https://www.amacad.org/news/new-evidence-waning -american-reading-habits.

16. Dana Gioia, commencement speech, Stanford University, Stanford, CA, June 17, 2007, available at "Gioia to Graduates: 'Trade Easy Pleasures for More Complex and Challenging Ones,'" *Stanford Report*, June 17, 2007, https://news.stanford.edu /news/2007/june20/gradtrans-062007.html.

17. Gioia, "Trade Easy Pleasures."

18. Colleen Carroll Campbell, *The Heart of Perfection: How the Saints Taught Me to Trade My Dream of Perfect for God's* (New York: Howard, 2019), 21.

19. Campbell, *Heart of Perfection*, 22.

20. Dante Alighieri, *Paradise* 3.13.16–18, trans. Anthony Esolen (New York: Modern Library, 2007).

21. Dorothy Day, *On Pilgrimage* (Grand Rapids: Eerdmans, 1999), 100–101.

Chapter 1: Holy Foolishness

1. Ralph Wood, "We're All Monsters: Ralph Wood on the Good, the Bad, and the Human," *The Table Podcast*, Center for Christian Thought, May 6, 2019, https://cct .biola.edu/were-all-monsters-ralph-wood.

2. G. K. Chesterton, *What's Wrong with the World?* (New York: Dodd, Mead, 1912), 48.

3. Frederick Buechner, *Beyond Words: Daily Readings in the ABC's of Faith* (San Francisco: HarperSanFrancisco, 2004), 156.

4. Maria Skobtsova, *Essential Writings*, ed. Helene Klepnin-Arjakovsky, trans. Richard Pevear and Larissa Volokhonsky (Maryknoll, NY: Orbis Books, 2002), 57.

5. Leonid Ouspensky and Vladimir Lossky, *The Meaning of Icons* (Crestwood, NY: St. Vladimir's Seminary Press, 1969), 36.

6. Ouspensky and Lossky, *Meaning of Icons*, 38.

7. Ouspensky and Lossky, *Meaning of Icons*, 36.

8. Eugene Vodolazkin, "The New Middle Ages," *First Things*, August 2016, https://www.firstthings.com/article/2016/08/the-new-middle-ages.

9. Vodolazkin, "New Middle Ages."

10. Vodolazkin, "New Middle Ages."

11. John Chryssavgis, *In the Heart of the Desert: The Spirituality of the Desert Fathers and Mothers* (Bloomington, IN: World Wisdom, 2003), 20.

12. Eugene Vodolazkin, *Laurus*, trans. Lisa C. Hayden (London: Oneworld, 2015), 296–97.

13. Vodolazkin, *Laurus*, 90.

14. Vodolazkin, *Laurus*, 143.

15. Vodolazkin, *Laurus*, 146.

16. Vodolazkin, *Laurus*, 302.

17. Fyodor Dostoevsky, *Notes from Underground*, trans. Richard Pevear and Larissa Volokhonsky (New York: Vintage, 1994), 129–30.

18. C. S. Lewis, "The Weight of Glory," in *The Weight of Glory and Other Addresses*, ed. Walter Hooper (1949; repr., San Francisco: HarperOne, 2001), 26.

19. Vodolazkin, *Laurus*, 30.

20. C. S. Lewis, preface to *Essays Presented to Charles Williams*, ed. C. S. Lewis (London: Oxford University Press, 1947), xiv, quoted in Philip Zaleski and Carol Zaleski, *The Fellowship: The Literary Lives of the Inklings* (New York: Farrar, Straus & Giroux, 2015), 340.

21. Vodolazkin, *Laurus*, 223.

22. In the prolegomenon, the narrator suggests that people think Arseny has the elixir of immortality (Vodolazkin, *Laurus*, 4). But when they come to seek it, he points them to the sacraments in the church (316).

23. Vodolazkin, *Laurus*, 90.

24. Vodolazkin, *Laurus*, 228–29.

25. Vodolazkin, *Laurus*, 5.

26. Vodolazkin, *Laurus*, 308.

27. Vodolazkin, *Laurus*, 309.

28. Vodolazkin, *Laurus*, 339.

29. Vodolazkin, "New Middle Ages."

30. Vodolazkin, *Laurus*, 352.

31. Vodolazkin, *Laurus*, 309.

32. Vodolazkin, *Laurus*, 143.

33. Vodolazkin, *Laurus*, 330.

34. Vodolazkin, *Laurus*, 3.

35. Dionysius the Areopagite, *Ecclesiastical Hierarchy* 2.3.8 (Patrologia Graeca 3:437), quoted in Ouspensky and Lossky, *Meaning of Icons*, 38.

36. Vodolazkin, *Laurus*, 330.

37. Vodolazkin, *Laurus*, 32–33.

38. Vodolazkin, *Laurus*, 210–11.

39. "Venerable Arsenius the Great," Orthodox Church in America, accessed April 30, 2021, https://www.oca.org/saints/lives/2015/05/08/101328-venerable-arsenius-the -great.

Chapter 2: Communion of Saints

1. John Wesley, preface to *Hymns and Sacred Poems* (London: Strahan, 1739), viii.

2. Elie Wiesel, *Night*, trans. Marion Wiesel (New York: Hill and Wang, 2006), 110–11.

3. C. S. Lewis, *The Abolition of Man* (1943; repr., New York: HarperCollins, 2001), 24–25.

4. Lewis, *Abolition of Man*, 25.

5. C. S. Lewis, *Out of the Silent Planet* (1938; repr., New York: Scribner Classics, 1996), 152.

6. C. S. Lewis, preface to *That Hideous Strength* (1945; repr., New York: Scribner Classics, 1996), 7.

7. George Orwell, "The Scientists Take Over," *Manchester Evening News*, August 16, 1945, reprinted in *The Complete Works of George Orwell*, ed. Peter Davison (London: Secker & Warburg, 1998), 17:250–51.

8. Orwell, "The Scientists Take Over."

9. Lewis, preface to *That Hideous Strength*, 7.

10. Lewis, *That Hideous Strength*, 99.

11. Lewis, *That Hideous Strength*, 100.

12. Lewis, *That Hideous Strength*, 242.

13. Lewis, *That Hideous Strength*, 245.

14. Lewis, *That Hideous Strength*, 53.

15. Lewis, *That Hideous Strength*, 52.

16. Lewis, *That Hideous Strength*, 341.

17. Lewis, *That Hideous Strength*, 68.

18. Lewis, *That Hideous Strength*, 40.

19. Lewis, *That Hideous Strength*, 59.

20. Lewis, *That Hideous Strength*, 40.

21. Lewis, *That Hideous Strength*, 215.

22. Lewis, *That Hideous Strength*, 220.

23. Lewis, *That Hideous Strength*, 243–44.

24. Lewis, *That Hideous Strength*, 127.

25. Hannah Arendt, *Eichmann in Jerusalem: A Report on the Banality of Evil* (New York: Viking Press, 1963).

26. Lewis, *Abolition of Man*, 77.

27. Lewis, *That Hideous Strength*, 170.

28. Lewis, *That Hideous Strength*, 221.

29. Lewis, *Abolition of Man*, 77.

30. C. S. Lewis, *Surprised by Joy: The Shape of My Early Life* (New York: Harcourt Brace, 1955), 133.

31. Lewis, *Surprised by Joy*, 134.

32. Lewis, *That Hideous Strength*, 313.

33. Lewis, *That Hideous Strength*, 60.

34. Lewis, *That Hideous Strength*, 149.

35. Lewis, *That Hideous Strength*, 139–41.

36. Lewis, *That Hideous Strength*, 231.

37. One of St. Anne's frustrating "old-fashioned" morals is that Jane must submit to her husband. Jane grows indignant that she must ask Mark's permission to join the group at St. Anne's. When she protests, Ransom responds, "Equality is not the deepest thing, you know" (Lewis, *That Hideous Strength*, 145). Yet Ransom forms an egalitarian home where the lower-class Maggs stands equal with Jane and the Dimbles, where he, as director, acknowledges that he never called the group together,

but they all submit to the calling of Maleldil. Many female readers find Jane untenable and even annoying as a character. While I agree that Jane should discuss her decision to join St. Anne's with Mark, he should just as much have asked her permission to join N.I.C.E., an equality omitted from the narrative. Granted, Lewis wrote this novel prior to his marriage to Joy Davidman, so one could hope that her influence would have altered his perception of Jane's role and character.

38. Lewis, *That Hideous Strength*, 285.

39. Lewis, *That Hideous Strength*, 41.

40. Lewis, *Abolition of Man*, 74.

41. Lewis, *That Hideous Strength*, 343.

42. Lewis, *That Hideous Strength*, 318.

43. Lewis, *That Hideous Strength*, 369.

44. C. S. Lewis, *Letters to Malcolm, Chiefly on Prayer* (New York: HarperOne, 2017), 18–19.

45. Lewis, *That Hideous Strength*, 369.

Chapter 3: Creation Care as a Holy Calling

1. John G. Neihardt, ed., *Black Elk Speaks* (Lincoln: University of Nebraska Press, 2014), 15–16.

2. "In 1979, I proclaimed Saint Francis of Assisi as the heavenly Patron of those who promote ecology. He offers Christians an example of genuine and deep respect for the integrity of creation. As a friend of the poor who was loved by God's creatures, Saint Francis invited all of creation—animals, plants, natural forces, even Brother Sun and Sister Moon—to give honour and praise to the Lord. . . . It is my hope that the inspiration of Saint Francis will help us to keep ever alive a sense of 'fraternity' with all those good and beautiful things which Almighty God has created. And may he remind us of our serious obligation to respect and watch over them with care, in light of that greater and higher fraternity that exists within the human family." John Paul II, "For the Celebration of the World Day of Peace," Vatican, January 1, 1990, http://www.vatican.va/content/john-paul-ii/en/messages/peace/documents/hf_jp-ii_mes_19891208_xxiii-world-day-for-peace.html.

3. G. K. Chesterton, *St. Francis of Assisi*, in *St. Thomas Aquinas, St. Francis of Assisi* (San Francisco: Ignatius, 2002), 259.

4. Chesterton, *St. Francis of Assisi*, 258.

5. Norman Wirzba, *From Nature to Creation: A Christian Vision for Understanding and Loving Our World* (Grand Rapids: Baker Academic, 2015), 3.

6. Cormac McCarthy, *The Road* (New York: Knopf, 2006), 2.

7. McCarthy, *The Road*, 230–31.

8. Wendell Berry, "Imagination in Place," in *Imagination in Place: Essays* (Berkeley, CA: Counterpoint, 2011), 15.

9. Wendell Berry, *Life Is a Miracle: An Essay against Modern Superstition* (Washington, DC: Counterpoint, 2000), 137–38.

10. J. R. R. Tolkien, "On Fairy-Stories," in *The Monsters and the Critics and Other Essays*, ed. Christopher Tolkien (London: HarperCollins, 1997), 117.

11. Tolkien, "On Fairy-Stories," 117.

12. Tolkien, "On Fairy-Stories," 118.

13. Mentioned in Philostratus, *Life of Apollonius of Tyana* 5.14, trans. F. C. Conybeare, 1912, available at https://www.livius.org/sources/content/philostratus -life-of-apollonius/philostratus-life-of-apollonius-5.11-15/#5.14.

14. C. S. Lewis, letter to Delmar Banner (T), November 30, 1942, *The Collected Letters of C. S. Lewis*, ed. Walter Hooper (San Francisco: HarperSanFrancisco, 2004), 2:528, quoted in Holly Ordway, *Tolkien's Modern Reading: Middle-Earth Beyond the Middle Ages* (Park Ridge, IL: Word on Fire Academic, 2021), 65.

15. Walter Wangerin Jr., afterword to *The Book of the Dun Cow*, 25th anniv. ed. (San Francisco: HarperSanFrancisco, 2003), 243.

16. Wangerin, *Book of the Dun Cow*, 23.

17. In his defense of Tolkien's *The Lord of the Rings* against the charges of "allegory," Lewis writes, "My view [would] be that a good myth (i.e. a story out of which ever varying meanings will grow for different readers and in different ages) is a higher thing than an allegory (into which *one* meaning has been put). Into an allegory a man can put only what he already knows: in a myth he puts what he does [not] yet know and [could] not come to know any other way." Lewis, letter to Father Peter Milward, September 22, 1956, in *Letters of C. S. Lewis*, ed. W. H. Lewis (San Diego: Harvest Books, 1966), 458.

18. J. R. R. Tolkien, foreword to *The Fellowship of the Ring* (New York: Houghton Mifflin, 1965), 7.

19. Wangerin, afterword to *Book of the Dun Cow*, 246.

20. Wangerin, *Book of the Dun Cow*, 22.

21. Chesterton, quoted by Joseph Pearce, introduction to *St. Francis of Assisi* by Chesterton, in *St. Thomas Aquinas, St. Francis of Assisi*, 186.

22. Wangerin, afterword to *Book of the Dun Cow*, 244.

23. Wangerin, *Book of the Dun Cow*, 23.

24. Wangerin, afterword to *Book of the Dun Cow*, 244.

25. *The Aberdeen Bestiary*, University of Aberdeen, folio 39R, accessed September 7, 2021, https://www.abdn.ac.uk/bestiary/ms24/f39r.

26. J. R. R. Tolkien, "Beowulf: The Monsters and the Critics," in *The Monsters and the Critics*, 19–20.

27. Wangerin, *Book of the Dun Cow*, 24.

28. John Milton, *Paradise Lost* 10.507–9 (New York: Norton, 1993): "On all sides, from innumerable tongues / A dismal universal hiss, the sound / Of public scorn."

29. Matthew Dickerson and David O'Hara classify four evils in *The Book of the Dun Cow* and describe the basilisks as temptations. Dickerson and O'Hara, *From Homer to Harry Potter: A Handbook on Myth and Fantasy* (Grand Rapids: Brazos, 2006), 220.

30. Wangerin, *Book of the Dun Cow*, 11.

31. Wangerin, *Book of the Dun Cow*, 138.

32. Wangerin, *Book of the Dun Cow*, 12.

33. Steven Bouma-Prediger, *For the Beauty of the Earth: A Christian Vision for Creation Care*, 2nd ed. (Grand Rapids: Baker Academic, 2010), 88.

34. Wangerin, *Book of the Dun Cow*, 24.

35. Bouma-Prediger, *For the Beauty of the Earth*, 89.

36. Wangerin, *Book of the Dun Cow*, 89.

37. Wangerin, *Book of the Dun Cow*, 82.

38. Wangerin, *Book of the Dun Cow*, 144.

39. Wangerin, *Book of the Dun Cow*, 156, 171.

40. Wangerin, *Book of the Dun Cow*, 138.

41. Wangerin, *Book of the Dun Cow*, 146.

42. Wangerin, *Book of the Dun Cow*, 147.

43. Wangerin, *Book of the Dun Cow*, 147.

44. Johannes Kepler, *The Harmony of the World*, book 4, trans. Alistair Matheson Duncan, E. J. Aiton, and J. V. Field (Philadelphia: American Philosophical Society, 1997).

45. Josef Pieper, *Only the Lover Sings: Art and Contemplation*, trans. Lothar Krauth (San Francisco: Ignatius, 1990), 47.

46. J. R. R. Tolkien, "Ainulindalë: The Music of Ainur," in *The Silmarillion*, 2nd ed., ed. Christopher Tolkien (New York: Houghton Mifflin, 2001), 15.

47. C. S. Lewis, *The Magician's Nephew* (New York: Harper, 1955), 116.

48. Lewis, *Magician's Nephew*, 116–17.

49. Lewis, *Magician's Nephew*, 117.

50. Wangerin, *Book of the Dun Cow*, 148.

51. Wangerin, *Book of the Dun Cow*, 241.

52. Augustine, *Confessions* 1.1, trans. Henry Chadwick (Oxford: Oxford University Press, 1992), 3.

53. Jürgen Moltmann, *God in Creation: A New Theology of Creation and the Spirit of God*, trans. Margaret Kohl (Minneapolis: Fortress, 1993), 277.

54. Wangerin, *Book of the Dun Cow*, 140–44.

55. Translation from Steven Bouma-Prediger, *For the Beauty of the Earth*, 106–7.

Chapter 4: Liberating Prophets

1. Seamus Heaney, *The Cure at Troy: A Version of Sophocles' "Philoctetes"* (New York: Farrar, Straus & Giroux, 1991), 77.

2. Walter Brueggemann, *The Prophetic Imagination*, 40th anniv. ed. (Minneapolis: Fortress, 2018), xxxiv.

3. Howard Thurman, *Jesus and the Disinherited* (Boston: Beacon, 1996), 12.

4. Thurman, *Jesus and the Disinherited*, 12.

5. Thurman, *Jesus and the Disinherited*, 3.

6. Brueggemann, *Prophetic Imagination*, 113.

7. Brueggemann, *Prophetic Imagination*, 18.

8. Brueggemann, *Prophetic Imagination*, 4.

9. Brueggemann, *Prophetic Imagination*, 6.

10. Brueggemann, *Prophetic Imagination*, 39.

11. Julia Alvarez, "A Postscript," in *In the Time of the Butterflies* (New York: Plume, 1995), 324.

12. Brueggemann, *Prophetic Imagination*, 40.

13. Brueggemann, *Prophetic Imagination*, 5.

14. In Josephus's account, Moses is a general who conquers Ethiopia. Scholars think Hurston drew from Josephus's *Antiquities of the Jews* for her version of Moses.

15. Brueggemann, *Prophetic Imagination*, 16.

16. Zora Neale Hurston, introduction to *Moses, Man of the Mountain* (New York: Harper, 1939), xxiv.

17. Andrew Delbanco, "The Political Incorrectness of Zora Neale Hurston," *Journal of Blacks in Higher Education* 18 (Winter 1997–1998): 103–8.

18. Zora Neale Hurston, "How It Feels to Be Colored Me," *The World Tomorrow*, May 1928, available at https://www.casa-arts.org/cms/lib/PA01925203/Centricity /Domain/50/Hurston%20How%20it%20Feels%20to%20Be%20Colored%20Me.pdf.

19. In her autobiography *Dust Tracks on a Road* (Chicago: University of Illinois Press, 2008), 206, Hurston claims, "Negroes are supposed to write about the Race Problem. . . . I was and am thoroughly sick of the subject. My interest lies in what makes a man or a woman do such-and-so, regardless of color."

20. Alice Walker, introduction to *I Love Myself When I Am Laughing . . . And Then Again When I Am Looking Mean and Impressive: A Zora Neale Hurston Reader*, ed. Alice Walker (New York: Feminist Press at CUNY, 2020), 176.

21. Hurston, letter to Edwin Grover, October 12, 1939, quoted in Robert J. Morris, "Zora Neale Hurston's Ambitious Enigma," *CLA Journal* 40, no. 3 (March 1997): 310.

22. Roberts played Moses a few decades before Charlton Heston (and later, of course, Christian Bale) reprised the role.

23. Hurston, introduction to *Moses, Man of the Mountain*, xxiv.

24. Brueggemann, *Prophetic Imagination*, 6.

25. Hurston, *Moses, Man of the Mountain*, 5.

26. Delbanco, "Political Incorrectness," 104.

27. Hurston, *Moses, Man of the Mountain*, 1.

28. Brueggemann, *Prophetic Imagination*, 12.

29. Hurston, *Moses, Man of the Mountain*, 12.

30. Hurston, *Moses, Man of the Mountain*, 67.

31. Esau McCaulley, *Reading While Black: African American Biblical Interpretation as an Exercise in Hope* (Downers Grove, IL: IVP Academic, 2020), 33.

32. Hurston, *Moses, Man of the Mountain*, 68.

33. Hurston, *Moses, Man of the Mountain*, 62.

34. Hurston, *Moses, Man of the Mountain*, 68.

35. Hurston, *Moses, Man of the Mountain*, 73–74.

36. Hurston, *Moses, Man of the Mountain*, 238.

37. Brueggemann, *Prophetic Imagination*, 82.

38. Hurston, *Moses, Man of the Mountain*, 282.

39. Thurman, *Jesus and the Disinherited*, 11.

40. Thurman, *Jesus and the Disinherited*, 23.

41. Thurman, *Jesus and the Disinherited*, 11.

42. Lauren LeBlanc, "Julia Alvarez on New Book 'Afterlife' and Why Writing about Grief Requires Brevity," *Observer*, April 7, 2020, https://observer.com/2020 /04/julia-alvarez-interview-afterlife-writing-about-grief.

43. Henry David Thoreau, *Walden* (London: Dover, 1995), 59.

44. Alvarez, *In the Time of the Butterflies*, 58.

45. Brueggemann, *Prophetic Imagination*, 89.

46. Alvarez, *In the Time of the Butterflies*, 58–59.

47. Alvarez, *In the Time of the Butterflies*, 86.

48. Alvarez, *In the Time of the Butterflies*, 39.

49. Alvarez, *In the Time of the Butterflies*, 78.

50. Alvarez, *In the Time of the Butterflies*, 75.

51. Alvarez, *In the Time of the Butterflies*, 153.

52. Alvarez, *In the Time of the Butterflies*, 162.

53. Alvarez, *In the Time of the Butterflies*, 163.

54. Alvarez, *In the Time of the Butterflies*, 168.

55. Alvarez, *In the Time of the Butterflies*, 201.

56. Brueggemann, *Prophetic Imagination*, 99.

57. Alvarez, *In the Time of the Butterflies*, 216.

58. Alvarez, *In the Time of the Butterflies*, 239.

59. Alvarez, *In the Time of the Butterflies*, 230.

60. Alvarez, *In the Time of the Butterflies*, 241.

61. Alvarez, *In the Time of the Butterflies*, 277.

62. Alvarez, *In the Time of the Butterflies*, 238.

63. Alvarez, *In the Time of the Butterflies*, 308.

64. Alvarez, *In the Time of the Butterflies*, 318.

65. Alice Walker, "The Civil Rights Movement: What Good Was It?," in *In Search of Our Mothers' Gardens: Womanist Prose* (New York: Harcourt, 1983), 124–25.

66. Walker, "Civil Rights Movement," 125.

67. Walker, "Civil Rights Movement," 128–29.

68. "Pope Francis Explains Prayer and the Communion of Saints," *America*, April 7, 2021, https://www.americamagazine.org/faith/2021/04/07/pope-francis-explains-commmunion-saints-prayer-240398.

69. Alvarez, *In the Time of the Butterflies*, 313.

70. Hurston, *Moses, Man of the Mountain*, 268.

71. Fannie Lou Hamer, "I'm Sick and Tired of Being Sick and Tired," speech, Williams Institutional CME Church, Harlem, New York, December 20, 1964, in *The Speeches of Fannie Lou Hamer*, ed. Maegan Parker Brooks and Davis W. Houck (Jackson: University Press of Mississippi, 2011), 62–63.

Chapter 5: Virgin, Bride, Mother

1. Dorothy Day, *On Pilgrimage* (Grand Rapids: Eerdmans, 1999), 76.

2. Sigrid Undset, "Some Reflections on the Suffragette Movement" (1912), in *Sigrid Undset on Saints and Sinners: New Translations and Studies*, ed. Deal W. Hudson, Proceedings of the Wethersfield Institute 6 (San Francisco: Ignatius, 1993), 201.

3. Weymouth New Testament translation, 1903.

4. Cynthia Westfall, *Paul and Gender: Reclaiming the Apostle's Vision for Men and Women in Christ* (Grand Rapids: Baker Academic, 2016), 133.

5. O'Connor, letter to "A" (Betty Hester), November 25, 1955, in *The Habit of Being: The Letters of Flannery O'Connor*, ed. Sally Fitzgerald (New York: Farrar, Straus & Giroux, 1979), 119.

6. Natalie Carnes, *Motherhood: A Confession* (Stanford, CA: Stanford University Press, 2020), 3.

7. Sigrid Undset, *Kristin Lavransdatter*, trans. Tiina Nunnally (New York: Penguin, 2005), 1071.

8. Undset, *Kristin Lavransdatter*, 35.

9. O'Connor, letter to Sister Mariella Gable, May 4, 1963, in Fitzgerald, *Habit of Being*, 517.

10. Undset, *Kristin Lavransdatter*, 36.

11. Undset, *Kristin Lavransdatter*, 34.

12. Gerard Manley Hopkins, "The Leaden Echo and the Golden Echo," accessed September 7, 2021, available at https://hopkinspoetry.com/poem/the-leaden-echo -and-the-golden-echo.

13. Undset, *Kristin Lavransdatter*, 34.

14. G. K. Chesterton, *Where All Roads Lead*, in *The Collected Works of G. K. Chesterton*, ed. James J. Thompson Jr. (San Francisco: Ignatius, 1990), 3:39.

15. Robert Hugh Benson, *The Friendship of Christ*, 1912, available at https:// catholicsaints.info/the-friendship-of-christ-by-father-robert-hugh-benson.

16. Benson, *Friendship of Christ*.

17. Undset, *Kristin Lavransdatter*, 142.

18. Undset, *Kristin Lavransdatter*, 141.

19. Edith Stein, *Essays on Woman: The Collected Works of Edith Stein*, 2nd ed., ed. Lucy Gelber and Romaeus Leuven, trans. Freda Mary Oben (Washington, DC: Institute of Carmelite Studies, 2017), 2:94.

20. Undset, *Kristin Lavransdatter*, 230.

21. Undset, *Kristin Lavransdatter*, 142.

22. Undset, *Kristin Lavransdatter*, 230.

23. Thérèse of Lisieux, letter to Céline, October 14, 1890, in *Letters of St. Thérèse of Lisieux*, vol. 2, *1890–1897* (Washington, DC: ICS Publications, 1988), 709–10.

24. Alice von Hildebrand, *The Privilege of Being a Woman* (Naples, FL: Sapientia Press of Ave Maria University, 2002), 92.

25. Undset, *Kristin Lavransdatter*, 445.

26. Undset, *Kristin Lavransdatter*, 401.

27. Undset, *Kristin Lavransdatter*, 361.

28. Undset, *Kristin Lavransdatter*, 401.

29. Undset, *Kristin Lavransdatter*, 364.

30. Undset, *Kristin Lavransdatter*, 366.

31. *Meditations on the Life of Christ*, trans. and ed. Sarah McNamer (Notre Dame, IN: University of Notre Dame Press, 2018): "And as our Lady was meditating on this desire [to see the Son of God in human flesh], in an instant, by divine dispensation, the Son of God was born, leaving the womb of the Virgin Mother Mary without any trouble. And just as she did not feel him enter, in the same way, she did not feel him exit" (23).

32. Undset, *Kristin Lavransdatter*, 364.

33. This translation comes from Jerome's Vulgate: "Tecum principium in die virtutis tuae in splendoribus sanctorum: ex utero, ante luciferum, genui te." English translation from Eugene F. Rogers Jr., *After the Spirit: A Constructive Pneumatology from Resources Outside the Modern West* (Grand Rapids: Eerdmans, 2005). Rogers explains, "Since the psalm was, furthermore, taken to assert the preexistence of the Son with the Father before creation, the womb in question was not the earthly womb of Mary, but the preexistent origin of the Son in the substance of the Father" (115). The Hebrew is questionable and cannot be accurately translated. Robert Alter notes on this verse, "Many manuscripts read 'I gave you birth' . . . (a difference only of vocalization), but . . . the idea of giving birth to the king like (?) dew is puzzling." Alter, *The Hebrew Bible*, vol. 3, *The Writings* (New York: Norton, 2018), 265. What

might be puzzling to a Jewish scholar makes sense for Christian scholars in light of the Messiah coming.

34. Julian of Norwich, *Revelations of Divine Love*, trans. Elizabeth Spearing (London: Penguin, 1998), 141.

35. Tish Harrison Warren, "The Church Made Vagina Sculptures Long Before Nadia Bolz-Weber," *Christianity Today*, February 26, 2019, https://www.christianitytoday.com/ct/2019/february-web-only/nadia-bolz-weber-church-made-vagina-sculptures.html.

36. John Calvin, *Commentary on Isaiah*, vol. 3, *Isaiah 33–48*, trans. William Pringle (Grand Rapids: Christian Classics Ethereal Library), 238.

37. John Paul II, *Man and Woman He Created Them: A Theology of the Body*, trans. Michael Waldstein (Ann Arbor: University of Michigan Press, 2006), 322.

38. Gregory of Narek, *The Blessing of Blessings: Gregory of Narek's Commentary on the Song of Songs*, trans. Roberta Ervine, Cistercian Studies 215 (Kalamazoo, MI: Cistercian Publications, 2008), 62.

39. Garrett Green, *Imagining Theology: Encounters with God in Scripture, Interpretation, and Aesthetics* (Grand Rapids: Baker Academic, 2020), 140.

40. Undset, *Kristin Lavransdatter*, 394.

41. Undset, *Kristin Lavransdatter*, 438.

42. Undset, *Kristin Lavransdatter*, 450.

43. Undset, *Kristin Lavransdatter*, 970.

44. Simone Weil, *Letter to a Priest*, trans. A. F. Wills (New York: Putnam's Sons, 1954), 53.

45. Francis, "Homily of Holy Father Francis," Vatican, July 8, 2013, http://www.vatican.va/content/francesco/en/homilies/2013/documents/papa-francesco_20130708_omelia-lampedusa.html.

46. Undset, *Kristin Lavransdatter*, 1068.

47. Evelyn Birge Vitz, "The Legend of the Saints," in Hudson, *Sigrid Undset on Saints and Sinners*, 61.

48. Undset, *Kristin Lavransdatter*, 1074.

49. Undset, *Kristin Lavransdatter*, 1111.

50. Undset, *Kristin Lavransdatter*, 1113.

51. O'Connor, letter to Betty Hester, November 11, 1961, in Fitzgerald, *Habit of Being*, 453.

52. Undset, *Kristin Lavransdatter*, 1122.

53. Undset, "Some Reflections on the Suffragette Movement," 200.

54. Quoted by Mitzi M. Brunsdale, "Stages on Her Road: Sigrid Undset's Spiritual Journey," *Religion and Literature* 23, no. 3 (Autumn 1991): 83–96.

55. Undset, *Kristin Lavransdatter*, 1071.

56. Julian of Norwich, *Revelations of Divine Love*, 141.

Chapter 6: Contemplative and Active Life

1. Georges Bernanos, letter to Jorge de Lima, January 1942, quoted in Hans Urs von Balthasar, *Bernanos: An Ecclesial Existence*, trans. Erasmo Leiva-Merikakis (San Francisco: Ignatius, 1996), 199.

2. Hans Urs von Balthasar, *Prayer*, trans. Graham Harrison (San Francisco: Ignatius, 1986), 15.

3. Georges Bernanos, *Diary of a Country Priest*, trans. Pamela Morris (New York: Doubleday, 1954), 140.

4. Bernanos, *Diary of a Country Priest*, 18.

5. Bernanos, *Diary of a Country Priest*, 19.

6. Bernanos, *Diary of a Country Priest*, 4.

7. Bernanos, *Diary of a Country Priest*, 84.

8. Bernanos, *Diary of a Country Priest*, 80.

9. Bernanos, *Diary of a Country Priest*, 81.

10. Bernanos, *Diary of a Country Priest*, 82.

11. Bernanos, *Diary of a Country Priest*, 180.

12. Bernanos, *Diary of a Country Priest*, 188.

13. Bernanos, *Diary of a Country Priest*, 163.

14. Bernanos, *Diary of a Country Priest*, 188.

15. Bernanos, *Diary of a Country Priest*, 202.

16. Bernanos, *Diary of a Country Priest*, 82.

17. Kurt F. Reinhardt, *The Theological Novel of Modern Europe: An Analysis of Masterpieces by Eight Authors* (New York: Frederick Ungar, 1969), 118.

18. Aquinas, *Summa Theologiae* II-II.182.1–2, trans. Fathers of the English Dominican Province (1920), available at https://www.newadvent.org/summa/3182.htm #article1.

19. Gregory the Great, *Homilies* 2.2.15, in *The Growth of Mysticism: Gregory the Great through the Twelfth Century*, ed. Bernard McGinn, vol. 2. of *The Presence of God: A History of Western Christian Mysticism* (New York: Crossroad, 1999), 77.

20. Bernanos, *Diary of a Country Priest*, 9.

21. Bernanos, *Diary of a Country Priest*, 11.

22. Bernanos, *Diary of a Country Priest*, 120.

23. Bernanos, *Diary of a Country Priest*, 123.

24. Bernanos, *Diary of a Country Priest*, 124.

25. Josef Pieper, *Happiness and Contemplation*, trans. Clara and Richard Winston (Ann Arbor: University of Michigan Press, 1966), 72.

26. Bernanos, *Diary of a Country Priest*, 131.

27. Bernanos, *Diary of a Country Priest*, 132.

28. Bernanos, *Diary of a Country Priest*, 138.

29. Bernanos, *Diary of a Country Priest*, 140.

30. N. T. Wright, *After You Believe: Why Christian Character Matters* (New York: HarperOne, 2010).

31. Aelred of Rievaulx, *De institutione inclusarum*, quoted in Thomas Merton, *Contemplative Prayer* (New York: Image, 1969), 51.

32. Bernanos, *Diary of a Country Priest*, 11.

33. Bernanos, *Diary of a Country Priest*, 71.

34. Quoted in Walter Herbstrith, *Edith Stein: A Biography*, trans. Bernard Bonowitz (New York: Harper & Row, 1985), 71.

35. Flannery O'Connor, "The Fiction Writer and His Country," in *Mystery and Manners: Occasional Prose*, ed. Sally Fitzgerald and Robert Fitzgerald (New York: Farrar, Straus & Giroux, 1969), 35.

36. Friedrich Nietzsche, *On the Genealogy of Morality: A Polemic*, trans. Maudemarie Clark and Alan J. Swensen (Indianapolis: Hackett, 1998), 1.

37. George Herbert, "The Windows," accessed September 7, 2021, available at https://www.poetryfoundation.org/poems/50695/the-windows-56d22df68ff95.

38. Bernanos, *Diary of a Country Priest*, 124.

39. Bernanos, *Diary of a Country Priest*, 85.

40. O'Connor, *Mystery and Manners*, 226: "In us the good is something under construction."

41. Hans Urs von Balthasar, *Bernanos: An Ecclesial Existence*, 4th ed. (San Francisco: Ignatius, 1996), 261.

42. Bernanos, *Diary of a Country Priest*, 57.

43. Bernanos, *Diary of a Country Priest*, 208.

44. Bernanos, *Diary of a Country Priest*, 115.

45. Flannery O'Connor, *A Prayer Journal* (New York: Farrar, Straus & Giroux, 2013), 38.

46. Bernanos, *Diary of a Country Priest*, 65.

47. Bernanos, *Diary of a Country Priest*, 208.

48. Karl Rahner, "Christian Living Formerly and Today," in *Theological Investigations VII*, trans. David Bourke (New York: Herder and Herder, 1971), 15.

49. Balthasar, *Prayer*, 9.

50. Bernanos, *Diary of a Country Priest*, 180.

51. Bernanos, *Diary of a Country Priest*, 59.

52. Bernanos, *Diary of a Country Priest*, 194.

53. Bernanos, *Diary of a Country Priest*, 214.

54. Bernanos, *Diary of a Country Priest*, 232.

55. Bernanos, *Diary of a Country Priest*, 4.

56. Aelred, *De institutione inclusarum*, quoted in Thomas Merton, *Contemplative Prayer* (New York: Image, 1969), 51.

Chapter 7: Sharing in His Suffering

1. Mother Teresa, *No Greater Love* (Novato, CA: New World Library, 2010), 86.

2. Augustine, *Confessions* 8.7.17, trans. Henry Chadwick (Oxford: Oxford University Press, 2008), 145.

3. Flannery O'Connor, *A Prayer Journal* (New York: Farrar, Straus & Giroux, 2013), 33.

4. "Prior to Flannery O'Connor, this nation which Chesterton famously defined as a nation with the soul of a church, had produced no really major Christian writer." Ralph Wood, "We're All Monsters: Ralph Wood on the Good, the Bad, and the Human," *The Table Podcast*, Center for Christian Thought, May 6, 2019, https://cct.biola.edu/were-all-monsters-ralph-wood.

5. Graham Greene, *Ways of Escape* (New York: Simon and Schuster, 1980), loc. 44 of 4525, Kindle.

6. Greene, *Ways of Escape*, loc. 67 of 4525, Kindle.

7. Greene, *Ways of Escape*, loc. 185 of 4525, Kindle.

8. O'Connor, *Prayer Journal*, 4.

9. Léon Bloy, *The Woman Who Was Poor*, trans. I. J. Collins (New York: Sheed & Ward, 1939).

10. "I am so lukewarm as to need Bloy always to send me into serious thought." O'Connor, *Prayer Journal*, 35.

11. O'Connor, *Prayer Journal*, 35.

12. Graham Greene, *The Power and the Glory* (New York: Viking, 1972), 284.

13. Quoted in Ralph C. Wood, *Flannery O'Connor and the Christ-Haunted South* (Grand Rapids: Eerdmans, 2004), 215.

14. O'Connor, letter to "A" (Betty Hester), December 8, 1955, in *The Habit of Being: The Letters of Flannery O'Connor*, ed. Sally Fitzgerald (New York: Farrar, Straus & Giroux, 1979), 120–21.

15. O'Connor, letter to Louise Abbot, 1959, in Fitzgerald, *Habit of Being*, 354.

16. Lev Grossman and Richard Lacayo, "All-TIME 100 Novels," *Time*, October 16, 2005, https://entertainment.time.com/2005/10/16/all-time-100-novels/slide/all.

17. Greene, *The Power and the Glory*, 178.

18. Greene, *The Power and the Glory*, 176.

19. St. Jerome, *The Satirical Letters of St. Jerome*, trans. Paul Carroll (Chicago: Gateway Editions, 1956), 5.

20. Flannery O'Connor, *The Violent Bear It Away*, in *The Collected Works*, ed. Sally Fitzgerald (New York: Library of America, 1988), 341.

21. O'Connor, letter to Betty Hester, July 25, 1959, in Fitzgerald, *Habit of Being*, 343.

22. O'Connor, *The Violent Bear It Away*, 478.

23. O'Connor, *The Violent Bear It Away*, 479.

24. Graham Greene, *The End of the Affair* (New York: Penguin, 1991), 95.

25. Greene, *The Power and the Glory*, 176.

26. Greene, *The Power and the Glory*, 95.

27. Dorothy Day, *On Pilgrimage* (Grand Rapids: Eerdmans, 1999), 75–76.

28. Day, *On Pilgrimage*, 76.

29. Day, *On Pilgrimage*, 77.

30. Dietrich Bonhoeffer, *Life Together*, trans. John W. Doberstein (New York: Harper & Row, 1954), 20.

31. O'Connor, letter to Louise Abbot, 1959, in Fitzgerald, *Habit of Being*, 354.

32. Flannery O'Connor, "Greenleaf," in *Collected Works*, ed. Sally Fitzgerald (New York: Library of America, 1988), 506.

33. O'Connor, "Greenleaf," 507.

34. O'Connor, "Greenleaf," 505.

35. O'Connor, "Greenleaf," 507.

36. Greene, *End of the Affair*, 120.

37. Greene, *End of the Affair*, 120–22.

38. Greene, *End of the Affair*, 120.

39. Brian S. Hook and R. R. Reno, *Heroism and the Christian Life: Reclaiming Excellence* (Louisville: Westminster John Knox, 2000), 2.

40. Greene, *The Power and the Glory*, 268.

41. William James, *The Varieties of Religious Experience*, ed. Martin E. Marty (New York: Penguin, 1982), 373.

42. Flannery O'Connor, "Introduction to *A Memoir of Mary Anne*," in *Mystery and Manners: Occasional Prose*, ed. Sally Fitzgerald and Robert Fitzgerald (New York: Farrar, Straus & Giroux, 1969), 227.

43. Greene, *The Power and the Glory*, 268.

44. Greene, *The Power and the Glory*, 269.

45. O'Connor, *The Violent Bear It Away*, 412.

46. O'Connor, *The Violent Bear It Away*, 413.

47. O'Connor, *The Violent Bear It Away*, 414.

48. O'Connor, *The Violent Bear It Away*, 415.

49. Greene, *The Power and the Glory*, 284.

50. Greene, *The Power and the Glory*, 291.

51. Greene, *End of the Affair*, 190.

52. O'Connor, letter to Louise Abbot, May 28, 1964, in Fitzgerald, *Habit of Being*, 581.

53. O'Connor, letter to Elizabeth and Robert Lowell, March 17, 1953, in Fitzgerald, *Habit of Being*, 57.

54. O'Connor, letter to Betty Hester, June 28, 1956, in Fitzgerald, *Habit of Being*, 163.

55. Greene, *The Power and the Glory*, 95.

56. Miguel de Unamuno, *Selected Works of Unamuno*, vol. 4, *The Tragic Sense of Life in Men and Nations*, trans. Anthony Kerrigan and Martin Nozick (Princeton: Princeton University Press, 2021), 226–27.

Chapter 8: *Ars Moriendi*

1. Mary Oliver, "The Summer Day," in *New and Selected Poems* (Boston: Beacon Press, 1992), 94.

2. Muriel Spark, *Memento Mori* (New York: New Directions, 2014), 1.

3. Lydia Dugdale, *The Lost Art of Dying Well* (New York: HarperOne, 2020), 147.

4. Christopher P. Vogt, *Patience, Compassion, Hope, and the Christian Art of Dying Well* (Lanham, MD: Rowman & Littlefield, 2004), 98.

5. Flannery O'Connor, "A Temple of the Holy Ghost," in *The Collected Works*, ed. Sally Fitzgerald (New York: Library of America, 1988), 243.

6. Dante Alighieri, *Paradise* 3.17.55–57, trans. and ed. Anthony M. Esolen (New York: Modern Library, 2004).

7. Countee Cullen, "The Black Christ," in *The Black Christ and Other Poems* (New York: Harper & Brothers, 1929), 69.

8. James Cone, *The Cross and the Lynching Tree* (Maryknoll, NY: Orbis, 2011).

9. Ernest J. Gaines, *A Lesson before Dying* (New York: Vintage, 1994), 3.

10. Gaines, *A Lesson before Dying*, 7–8.

11. Gaines, *A Lesson before Dying*, 21.

12. Gaines, *A Lesson before Dying*, 31.

13. Dugdale, *Lost Art of Dying Well*, 29.

14. Gaines, *A Lesson before Dying*, 194.

15. Gaines, *A Lesson before Dying*, 191.

16. Gaines, *A Lesson before Dying*, 193.

17. Gaines, *A Lesson before Dying*, 193.

18. Gaines, *A Lesson before Dying*, 193.

19. George MacDonald, *An Anthology: 365 Readings*, ed. C. S. Lewis (1946; repr., San Francisco: HarperSanFrancisco, 2001), 75.

20. Gaines, *A Lesson before Dying*, 223.

21. Gaines, *A Lesson before Dying*, 224.

22. Gaines, *A Lesson before Dying*, 233.

23. Gaines, *A Lesson before Dying*, 254.

24. Gaines, *A Lesson before Dying*, 254.

25. Gaines, *A Lesson before Dying*, 255.

26. O'Connor, letter to "A" (Betty Hester), June 28, 1956, in *The Habit of Being: The Letters of Flannery O'Connor*, ed. Sally Fitzgerald (New York: Farrar, Straus & Giroux, 1979), 163.

27. Walker Percy, "Questions They Never Asked Me," in *Signposts in a Strange Land*, ed. Patrick Samway (New York: Farrar, Straus & Giroux, 1991), 417.

28. Walker Percy, *The Last Gentleman* (New York: Farrar, Straus & Giroux, 1966), 244.

29. Percy, *Last Gentleman*, 210.

30. Percy, *Last Gentleman*, 390.

31. Percy, *Last Gentleman*, 401.

32. Percy, *Last Gentleman*, 403.

33. Percy, *Last Gentleman*, 405.

34. Percy, *Last Gentleman*, 56.

35. Willa Cather, "On *Death Comes for the Archbishop*," letter to *Commonweal*, November 23, 1927, 374.

36. Cather, "On *Death Comes for the Archbishop*," 377.

37. Willa Cather, *Death Comes for the Archbishop* (New York: Vintage, 1990), 171.

38. Cather, *Death Comes for the Archbishop*, 286.

39. Cather, *Death Comes for the Archbishop*, 263.

40. Cather, *Death Comes for the Archbishop*, 263.

41. Cather, *Death Comes for the Archbishop*, 288.

42. Cather, *Death Comes for the Archbishop*, 259.

43. Cather, *Death Comes for the Archbishop*, 267.

44. Cather, *Death Comes for the Archbishop*, 169–70.

45. Leo Tolstoy, "The Death of Ivan Ilyich," trans. Lynn Solotaroff (New York: Bantam, 1981), 108.

Conclusion

1. C. S. Lewis, letter to Sister Penelope, July 9, 1939, in *Letters of C. S. Lewis*, ed. W. H. Lewis (San Diego: Harvest Books, 1966), 322.